TALES FROM A BARREN ROCK

Reminiscences of life in Hong Kong

EDITED BY

ROGER MEDCALF & ROD OLSEN

Tales from a Barren Rock

By Roger Medcalf and Rod Olsen

ISBN-13: 978-988-8843-57-2

© 2024 Roger Medcalf and Rod Olsen

HISTORY / ASIA / HONG KONG

EB212

Published in Hong Kong by Earnshaw Books Ltd.

PREFACE

In 1841, Hong Kong was denounced by the British Prime Minister Lord Palmerston as "a barren rock with nary a house upon it" that would "never be a mart for trade." He believed Britain had got a raw deal in the treaty under which the island was ceded by the Qing Empire. How wrong he was.

Many books have subsequently celebrated this great city, described by King Charles III as "one of the most successful societies on Earth". TALES FROM A BARREN ROCK seeks to give a portrait of the territory through the eyes of a cross-section of long-term residents. They relate stories that offer a sense of what the territory was and what it meant to those who lived here in the years leading up and beyond the handover to Chinese sovereignty in 1997.

The book's inception was somewhat prosaic. Journalist and publisher Jethro Roger Medcalf, resident for more than fifty years, read the book *Stories from the Royal Hong Kong Police: Fifty Accounts from Officers of Hong Kong's Colonial-Era Police Force* and thought, why not do a general interest version based on the same idea. He invited friends and acquaintances to write their reminiscences of life in the city they had grown to love, and the trickle of submissions soon become a flood. Knowing his weaknesses, Roger decided he had better have back-up and asked Rod Olsen, a fellow New Zealander with a stellar corporate background, to join as co-editor. Rod brought discipline to the team.

This book is published at a time when Hong Kong has in many ways changed from the place featured in these reminiscences. But this book aims in a small way to shine a light on the extraordinary facets of life on this once-barren rock while encouraging a quiet confidence that it has not lost its entrepreneurial flair nor its adaptability.

The writers found in these pages are a diverse bunch: former officials of the government and the Jockey Club, pilots, policemen, a naturalist, technology experts, bankers, a journalist, housewives, a church leader, businessmen, a lawyer, a private secretary to the Governor and Hong Kong's most admired animal welfare activist Jill Robinson. The stories cover a wide range of topics and styles. Clinton Leeks writes about the inner workings and personalities of Government House in the British era; Stuart McDouall describes dark days in the police force when an officer started shooting colleagues; Dave Newbery tells how a Cathay Pacific crew survived a bombing; Amanda White relates how friends got lured into the fringes of prostitution… and so on. Whatever their tastes, readers will find much to interest and amuse in these pages, presented as a homage to a great city.

Roger Medcalf
Rod Olsen
Hong Kong, January 2024

TABLE OF CONTENTS

01 At Home Away in Hong Kong—Sue Lavender 1

02 Displaced—Rachel Beresford-Davies 10

03 Memories of Government House—Clinton Leeks 17

04 Amanda and Jane—Amanda White 29

05 Tales from a Barren Rock—Professor Dr. Judith Mackay 36

06 Benevolent or Barking Mad—Jill Robinson 42

07 Desperation and Deliverance—Stuart McDouall 55

08 Shattering the Glass Ceiling—Evelyn Lam 65

09 St John's Cathedral: Do Ordinary Things with
Extraordinary Love—Stuart McDouall 79

10 Anti-Darkness Group versus Triads—Stuart McDouall 85

11 Cue Chaos—Steve Reels 103

12 Drunk as a Royal Skunk in First Class—
Mark Esterhuizen 112

13 Insurance Man-cum-Preacher Builds Family of God—
John Snelgrov 117

14 Farmers' Boys Dream of Future Landings—
Colin Dyson 128

15 Guarding the Border: Nabbing Illegals, Spying on PRC
and Recoiling from Snakes—Mike Sharp 133

16 Is Flying for a Living Dangerous?—David Newbery 140

17 Light Aircraft Flying: Best Fun You Can Have With Your
Clothes On 146

18 Murderer with a Double Life—Guy Sanderson Shirra 158

19 One Spare—Chris Emmett 162

20 The Hokey Pokey Squad—Barry J Smith 168

21	You've Found What? — Barry J Smith	177
22	Rising Damp — Mike Tinworth	185
23	Raining Fire in the Sky — Mark Esterhuizen	192
24	The Body in the Sack — Guy Sanderson Shirra	195
25	The Four Peaks & Captain Barbecue — Lynn Seymour	200
26	Here's US$25,000, Now Let's Get Out of Here — Mark Esterhuizen	202
27	Nine Lives of the Chinese White Dolphin — Clinton Leeks	205
28	Rambles in the Islands with Butterfly Nets and a Podgy Misfit — GT Reels	216
29	Wonderland — Rachel Beresford-Davies	237
30	Lai Chi Wo: Remote Walled Village — Lynn Seymour	245
31	Drug Money Laundering: the Hong Kong Connection — Stuart McDouall	248
32	A Muslim Discovers Freemasonry — Noorie Razack	256
33	Confrontation — Guy Sanderson Shirra	266
34	Touch and Go — Mike Tinworth	279
35	Jockey Club — Stuart Smith	284
36	The Chater Collection Mystery — Edited by Stuart McDouall	297
37	Via Imperial: Pilgrimage into the Unknown — Rod Olsen	309

At Home Away in Hong Kong

Sue Lavender

The mobile rang, as it inevitably does in Hong Kong.

"Are you at home, Susan?" the client asked.

"Far from it," I replied.

It was Good Friday 2006. Despite the public holiday, like many corporate lawyers, I was huddled over my office desk, chin bent un-ergonomically to my shoulder supporting the mobile, while using one hand to reply to an e-mail and picking up the landline, which had just started ringing, with the other.

Good Friday is the day of doubts, rejection, crucifixion, flagellation and atonement for sins, so the client's question brought my own suppressed doubts to the surface. Where was I? How did I get here? Why wasn't I at home?

All I had known when I left Montreal in 1992 was that I had to get away, away from the vast white expanse of space, the snow on my skin, the ice in my veins, icicle tears, numbed frozen fingers, the numbed void in my heart. No more futile trying to make a hopeless relationship work; no more digging out after a snow storm only to see a snow truck emerge from nowhere and dump a mountain of packed snow on my car, making me start all over again, time after time; no more frozen car door locks that keys just can't open, ignitions that just won't start; no more trying to jump start an unrequited love; no more six-lane highways of skidding, criss-crossing cars and hearts; no more "colleagues" sabotaging a disastrous career; no more salting the driveway;

no more salt on my wounds; no more broken bones, no more. broken heart. *"Mon pays ce n'est pas un pays, c'est l'hiver"* ("My country is not a country, it is winter.") the poet said of Quebec. No more slipping and sliding, I must change more than lanes, I must change my life. I had no option. I was a refugee.

So, like the proverbial Owl and Pussycat, I left. I came here and found the sun. I fell for this 'borrowed place', which was nearing its expiry date, as soon as I touched down at Kai Tak airport, between the South China Sea on one side and Kowloon's ubiquitous washing lines on the other, a first taste of Hong Kong's sympathetic schizophrenia.

The next morning I took my first bus ride down Nathan Road to reach my Kowloon office at UNHCR (United Nations High Commissioner for Refugees). It was to be the base from which I would travel to Hong Kong's many refugee camps on its outlying islands and the Kowloon peninsula in order to report on the asylum claims of the Vietnamese boat people who were seeking refuge in Hong Kong in large numbers at that time. (My UNHCR contract was for six months but I've been here 29 years at time of writing in 2021.)

My office at UNHCR was in the Yaumatei carpark building. Yes, an office in a carpark. What's more, this building had a highway running through it—the Gascoigne Road Flyover and vehicles (more types than I could have ever imagined in the land of four-wheel drive and snow tyres), all vying for space on the streets and the pavement. The crowded buildings also caught my eye, crammed so closely together that their multitudinous giant signs of seemingly dancing Chinese characters conspired with flowerpots and underwear drying on clotheslines to obscure the names of the little side-street arteries leading off the governor's highway, Nathan Road.

I took lots of trips on Hong Kong double-decker buses that

brought back memories of the first home I had abandoned many decades earlier to immigrate to Canada, but, in typical Hong Kong-style, these buses could not be just plain red or just plain any-one-color. Instead, every inch of them was covered with pictorial and written advertising in elegant Chinese characters and in more colors than Joseph's biblical coat.

On my first weekend in Hong Kong, I rode the bus southwards from the top of Kowloon's Boundary Street frontier, the former limit of British territory before the New Territories were leased to the United Kingdom for 99 years in 1898. I sat up front on the upper deck, expecting to see the famous "Fragrant Harbor" eventually appear before me, but as we reached Tsim Sha Tsui, I wondered if I was on the wrong bus. Where was it? I could not have guessed that Hong Kong's prime vista would be surreptitiously tucked away from view behind its Space Museum. Nevertheless, when I finally managed to find it, it simply took my breath away. The smelly "fragrance" of Victoria Harbor was one of Hong Kong's many contradictions I would discover, but to me it smelled better than any Parisian perfume. I rode the Star Ferry's appropriately named Morning Star to cross the harbor. By the time I reached the Hong Kong side I had no doubt that I was home.

I walked to Blake's Pier and sat down to look back across the harbor at Kowloon. I took in the sights and smells of the harbor with every pore of my body. Directly in front of me I saw various vessels of all shapes and sizes: ocean liners, container ships, ferries of all kinds, not least the Star Ferry, sailing back and forth between Kowloon and Hong Kong Island, and tiny sampans, loading up with mysterious cargo.

I could also clearly see Kowloon's high-rise buildings, glimmering in the sun, planes zooming low into Kai Tak, too close for comfort to the residential blocks visible in the distance behind the old Kowloon Canton Railway Clock Tower, and behind all of them, the Eight Dragon Hills. I imagined the ninth dragon, the Song Dynasty's Emperor Bing, holding sway above them as he gave Kowloon its name, "Nine Dragons", to include himself.

My work as a UNHCR lawyer took me to various parts of the territory and allowed me to appreciate its many contrasts: its co-existing Chinese and Western cultures, its ancient traditions and modern business environment, the tranquillity of the outlying islands, as peaceful as Hong Kong Island is restless and noisy. I lived on Lantau Island, the largest island in the archipelago, paradoxically larger than Hong Kong Island itself — yet another Hong Kong contradiction.

In those early years there were many happy times during which I relished the varied delights of steamy dim sum parlour trolleys, raft rides from Lantau to Tai O village, Lamma typhoon gin parties, boozy junk trips, tequila BBQs and mud-wrestling at Lantau's infamous Frog and Toad pub, lemon chicken Sunday lunch at Mr Chan's place on Peng Chau island, the Cheung Chau Bun Festival and, best of all, the serenity of the many different boat rides on the South China Sea that Hong Kong offered. Island-hopping was my favourite activity — part of my work and also my recreation at weekends.

I knew my job at UNHCR could not last forever and China experience had become necessary. I would have to reinvent myself to survive. So after obtaining a post-graduate diploma in Chinese law from the University of Hong Kong, I moved temporarily to Beijing in the mid-nineties to study Mandarin and work for the representative office of the first Italian law firm to set up in mainland China. My feeling of "Hong Kong home" was intensified by this move. I felt homesick for my *Dong fang zhi zhu* (Pearl of the East). When asked where I came from, I replied unequivocally *"Wo shi xiang gang ren"* ("I'm a Hong Konger").

There was a sense of strengthened belonging when I eventually returned to Hong Kong not long before the 1997 Handover.

Instead of UNHRC's Yaumatei carpark building office and travel all over Hong Kong, by the end of the 20th Century I had become a permanent fixture in a Central high-rise corporate law firm. Living on an outlying island was no longer practical and anyway, Lantau was no longer an unconnected island. It had been attached to the Kowloon peninsula by road and bridge to serve the new Chek Lap Kok Island airport. I moved to the Mid-Levels on Hong Kong Island. After all, it "saves time" and is "so much more convenient".

Though it's nowhere near as beautiful.

I now had to face the inevitable. My life had permanently shifted to Hong Kong. Severing ties with Canada had been pushed to the back of my mind: "this year, next year, sometime, never", but I knew upon return from Beijing that I must do it. I had a permanent job now, no longer the non-committal temporary ones of the past. So I flew to Montreal and, heart-breaking though it was, I disposed of the remnants of my material existence there.

Facing the port of old Montreal, on the St Lawrence River, a statue of Mary stands atop the Church of Notre Dame de Bonsecours. She was a fellow wandering Montrealer, Leonard Cohen's *Our Lady of the Harbor*, stretching her arms out towards the sea to welcome returning sailors. I looked up and said goodbye to her somewhat nostalgically. After all, I had always liked her. She had always welcomed me back like those sailors. I also nostalgically imagined Leonard on the balcony of a Montreal walk-up apartment, muttering the words of some new song. Of course, in fact he was long gone — to a Zen Buddhist monastery in California around the time I had gone to Beijing.

Anyway, it was over. I was free, but as Janis Joplin knew only too well, *"Freedom's just another word for nothing left to lose."*

TALES FROM A BARREN ROCK

I was free to return home to a smelly harbor, which I could only vaguely glance at if I strained my head uncomfortably over the top of my computer and squinted through the reflecting glass of my 24th floor office window — that is if I had time to look up from the frenetic, never-ending work before me on the screen. "24": doesn't that mean "easy death" in Cantonese?

On occasion, when the haze was not too strong, I might also catch a glimpse of the harbor from my tiny shoe-box apartment window, just a thin blue thread between two high-rises, barely visible through the Mid-Levels mist. Did I give up the oxygen, space and security of Canada for this? Where had the island-hopping gone? Had the boat rides turned Cinderella-like into smoky, gridlocked Central cab flag-falls? Had Montreal's snow and ice and the perils of digging out and cranking up a frozen ignition simply morphed into small spaces, mold and mist, mobiles, computers, contracts and clients? *Plus ça change?* Had Hong Kong drawn me to itself like a siren and, now that I had no other home to return to, was it suffocating me in its smog and corporate law without mercy?

What or where is "home" exactly, anyway? I asked myself. Is it that nuclear place in one's life, "domicile" in legal terms? (I always thought it strange that the stony heartless taxman analyses where the psychological nucleus of an individual's life is in order to stab him with his taxes there!) The word "home" is ambiguous. "Home" is a simple noun, but it is also an expression of the dative case, a direction. We go "home", not "to home"; the computer's "home" key moves us "home" to the beginning of the line, back to where we started. *"Grow where you're planted?"* Snails carry their homes around on their backs. I thought mine was in my backpack when I arrived in Hong Kong, but did it slip away, just as Aeneas left the flames of fallen Troy and headed for Rome. Can reaching one's destination take on such overriding importance that everything else is lost along the way? And what about being "at home"? Was Aeneas "at home" in Rome? Rome was not his home.

Those were my thoughts on Good Friday 2006, but Good Friday paves the way for Easter Sunday, day of repentance, forgiveness, reconciliation, resurrection and catharsis. So, two days later, on Easter Sunday evening, I returned to look at Victoria Harbor again, from a fresh angle, from the opposite side this time, sitting on the Kowloon-side, looking over at Hong Kong Island.

The Peak no longer dominated the Island's landscape as it did when I first arrived on the Barren Rock. The International Finance Center skyscraper had taken care of that. The increased haze made it more difficult to see the other side of the harbor. Blake's Pier, my first harbor-viewing point in 1992, was gone. There were fewer of those characteristic "look at me" flamboyant commercial signs defiantly invading the night skyline with their multi-colored neon lights. The harbor was narrower than it used to be as land reclamation had been advancing rapidly. The new wing of the Hong Kong Convention and Exhibition Centre, jutting out like a peninsula from Wanchai, was just one example of the encroachment of artificial land into the sacred realm of Neptune. One day, I swear we'll walk across from Kowloon to Hong Kong.

There were also changes not physically visible across the breadth of the harbor but which I could see in my mind's eye, like the less-ostentatious buses, now clad only in the drab colors of their corporate livery. Thank goodness the trams were still brightly decorated as they continued to defy more advanced forms of transport, doggedly ploughing their way across Hong Kong Island's northern horizontal strip. Despite all the changes, Hong Kong itself remained beautiful, as it still is now, after all this time.

How we see things is essentially a matter of perspective: like the difference between the views from the Hong Kong side and the Kowloon side: both beautiful yet different. The images I saw before me on that Easter Sunday evening in 2006 no longer blotted out a life I wanted to leave behind, as my first view of the harbor had done so many years before. I felt at peace with Montreal again now, viewed through the prism of Hong Kong. Central's gleaming skyscrapers made me think of downtown Montreal. The Peak recalled Montreal's "mountain", Mount Royal, the city's majestic backdrop, gracefully reclining behind Montreal's business district. The Star Ferry bustling to and fro between Kowloon and Hong Kong reminded me of the central interchange station of Montreal's underground, the Metro, seamlessly connecting the island of Montreal from north to south as well as east to west. The Convention Center's new wing still makes me think of Montreal's own low-rise architectural crustacean, the Olympic Stadium, built but unfinished, for the 1976 Olympics.

I looked at the little sampans, tiny but so resilient, bobbing up and down in front of me as they were being filled with different varieties of cargo and passengers. I thought of the little boats that had carried the Vietnamese asylum-seekers here — my reason for coming to Hong Kong. I imagined a little sampan transporting me back to that other island harbor, back to the forgiving, ever-welcoming arms of Notre Dame de Bonsecours and bringing Leonard Cohen's Suzanne her precious cargo of "*tea and oranges that come all the way from China*" for her to take home and serve to her guests in her safe, cozy little eyrie overlooking the St Lawrence River.

Victims of globalisation or simply of broken dreams, many of us must, snail-like, carry our homes with us to make ourselves at home wherever we are. We must accept that we inevitably change through life and so home changes too, for better or worse, even though we also continue to carry with us the love we will always bear for all the places we have ever called home.

I rode the Star Ferry back to my office Hong Kong side. My Easter Sunday musings were soon interrupted by a call on my mobile:

"Where are you?" the irritated partner from my law firm asked.

"I'm home," I replied.

DISPLACED: AN EXPAT ESTRANGED

Rachel Beresford-Davies

It is the late 1980s. I am twenty years old and have spent a year or so ping-ponging between England and my childhood home, Hong Kong. After almost twelve years, my parents are trying to decide at what point to cut the cord of their expat existence and return to the UK, and having spent a year or so of real life there, I'm of the opinion the answer is "not yet". There seems to be no me-shaped slot in either country, and really, I am neither one place nor the other. A kind of temporary displacement. In any case, my brother has just become engaged to Li Kam, a powerful yet soft-spoken Cantonese girl we all approve of, and today we are to be initiated into her family.

The scene: a circular table is laid with a white linen cloth and ten pairs of ornate chopsticks, the tips of which rest gently on small bamboo steps made from porcelain. Next to them are ten hand-painted china spoons and as a concession to our Western ineptness, three stainless steel forks for my parents and me.

To celebrate my brother Simon's engagement to Li Kam, an extravagant banquet has been laid on by her family at their pig farm in Hong Kong, just a spit from the border of China. Kam's parents look small and ancient, her mother dressed head to toe in black, her father in gray. They both have the tanned, leathery skin of farmers, and their faces are so lined that it's impossible to discern their expression. My parents and I smile awkwardly, feeling like giants among these delicate yet robust people. We try our best to look relaxed as Kam and her family chat away, often all at the same time. Their jangling words rebound off the walls of the sparsely furnished dining room, painted bright white and with a gleamingly clean tiled floor. My brother joins in now and then in Cantonese, which in turn has to be translated by Kam for her parents.

"They speak some sort of Hakka dialect. It's unintelligible," Simon tells me by way of explanation, when I ask why they don't understand him. It's literally Chinese whispers.

Kam's mother gestures for us all to sit down, laughing and nodding energetically as she points to the forks. We nod back and laugh too, watching as one of Kam's three brothers delivers a steaming bowl of something dark and viscous to the center of the table. I like Chinese food, we all do, but my brother had been worryingly vague when questioned over what we might have, stressing only that the feast was considered a great honour, and on no account could we refuse any of the food offered.

I eye the dish suspiciously as Kam's mother ladles what appears to be some sort of sweet-smelling soup into mercifully small bowls. I can make out dark lumps lurking just beneath the meniscus, and then something oval shaped and slightly paler than the rest of the mixture plops up into the bowl. Kam smiles serenely. My brother looks determined.

"Gosh. What's... this?" my father stammers, his fixed grin starting to look rictus-like.

"Sweet date soup with boiled egg, a traditional fertility dish," Kam explains.

I tear my gaze from the bowl placed in front of me to see Kam and her family watching us expectantly. They are waiting for one of us to initiate the meal. My mother is the first to take the plunge, presumably feeling some sort of responsibility for her son's future virility. She balances the egg on her china spoon, and with as much social grace as she is able to muster, bites it in half. A glossy trail of semi-cooked yolk runs down her chin, and it is all I can do not to gag. My family know how I feel about runny eggs. Simon is pointedly looking from me to my bowl, to the spoon in my hand, which I've halted a few inches from the soup. I take a deep breath and, foolishly, decide to follow my mother's tactic of getting the worst out of the way first and scoop the sticky oval onto my spoon. I dither a moment too long, panic slightly, and put the whole egg in my mouth. I have to puff my cheeks out to allow it some room and stop myself gagging. The date soup is cloyingly sweet and the egg bursts like a softened eyeball on my tongue. I chew hurriedly and ladle in some more of the syrupy liquid, suppressing every natural reflex in my body. Kam's brothers are taking their time over the soup, ingesting the eggs with blunt spoons and swirling the yolk elaborately through the dark liquid. They must think me a pig.

By the time I've swallowed down the last mouthful, I am perspiring slightly, but feeling strangely victorious. Nothing that is to come can be as bad as that, surely?

"What's up next?" I ask my brother, dabbing my top lip with a thin paper serviette. His brow creases slightly, and he looks as though he's about to tell me the cat's been run over.

"Abalone and sea cucumber," he says. My parents exchange glances and I decide there and then that should my other brother marry a Chinese girl (he did), I was already busy for their engagement banquet.

Things improve after the abalone, though. Each course is less alarming than the previous, and rice wine is passed around, which certainly helps as far as my father is concerned. My mother is chatting to Kam about wedding plans and Simon is happily stewing in the wine, leaning back on his chair and smiling benignly at everyone. Kam's brothers eat with relish, so much so that I have to look away. It's payback for my eating-the-egg-wrong misdemeanour.

"Would you like to see the farm?" Kam asks us. We would, grateful to walk off some of the unusual contents of our bellies. We push our chairs in and thank Kam's mother effusively, my father rubbing his stomach and making appreciative noises, which embarrasses my mother. I smile and nod at her, repeating the Cantonese words doh-cher and ho-sik, even though I know she speaks a different dialect. Twelve years and that's pretty much all I can offer.

As we step out onto the terrace, two medium-sized, chunky dogs, their tails curled up over their backs, move towards us. They are typical of the wild dogs that roam around the New Territories, but these are well fed and semi-tame. Kam's brother barks something urgent at them and they step back, looking sullen, then follow us as we head down a roughly made narrow concrete path towards a large pond. I'm not sure why there is a pond or why we are being shown it. This whole place feels a lifetime away from the cool-aired plazas of Central and Tsim Sha Tsui I usually inhabit at weekends. Everyone is playing Chinese whispers again, but I'm trying to make friends with the dogs. They keep trotting within a few feet of me, stopping, then jumping away like I've shooed them, which I haven't.

Eventually, we move away from the pond, me still none the wiser about it, and head towards the stinking pig sheds. There are grunting noises of all pitches coming from within, overlaid every now and again by blasts of urgent piggy shrieks. We are still traversing the narrow path, which keeps us just a few inches above the foul-smelling mud spread out like milk chocolate butter cream beneath us.

The smell inside the pig shed is unholy. My mother has dispensed with all etiquette now and has her hand clamped like an oxygen mask over her mouth and nose. She looks like she's going to be sick. The surprisingly enormous pigs lie on top of metal rails in narrow pens, bloated and immobilised. Many of them have a litter of piglets, which occupy an adjacent stall. They are given the luxury of a concrete floor and some hay. They can reach the teats of the mother through the bars and some of them are feeding, while others tussle around like puppies in the straw. This is all too real for me. I'm concerned for the poor mothers — they can't even stand. Kam's father is explaining again, and my father has adopted his army stance — chin in one hand, the other arm folded across his abdomen supporting his bent elbow, leaning back slightly from the waist, his weight all in one leg, the other bent a little. I've seen this posture a hundred times at family gatherings, parties. He's really *trying*. If I had waited to hear Kam's translation, I'd have heard that the mothers have to be separated from the piglets for a short time, otherwise they will crush them, or, horror of horrors, eat them. But I turn and walk straight through the shed and out of the door at the other end, looking for the dogs.

Later that evening, back home on the fourteenth floor of our Tsim Sha Tsui flat, we slump into wicker-framed furniture and watch telly. Simon has claimed top spot — the revolving, bowl-shaped chair, closest to the set. It swallows him up, the overly stuffed cushions blocking all but the tip of his nose from the rest of us crowded onto the corner sofa. He is almost, but not quite, subsumed. Our cats, loud and rangy, spread themselves long over the parquet flooring by the open balcony doors, like two black and white draft excluders.

We are watching the news. Most of the coverage is focused on political protests in China. Flickering images showing crowds of young men holding hastily made flags and banners. Scraps of red and white material displaying black calligraphy fluttering over scores of heads. I have no idea what the slogans say, and the newsreader's droning voice, like a low-flying plane, never manages to cut through my apathy. I'm too busy thinking about what I'll wear to Joe Banana's on Saturday night, and whether we have any Cheez Ums or BBQ crisps in the cupboard. I'm trying to listen, but I keep thinking about the pigs, and up here in our twilight filled flat, with the neon rainbow lights of Kowloon and Hong Kong framed in our balcony doors, it's difficult to focus. I'm aware, dimly, that there is an emotion shared among the people of the place I call home, the place I have grown and developed in, that I have not bothered to understand and am in no way part of. Somehow, I am submerged and removed at the same time. My mother asks if anyone wants something from the fridge, and I unfold my legs from beneath me and trail after her into the kitchen, looking for Cheez Ums and a carton of lemon tea.

We didn't know it at the time, but within three months my parents and I would leave Hong Kong for good. After a lifetime of travel, my parents would settle into a quiet routine in the Hampshire countryside. They at least adhered to the romanticised version of English life we had all adopted. I would accept a hum-drum job on a gloomy industrial estate, sending my body to work while my head stayed in the clouds, all the while nurturing the suspicion that I had somehow, somewhere, missed my turn.

My brothers would stay on in Hong Kong, Simon squeezing our wicker furniture into his cozy marital home deep in the New Territories, along with our two cats. It was a short-lived displacement for them. Their pampered indoor lives had in no way prepared them for the roaming packs of angry-mouthed village dogs. They barely lasted three months.

Simon and Kam would go on to have a daughter, a placid

thing with the kind of beauty only Eurasian children possess. When she was born, Kam's family told them never mind, next time they would be blessed with a son, but they never had another child. A part of me would forever feel that I was in some way responsible. I'd eaten my symbolic sticky egg, but as with so many things in my unreal expat life, I had been looking in a different direction, and entirely missed the significance.

Memories of Government House

Clinton Leeks

A colonial government house is a strange beast. We all know what a house is, whether it's a "two-up-two-down" with an outside privy, or a rather bigger affair like, say, Castle Howard, the TV setting for *Brideshead Revisited*. We may even think we know what a colonial government house is, if we've seen, say, the film *Viceroy's House* with the Mountbattens and thousands of servants and soldiers all clubbing together in Delhi to decide how to carve up a subcontinent.

But it's actually a bit more complicated than that. Rather like those Russian babushka nested dolls, a government house plays several key but different roles, one laid inside another inside another, as it were.

First, it is a ceremonial building. It represents the governing power in the land. Hence, in Hong Kong's case, there are the beautiful gardens, sentries, flagpoles, the tower added by the Japanese occupiers in World War II (our government house had always been a bit of a mongrel) and the nice big ballroom for grand formal events like concerts and investitures. Even the tennis courts were added, it was rumoured, so the Governor could make a swift aerial getaway should the natives turn really shitty: shades of Saigon in 1975.

Second, it is a home—for the Governor and his wife, or even their family. They have to live there, as normally as possible, with some privacy. And occasionally they'll even have guests to stay.

Third, and here's the catch, it is a political office, in other words, a department of the Hong Kong Government. The office is there to carry out the instructions of the Governor. A stream of paper (not email, back in my day) came into Government House, was processed by the office, often needed the Governor's approval quickly and then went out again. Most of this paper went "up and down the hill" between the house on Upper Albert Road and the Government Secretariat on Lower Albert Road. With a strong arm and not too much interest in document security one could have thrown the offending document, tied to a helpful stone, from the Government House verandah and into the office window of some unlucky civil servant snoozing quietly in the offices below, but no, it (without the stone, sadly) went by van, of course. Some might feel the overall layout was rather like that in Hitchcock's *Psycho*, with the rooms of the motel down below at street level as the business end of the enterprise and the owners up in their old gothic house above. Just as a metaphor, you understand. Though, come to think of it, one Governor was nicknamed Mac the Knife.

And because it was a political office, supporting the head of the government and acting as part of the umbilical between the colony and its mother ship 6,000 miles away, there were all the paraphernalia of proper government—security, procedures, communications, cars and so on.

And just to complete the confusion, sometimes the guests who came to stay were very important, with their own political jobs to do. Such as the Governor's boss, the Foreign and Commonwealth Secretary, or a British ambassador from somewhere nearby and allegedly civilised. Then, mercifully, we had a second office, which they (and any hangers-on they'd brought along) could use, too.

So, what did all this mean? Well, being it was and we were

British, it meant a mess. But being a British mess, we somehow always got through it more or less intact, surmounting every crisis at five minutes to midnight and with our fragile sanity sort of preserved. (There were some staff who eventually left Government House for new pastures, showing clear signs of premature dementia, but one always felt that that merely strengthened their qualifications for their next posting.) But first, the layout of Government House.

The main rooms
There was of course the Governor's study, reached by a long walk from the front hall (it was in the front hall that Admiral Harcourt took the Japanese Garrison's surrender in September 1945). It was a large room, though closely overlooked after 1989 by IM Pei's new Bank of China building with its chopstick aerials, which must have complicated things if anyone there had a telescope. The study had a long cabinet-style table where the Governor chaired his Friday meetings with the government policy branch secretaries.

Beside the study was the private office where the political staff worked, under the feeble guidance of a private secretary. There was a police aide-de-camp, or ADC, for ceremonial stuff, a personal assistant for the Governor's letters and appointments, and a very pretty assistant private secretary. And there was a walk-in safe, and a huge white board, of which more below.

There were separate offices adjacent for the social secretary and the housekeeper. And a hugely long old-style male row of urinals and WCs, such as would have graced the old Foreign Correspondents Club. There must have been a ladies' WC too. And the Governor had his own private loo ensuite in his study — for such are the emblems of true power in public service.

There was, as I've said, a second duplicate private office in the basement for any visiting bigwigs.

Then, of course, there was a large reception room, a dining room, a spectacular ballroom, umpteen bedrooms upstairs and the government cypher and communications team, and house switchboard, in the basement. Lots of outbuildings, staff quarters and garages. And a gorgeous garden.

The colonial mess

"Mess" is a wonderful English word, because it means so many things. It is significant that a favourite British pudding is allegedly an "Eton Mess", Eton having provided twenty percent of our (often worst) British Prime Ministers over the past 300 years. And messes are what we sometimes had, largely through the different roles Government House had to perform, all at the same time. A few examples:

Politics is about "being in the room". This gets harder when the room you want to be in is inside someone else's (very ornate) house. I always remember a certain Financial Secretary who went off on leave, so missing a crucial Government House chat that decided we needed a new airport, and fast. He returned from leave looking suitably bronzed but also some HK$200 billion poorer, as he was the one who'd have to find the money for it. Or the British ambassador who left Government House one evening for drinks with his old rugby mates, returning in the wee hours to find over breakfast that Sino-British relations over Hong Kong's future had mysteriously taken a giant but inconvenient leap in his hazy absence.

There were odd guests, too. The revered BBC foreign correspondent who came to cocktails paralytically drunk, passed out as he entered the reception room and was quietly picked up, put in a Government House car and driven off home. Henry Kissinger, whom I expected to "talk China", was especially proud to show the Governor a fine pair of brogues he had just bought in the Mandarin Arcade. Or the member of the House of Lords who accepted a cup of tea from the Governor, examined it suspiciously and at length, and then stirred it with the biro with which he was writing copious notes. Or the tiresome MP who absolutely insisted at the height of Hong Kong's 1989 crisis that his particular rank required that the Governor give him a private audience on a Saturday afternoon. Or the head of the government think tank who used to regularly pop in, pour bucket loads of flattery over us all and then ask to see the Governor. I amiably asked him to stop all the flattering, saying I knew him too well. He grinned and said, "Clinton, I always shovel it on with a trowel. And when I see the growing sense of pain in their eyes... then I shovel it on some more."

Conversely, some wonderful guests passed through. Their Royal Highnesses, the Prince and Princess of Wales, on the way to HM Yacht Britannia, and sadly in due course to the divorce courts. For an impressionable young man, once you gazed up into her face (and you did gaze up, as she was a tall lady) you never forgot — and indeed, probably never again washed the hand that had lightly shaken hers. Or there were the two nubile daughters of the King of Bhutan who came to stay. They would occasionally saunter through the Private Office. The aide-de-camp's head was invariably seen to hit his desk on such occasions.

Or there was the mysterious business card that was discovered in the porch way one morning. It belonged to a visiting French diplomat by the look of it, as he had also written his name and current hotel in the visitors' book. The right-hand end of the card was neatly folded over, about one-eighth of an inch. An investigation was at once launched — was it a coded signal? A declaration of war? A threat of assassination? The French were capable of anything. The Director of Protocol was summoned, and tasked to investigate. It turned out that in the faded genteel world pre-World War II, leaving such a card meant, "I have called to pay my respects. If you wish to meet me, I have left my contact details."

How wonderfully and delightfully old-fashioned. You read it here first.

And communications were slightly chaotic. The domestic staff wheeled files and letters around Government House on ornate trolleys, such as you'd otherwise see bringing you lunch at the Mandarin Grill. And having got rid of the files, at noon sharp they'd reappear in the private office with the same trolley to offer pre-lunch drinks. Doubtless there was an era when all would have had a stiff G&T to keep away malaria. But by the late 1980s if the Governor was in it was usually just a refreshing Virgin Mary. But the treat lay beside it... a huge plate of cheese straws, in truth, the main consolation for working at Government House. To die for.

Communications raised other challenges beside the trolleys. The usual quota of card-carrying nutcases would ring the switchboard and ask to have the opportunity to advise the Governor directly on matters of state. We had one or two impersonators for the likes of Mrs Thatcher and Deng Xiaoping (neither very good ones). More troublesome was the anonymous character who kept speed-dialling Government House for days on end. We only found out because the Governor was at the weekend lodge at Fanling one day and tried to ring Government House but couldn't get through. Why? Because the operator was being driven mad by the endless ringing and had abandoned his post. The Governor was not amused...

So the massed ranks of the police force were told to track the nutcase down and nick him pronto. Which they duly did, and reported to the ADC, who in turn proudly reported to the Governor that this most dangerous of criminals had been apprehended, in a rare policing triumph. Returning to his desk, the ADC received an angry call from the switchboard that the calls had restarted. He rang the police station. "No, sir, we have him under arrest here."

"Where?" "He's in a cell. He asked for a telephone to call his solicitor. Oh... wait a minute." And yes, there he was, in his cell, ringing and re-ringing Government House. Sigh.

The Private Secretary had a link to the Governor's main telephone, so that he could listen in or take over the call once the Governor had finished. He also had an intercom to the Governor to be summoned or otherwise instructed to act. Sometimes it didn't work so well. The late Sir YK Pao rang up one Saturday morning, excited that as Dragonair Chairman he had done a deal with Cathay that Beijing had blessed and which would simultaneously solve a Sino-British standoff over air service links between Hong Kong and the PRC and between Beijing and London. Air services are to the uninitiated (i.e., me) the equivalent of understanding the 19th Century Schleswig-Holstein question (if you understood it, you were either dead, or mad). And Sir YK had an amazing accent, which excitement merely turbo-charged. And while eavesdropping, I was simultaneously sorting out some other problem at my desk. Eventually, he rang off and the intercom buzzed. I assumed the Governor would tell me what on earth he had been saying. Instead, "Right. You got all that. Send an immediate telegram to London." Ah, well, up to a point, Lord Copper. So began a painstaking piece of detective work with the Economic Services Branch to piece together what YK ought to have said had I been listening, and what the air service problem we were allegedly solving actually was. All to be done by five minutes ago. Somehow with the help of the massed ranks of the government I found out and wrote a telegram that the Governor approved. At such times the Hong Kong Civil Service truly was a wonderful machine.

Then there were the uniforms. As I've said, Government House was part ceremonial and part hard work. All the domestic staff had nice smart winter black and summer white uniforms, both with nice red trim. The ADC had to wear his formal police dress uniform on special occasions. These two fountains of power, the ceremonial and the political, mingled ultimately in the person of His Excellency, the Governor. He had a whole walk-in wardrobe upstairs and a series of beautiful Gilbert and Sullivan uniforms required for every occasion, from investitures through parades to annual degree ceremonies at all the universities (he being chancellor of each of them). I actually had huge admiration for the way he coped with all this, given what else he had to remember while donning his sword, breeches, boots and ostrich feather hat. For some reason the Empire on Which the Sun Never Sets was also addicted to white, always an invitation to disaster. And it took a while to get kitted up – up to an hour. So a new and particularly thoughtful domestic decided to boot-black the leather of the Governor's sword belt and scabbard just before the Governor came in to kit up in his pristine colonial whites. Somehow the ADC spotted the servant's hands, which were covered in black polish, just as the Governor reached for the belt, sword and scabbard. As if tackling a hidden assassin, the ADC launched himself at the offending belt, and other accoutrements and seized them just before they came to rest against the white gubernatorial tunic and breeches. It was cleaned up and the domestic was led away quietly, gibbering on the cliff-edge of a spectacular nervous breakdown. For such was ever the nature of service in the house of the Queen's Representative.

The routine

"Events, Dear Boy, events," as Harold Macmillan may have said, which sort of kept us sane. Each day had to be properly planned, in roughly fifteen-minute segments. But that was simply to equip oneself for the unexpected... which invariably happened... and try to find time for the Governor and private office to deal with it. The famous white board held particular terror. The Governor's commitments as known for the day would mysteriously appear on it in advance, as if by magic—and by magic would sometimes change. A post-mortem would then take place as to where the new event came from and who was planning it—rather like a crime scene with a body found in an old country house. And we lacked a butler to blame. The same white board process in parallel took place for the good lady wife of the Governor, who quite rightly had her own official programme.

The other tyranny was the Government House safe, a walk-in job probably as big as a flat in some Mark 1 housing estates. All papers would go in there last thing in the evening before the Private Office closed up. It had an alarm inside, and a combination lock straight out of Ian Fleming. So, you triggered the alarm, walked out and set the combination, all within a short fixed time frame. I found out one evening what happened if you didn't. The huge safe door just would not close. As I wrestled with it eventually what seemed to be the whole riot squad from Central Police Station appeared at my office door. At this point I found I had earlier dropped a biro cap in the doorway gap, blocking the safe door. Job done. But I can't say the HK *Hawaii 5-0* team peering down at me were hugely impressed with my document security.

So what was the routine? Mondays were hell, as there was a weekend of telegrams to catch up on, then meet the Governor and agree how to handle them, then have weekly Monday "morning prayers" with the private office staff present, to plan the week. And all of that was by 9:30 a.m. At that time on a Monday the Chief Secretary and Financial Secretary would jointly meet the Governor in his study, to review HK politics and any imminent or very recent events and agree plans. As I have mentioned above, it was important for the Financial Secretary to be there as most plans inevitably involved spending money and he had to protect his (not exactly empty) piggy bank. He used to sometimes complain to me we were spending too much. I used to gently remind him he was grumbling to the wrong person.

Tuesdays were Exco days and a huge four-hour agenda for the Governor to chair his way through, a program which he'd had to digest fully the previous weekend.

Wednesday was Legco day. Until 1991, the Governor presided over Legco meetings which could go on for ten hours—I kid you not. And outside were plenty of people eager to tell lawmakers they were getting it wrong, such as the pig farmers who held a huge rowdy protest involving piglets and rural equipment surrounding the Governor's limousine in 1988. Legco could otherwise be appallingly dull. And as the President, the Governor was the only person in the chamber who could not fall asleep.

Thursdays were for outside visits to see stuff—the border, a new school or hospital, maybe a degree ceremony or a parade.

Friday mornings were for the Governor's weekly collective meeting with all the main branch heads, also known as the Governor's Security Committee. Quite a lot got done here, largely because it being Friday everyone was keen to get back to their office. They would gather nervously in the private office, awaiting the signal to go in. The more experienced ones would confidently sidle up to me to tell me a joke or ask what sort of mood the Governor was in. If I didn't like the one who was asking the question, I'd say sombrely that the Governor was in a foul mood and that they personally must be prepared to receive a total bollocking. The highpoint came one Friday when, while all were loitering, my beautiful assistant rose from behind her desk and went over to the photocopier. She was wearing a leather micro-skirt so far as I could discreetly tell. The whole overwhelmingly male audience fell dumb in reverence. Silence was broken only by the sound emanating from one branch secretary, who was addicted to identity bracelets and gold chains. He quivered at the sight of her, and all one could hear in the room was a lascivious tinkling noise. Government House briefly became a Swiss hillside.

Meetings did not always go well. It was decided Government House should host a farewell cup of tea to retiring heads of departments accompanied by their senior colleagues. People on the cusp of retiring seem to let themselves "go" somehow. The Governor at one such party reflected about the recent awful scenes of violence in Tiananmen Square on our TVs. The retiring head of department, a crusty old Scots expatriate, piped up, "Oh, I don't know. I was out here in 1956 doing national service with the army. We did far worse things when putting down the Double Tenth riots." He then proceeded to elaborate. The table fell wearily silent.

There were fewer of those retirement tea parties after that. But occasionally the truth would find its way out. One Friday the acting Attorney General came up to the usual morning meeting, a little nervous as he was standing in and had a lot to report about recent legal problems in Hong Kong. In a previous life he had sent me a humorously rude note about a presentation I had just finished giving to all heads of departments, including him. I had saved it. So as he nervously addressed the Governor and the whole room I arranged for a red folder labelled "Secret—Urgent" to be taken to him by a uniformed messenger. He apologised to the Governor and opened and read it immediately. All it said, in his own handwriting, was the very message he had passed to me years before. "Never heard so much shit in my life," it said. And that probably remains the best epitaph anywhere for the life of a long-suffering Hong Kong civil servant.

And then, finally there were Saturdays. A slightly more relaxed morning, clearing stuff "left over" from the week. Then at lunchtime, the Governor and his wife would head off to the weekend lodge at Fanling, and quiet would fall. Or even... they might stay the whole weekend there. Such weekends, in the quiet of a private office set in a very pretty and rather historical house like Government House, surrounded by beautiful gardens, were rather wonderful. For, despite all its complications and "events, Dear Boy, events" and despite Hong Kong's wider addiction to plate glass and steel modernity, Government House still remains the prettiest, most historical and in a way most magical building in the whole of Hong Kong.

AMANDA AND JANE
Amanda White

In September 1982, I'm in economy class, on my way to Hong Kong from Sydney. I'm smoking, as you do when you're an eighteen-year-old asthmatic (my good friend from school, Juliet, had convinced me at around age eleven that smoking menthol cigarettes was good for breathing difficulties). I'm taking a break after two terms at Sydney University, where I was studying science in order to become a civil engineer, just like my father. I hated the course, the lecturers (one of whom told me that "girls belong in arts"), the cliques, my lack of money and the overt sexism. My father, an inveterate drinker and (apparently) reformed womaniser had suggested I take a break and come and stay with him and his second wife in Hong Kong. He had moved there in 1977 to take up a big job with a global firm. With a level of impulse control I now realize is firmly embedded in the genes, at the age of 46 he had thrown away his highly paid job and decided to start a restaurant in Sai Kung, the (then) sleepy little Chinese fishing village that had become home to a certain type of expat. They moved out of the four-storey villa with pool in Tsam Chuk Wan and moved into a pokey little flat above the soon-to-be-restaurant, Ali Oli, overlooking Sai Kung's colorful square.

Due to boarding school, I had not lived with a parent for some time, and living in a small, chaotic flat with my brother and stepsister, both fifteen, stepmother, father (whose snoring shook the building's foundations) and an assortment of adored (by all of us) rescue animals, wore thin quite quickly.

The first order of business, therefore, was to get a job, the means to escape. I began working as a bartender in a local pub owned by a couple of dour Scots, Mike and Rob. It was only a few hundred metres from home, and with tips I was making some sort of living. I also learned some spectacular drinking games, including the Chinese game known as sahp-ngh yih-sahp, where my curated innocence allowed me to thrash opponents twice my age (the game is like a Chinese version of Scissors, Rock, Paper, only one must correctly guess the total number of fingers in order not to drink). After a while, I decided I needed extra shifts, and began working in an English-style pub in Tsim Sha Tsui, The Blacksmith's Arms.

December 1982

Making my way into TST each day, catching the MTR, walking through the crowded, neon-lit streets with all the strange smells Hong Kong had then felt truly exotic. Street food abounded, windows full of rows of cooked ducks, trays of all sorts of dried seafood, a random clothes market, a luxury watch shop a world away from a country girl's boarding school. The Blacksmith's Arms was somewhat incongruous, plonked in the middle. With its low ceiling, black wood interior, a permanent haze of smoke and a menu including Ploughman's Lunch and Steak and Kidney Pie, it felt like a bit of England.

I started my shift at 3:00 p.m., finishing at 2:00 a.m. for the grand rate of around US$1.80 per hour. The manager, Jimmy, a diminutive Chinese man in his forties who had no issue with skimming our tips (which we genuinely needed to survive) viewed breaks and meals as optional for the staff. I was "on the floor" waitressing, but quickly made friends with the bartender, Benny, a twenty-four-year-old Chinese with a smile that lit up the room. Benny looked after the waitresses, most of whom were gwei mois, and kept us supplied with drinks, snacks and cigarettes. The shifts were gruelling, running from table to table, keeping the punters' beer flowing, pretending to laugh at their sleazy jokes, all in cheap uncomfortable shoes that always led to aching feet.

It was at the Blacksmith's Arms that I first encountered another waitress, Jane, a twenty-three-year-old Brit. She was tiny, pale, and ethereally beautiful, with heavily lashed dark blue eyes and her dark hair cut very short, pixie style. She wore cool clothes and heavy makeup and spoke fluent Cantonese. I was in awe. I had been learning Cantonese and had giving directions, swearing and basic needs down pat, but she was in another league. We became firm friends, with me like a little sister to her. She took me under her wing, supervising my transformation from country bumpkin to cool city chick. She lived on San Miguel and cigarettes. I rarely witnessed her eating. Although only four years my senior, she seemed to have had an entire life. She was from Northern England where her parents ran a fish and chips shop. Jane was married at seventeen to the father of a family for whom she previously babysat. He had strange sexual needs and insisted his name be tattooed on her breasts, Christian name on one, surname on the other, encased in love hearts. At nineteen she had run off to Hong Kong with a Chinese man who worked in the murky world of casinos and then, to survive, I found out in time, became a prostitute.

January 1983
My father and his second family were becoming irritating. Regularly being at the receiving end of unwelcome lectures on smoking and drinking, I wanted to taste real independence ("I'm eighteen. I can do what I like!"). At Jane's behest, we moved

into a tiny flat in Tsuen Wan, right at the end of the MTR line, which was all we could afford. We were the only white people in the whole vast complex. Frankly, with her, *um*, supplemental income, she tended to subsidise me. I still think I'm possibly the only alumna from school who could add "pimp" to her résumé. My bedroom could only just accommodate a double mattress. The apartment was so high up, I remember it swaying in typhoons. We had rescued a kitten, Noodle, plucked mewling from a street bin, around three weeks old. When we weren't working in the pub, or out at other night spots, we were at home with Noodle, drinking San Miguel, smoking, watching videos like Michael Jackson's *Thriller* and nuclear horror, *The Day After*, and pondering how to better make ends meet.

Jane wasn't an obvious call girl. She had about four or five clients, all older Chinese men, late forties or fifties. They'd sometimes buy her things, like fancy brand handbags. But they'd mostly just take her out for dinner to some overpriced restaurant, then either take her to a hotel (or very occasionally to the flat), leaving her with around one or two thousand US dollars. This was an absolute fortune in my eyes. A few hours work for the same money I earned in more than a month. But I found the thought of it revolting.

Sometimes the men, with their friends, would ask her to bring a girlfriend. She assured me it was only to be company, strictly no sex required. In fact, she really never wanted me to do what she did; she was very clear about that, quite protective. I would turn up to dinner, laugh politely when required, then pocket a thousand dollars before peeling off back home to Noodle before whatever came next. I was frequently offered money to go further, but I had a boyfriend (Benny who didn't have a clue), and that extra step didn't sit well with me. The days after these outings, Jane and I would hit the shops, revelling in our new clothes and sipping cocktails in fancy bars, sometimes being sent bottles of champagne by men three times our age.

I frequently suggested to Jane that she try and give up the old men and learn some sort of trade, maybe secretarial school? She always scoffed. "That's not for me," she'd say, sipping her beer.

Despite finding this existence quite fascinating, I was getting a little worried about my future. I did not want to spend my life working in bars and definitely wanted to go back to university. I really wanted to study Chinese and was accepted into Hong Kong University, but by mid-1983 my father's restaurant adventure had cost him heavily and he was close to bankrupt. Supporting me was not an option. My mother back in Australia was lobbying for my return. Yet I couldn't quite see how to save the airfare.

August 1983

He seemed elderly, from my eighteen-year-old perspective. Chinese, probably fifties, short of stature, and completely loaded. He'd sit at the bar, sipping on an over-priced brand-name whisky, gazing at me. He always bought me drinks, left ridiculously large tips (i.e., enough for me to dine out if manager Jimmy didn't see). For mercenary reasons, I paid special attention to him, practicing my Cantonese and batting my eyelashes. He told me I was "ho leng" and that he would like to take me out. In Australia, a place where blonde hair, blue eyes and a suntan were (and still are) the main hallmarks of beauty, I was considered passably attractive. (I had alabaster skin, auburn hair and green eyes.) In Hong Kong, I was regularly told I was beautiful, even stopped on the street. He was persistent about wanting to take me out, name-dropping the most fashionable restaurants, and bragging about his sway in them. My shifts didn't end until 1:00 am, so I had a plausible reason for declining.

Then one day, he placed a red leather box with gold embossing on the bar. "For you," he said. "But why?" I asked, knowing full well this was Step 1 on the way to the world's oldest profession. "Just a present," he said innocently.

Curiosity got the better of me, and I opened the box. And there it was, a gold Cartier Tank Watch. It cost what I made in six months.

My New England boarding school prudery prevailed, and with a heavy heart I told him I couldn't possibly accept. He persisted, but so did I. When he started to put the box back in his bag I almost relented, but I stayed the path.

There were many more men making such propositions in my time in Hong Kong, but not long after that incident, Jane and I hatched a plan.

"All these old geezers would pay anything to sleep with you," she said (or words to that effect). "So, you can either do that, or trick them into thinking I will do instead."

January 1984

I'm in his apartment. It's somewhere on The Peak, Hong Kong's most luxurious address. It is large, dimly lit, with heavy, expensive antique Chinese furniture. It has a wine cellar and a spectacular view of the harbor. I am very drunk. He is reclining on an intricately engraved day bed. I am perched beside him, attempting to drink more whisky to blot out the sight before me. He is caressing my face, telling me I am beautiful. I find him repulsive. He is at least forty-five years older than I. He is Chinese, has thinning hair, wrinkly hands, jowls that wobble, and shedloads of money. I am nineteen and can barely afford to eat, let alone pay Noodle's vet bills.

My brain shifts into gear, albeit drunkenly, and I remember the game I must play. I step back. "I can't do this, Lawrence. I'm a virgin," This clearly makes him more excited. "Really," I say, "I feel sick. Can you call me a taxi? I can come back another time."

He's not happy, but then he appears to remember something. "I have something for you." He hands me an envelope.

"I will give you five times that if you return as promised," he says, pleased with his own cunning.

I make my way out to the taxi (he had his own car and driver, but not for me).

I finally arrive back in Tsuen Wan. We crack a San Miguel and open the envelope. Fifteen thousand dollars. Enough for airfare, a shopping trip and dinner at a fabulous restaurant. Jane and I toast each other she laughingly said she'd never sleep with him, which she had promised him if he gave me, a poor virgin, enough money to get home.

Sadly, neither of us ever saw Lawrence again.

Sadder still, I have not seen Jane since.

Tales from a Barren Rock

Professor Dr. Judith Mackay

I was born in a seaside town in Yorkshire while the Second World War was at its peak, schooled in Yorkshire, then graduated in 1966 as a medical doctor at the University of Edinburgh. I then made an impulsive decision to marry Dr John Mackay, a Scottish doctor already working for 3 years in Hong Kong, who was in Edinburgh on study leave. From the moment I saw him, I knew he was the man I would marry. John, being a cautious Scot, took a few weeks to move to the same position. I moved to Hong Kong in 1967. My first project was to spend nine months learning Cantonese.

Professionally, I was shocked to be paid 75% of a male doctor's salary, leading to Hong Kong being blacklisted in the British Medical Journal. This outraged me and led to a lifelong commitment to feminism.

From 1970 I worked 3 years in research on growth in Chinese children, involving home visits to families living in the old Kowloon Walled City, where I found nothing but courtesy and welcome. The study led to a change of weaning habits by introducing an alternative source of protein, which is why I am no longer taller than the local population on the MTR... I often muse 'if you only knew...'

I then worked at Queen Mary Hospital followed by the United Christian Hospital in Kwun Tong. The latter was then the only hospital serving a population of about three quarters of a million people, many living in the hillside squatter huts or in the early resettlement blocks. In the 1970s, many arrived at the hospital barefoot.

We had a maxim on our medical wards that we never admitted a non-smoker. Our male medical wards were full of patients admitted with tobacco-related illnesses—cancer, heart disease, lung disease—often at an incurable, end-stage. So, after 8 years at the UCH, I came to realise that health in Hong Kong would never be improved by curative medicine, only by preventive health. Time to move on.

I became active in public health education, wrote a weekly column for three years for the South China Morning Post on women's health, and appeared on television and radio programmes. I covered all manner of topics from cancer to mental health, from ageing to tobacco. When I suggested on RTHK that women were unfamiliar with their bodies and encouraged them to buy a hand mirror to look at their genitals, there was a report in the SCMP the next day that there had been a run on hand mirrors in HK!

Educating the public, especially women, was not well received by my own profession. I received personal threats from fellow doctors, with statements such as 'Beware. You have enemies in high places.' The doctors' disciplinary body, the Hong Kong Medical Council tried to silence me. I took the case all the way to the Appeals Court, won with a unanimous verdict and was awarded costs—the first time the courts had over-turned a verdict by the Medical Council in Hong Kong. But it took two years of my life and enormous stress to fight the case.

Women's issues

In 1985 I published the first survey on wife battering in Hong Kong (and in Asia), which found the pattern similar to the West. I then chaired the committee to set up the first refuge in Asia for battered women, Harmony House.

My interest in women and tobacco overlapped. I realised that smoking was a women's issue, in that the tobacco industry were advertising to women with promises of freedom and emancipation. When China asked me to help them organise the 10th World Conferences on Tobacco or Health in Beijing in 1997, I said I would do so on one condition—gender equity, in practice meaning equal men and women as plenary speakers, chairpersons and on committees. It worked. Since then, all World Conferences have adopted the principle of gender equity.

Few 'expatriate wives' worked for economic gain in Hong Kong in the last century, and there was hurtful criticism of me 'abandoning husband, family and home.' One prominent European male architect twisted a chain I was wearing around my neck at an event in the Hong Kong Club, lifting me off the ground to the extent I could hardly breathe, gleefully saying "Women will never be equal to men as they are not as strong."

John, remarkably for a man of his generation and upbringing, took my conversion to feminism calmly in his stride, and has never ceased to be supportive (and to make me laugh).

Tobacco

The final straw precipitating my change from curative medicine to prevention came from the tobacco industry itself, when they labelled me as 'entirely unrepresentative and unaccountable.' I was outraged.

Thus, since 1984, I have worked in tobacco control in most of the countries in the Asia-Pacific Region, and many in the Middle East. I work with every type of jurisdiction—kingdoms, communist states, and democracies. Surprisingly, my work is very similar irrespective of population, government or GDP. It is the same product, the same harm, the same obstacles (particularly the same tobacco industry), and the same actions that need to be taken.

One early success was in 1987 when I was instrumental in advising the Hong Kong government to ban the importation, manufacture and sale of smokeless tobacco: HK became only the second jurisdiction in the world to do so, in the face of considerable pressure from the US government.

Another success was when I gave evidence on behalf of the Thai government to a US Congressional Committee, upholding the right of the Thai Government to ban advertising of US cigarettes. When I arrived, the Immigration Officer didn't even bother to ask me why I had travelled to the USA — he said to me 'We know very well why you are here in the US,' which I found a bit chilling.

I became the first Executive Director of The Hong Kong Council on Smoking or Health (COSH) set up by Government in 1987, then left in 1989 to set up my own Asian Consultancy on Tobacco Control.

It was all-out war. The prospect of converting huge populations of existing Asian male smokers smoking local cigarettes to their product, plus inducing Asian women to start smoking, led a tobacco industry executive in 1998 to say *"You know what we want? We want Asia."* They thought they could gallop their Marlboro horse into Asia and it was theirs for the taking. But I was determined to stop them.

The tobacco industry and its supporters publicly threatened me with lawsuits, vilified me with names likening me to Hitler or a jihadist, and sent death threats. It got so bad that Geoffrey Barnes, 班乃信, then Secretary for Security in the HK Government offered me 24-hour police protection, which I refused. He then said that he would 'let it be known down the line" that if anything happened to me, the government would instigate a police enquiry. Since those early, lonely days, there has now been a sea-change in that tobacco control has become mainstream public health.

Hong Kong exemplified the 'Scream Test' when E-cigarettes and other new products were banned in 2022. One veteran legislator told me he had never seen such lobbying on any topic before. The Health Minister was smeared on all fronts.

Internationally, probably my biggest achievement was to instigate an internationally-binding convention on tobacco control. WHO's 'Framework Convention on Tobacco Control' (FCTC), entered into force in 2005, and is now ratified by 182 nations (including China, Hong Kong and Macau), making it one of the fastest track United Nations treaties of all time. Needless to say, it was bitterly opposed by the tobacco industry.

In the course of my work, I have been held to ransom in a cave in Halong Bay in Vietnam, held at gunpoint by Presidential guards in Mongolia, almost blown up with an ammunitions cache in Cambodia, but enjoyed the magic of seeing the Great Wall of China with no other person on it, the extraordinary event of being in China when Mao died, invited to North Korea, and meeting Kings, Queens, Empresses and Presidents.

It has been hard work, authoring a dozen health atlases, 300 papers, 600 lectures, and mentoring the next generation of tobacco control advocates.

I have been privileged to receive many awards ranging from the TIME 100 to the Hong Kong Silver Bauhinia Star. One of my most treasured awards comes from the tobacco industry itself which named me as 'one of the three most dangerous people in the world'.

Hong Kong is my home

We moved 'out of town' in 1971, after we received notification of a rental increase of HK$100 per month on our rented flat in

Kowloon. The same day we bought an old colonial bungalow on Clear Water Bay Road.

In 1971 it was pioneering stuff—only one other expat family in the area; we had to pump well water; the electricity supply often failed; many illegal immigrants ('IIs') trooped through the garden en route to south of Boundary Street in the 'touch base' policy; the single-access Clear Water Bay Road was often blocked for days by landslides in the worst typhoons, and our HK-side friends regarded visiting us as a major expedition into the deep unknown.

It turned out to be the second-best decision of my life. Our home has been a delight and an oasis for our whole family.

BENEVOLENT OR BARKING MAD

Jill Robinson

"You want to do what?" were the exasperated replies when I asked if they'd like a dog to visit and cheer up their patients in hospital wards, before the phone was cut off. Call after call followed to multiple hospitals, homes for the elderly and centers for the disabled, with the offer of providing "therapy" firmly rejected, until the matron of the Duchess of Kent Children's Hospital in Pok Fu Lam thought for a second before saying, "I've heard of animal therapy. You can have one hour, in the garden, with one dog."

After multiple rejections, it was a relief to have someone who realized that a therapy visit wasn't what some were thinking: bringing a dirty, smelly, unhygienic mutt into a sterile hospital environment and putting all the patients at risk, but instead providing a furry, much-loved companion who was more than guaranteed to put a smile on the faces of those who needed a very best friend.

And so, on a bright August day in 1991, with my old golden retriever Max plodding into the hospital grounds, I waited nervously for the nurses to lead out the young patients in their wheelchairs or beds.

Their smiles said it all, and the children confidently approached Max whose wise "counsel" and paw shakes were just what they needed. They brushed him and stroked him and gave him more treats than were good for him, and shyly smiled for pictures for a photographer from the South China Morning Post.

As Max patiently allowed them to bandage his paws as their own limbs were bandaged, I could see a nurse coming towards us wheeling a paraplegic boy in his bed. Without hesitation, Max walked over to the boy's bed, placed his huge golden paws onto the mattress as the boy's face lit up for Hong Kong, and Dr Dog was born.

That was all it took, one boy and one dog with a cold nose and a wagging tail. Just what the doctor ordered.

The next day, the picture and story in the SCMP told a different tale (tail?) than that of the past few weeks, and I couldn't answer the phone quickly enough as calls flooded in from people wanting to volunteer their dogs for this unique programme, or from hospitals and homes requesting a visit from the new canine doctors in town.

Dr Dog soon had well over a thousand dogs in the programme, some going on to flourish in mainland China, the Philippines, India, Malaysia, Japan and Taiwan. Everywhere, it was the same story as children clamoured to meet their furry friends, the elderly saved up their breakfast dim sum for treats, and doctors and nurses spoke warmly about the non-judgmental animals benefitting their patients and bringing unconditional love into their lives.

Some years later institutions such as City University would ask for visits, especially during exam times, so that the dogs could help to reduce pre- and post-examination nerves. They put no restrictions on the dogs at all and simply said they and the volunteers could go anywhere on campus they chose. There was obviously more to this than just seeing calmer students, considering that Hong Kong sadly sees quite a number of young suicides during this stressful time. Once again, dogs were proving their worth in society and showing the community how much more valuable they were than food.

Following the success of Dr Dog, it wasn't long before Professor Paws was born. Inspired by our then Education Director and now Board Chairperson Anneleise Smillie (daughter of long-standing Hong Kong vet and animal behaviourist Dr Cynthia Smillie), Professor Paws launched into schools rather than hospitals. His mission was and is to encourage children to enhance their reading abilities. Here, kids with reading problems simply read to the dogs. As much as it sounds a simplistic programme, the reality is anything but, as the reading material contains sound advice such as how to look after your own dog (or cat), how to approach dogs safely if you're not an animal owner, and wider lessons for protecting the environment and enhancing animal welfare.

This was a first in Hong Kong and another programme seen initially as novel and even a little risky. While scientific papers abound in the West confirming such initiatives work (and prove children with reading issues are far less embarrassed to read to a dog than a teacher), it took a while for the teachers and schools here to be convinced. However, the reaction from the students said more about the pilot programme than anything, and teachers realized dogs really were the cutting edge in the enhancement of language skills. It didn't even matter if the dogs fell asleep, we simply said that Professor Paws was just resting his eyes and the students were happy with this little white lie.

The dogs themselves, of course, need to be "bomb proof" for this programme and naturally for Dr Dog too. I want to pay enormous tribute to both the dogs and their remarkable owners, many of whom have been with us for years, ensuring the programmes run successfully and incident free. Only one "indiscretion" has occurred since both programmes began—at the paws of Hong Kong Governor Chris Patten's dogs, Whisky and Soda, who were inspired to join by the Governor's wife, Lavender. Even then, the incident occurred in the grounds of Government House when the over-exuberant terriers thought it a good idea to chase and nip the ankles of an unfortunate trader, rather than perform their solemn duty as therapists.

Now in its eighteenth year and headed by our Education Manager Karina O'Carrol, together with Marnie Yau and Cassy Mak, Professor Paws has also made it successfully to mainland China and has significantly boosted our pioneering programme there, "Friends... or Food".

While dog eating has been illegal in Hong Kong since 1950, of course, in China the consumption of dogs and cats has fallen into a very gray area indeed.

Since arriving in Hong Kong in 1985 and going on to document the trade in dogs and cats almost immediately, I've lost count of the number of foul live-animal markets visited in the time since.

The story is always the same. A melting pot of misery and disease, with trucks arriving from early morning to late at night carrying the stolen or stray victims of the trade. Cages stacked sometimes eight or nine high, and each crammed with up to six or eight dogs, the scene is out of the worst horror film imaginable.

It takes patience and a strong stomach to take pictures of such horrible scenes, and I've never left a market yet without crying behind the lens and apologising to every dog or cat as the shutter clicks. Once the trucks arrive at the market, the bartering and weighing begins, with traders pitching up to buy the "livestock" just arrived. The cages are hurled to the cement ground, with the animals inside screaming in agony as paws and tails and limbs are crushed. Sometimes the traders place large rubber tyres on the floor to lessen the impact, but even then the cages often bounce off the tyres and crash onto the ground with a sickening thud and howls of pain.

The slaughter is unbelievably cruel, too. The dogs are dragged out of their transport cages and placed into holding pens, looking miserably at bowls containing revolting and often rotting rice gruel, simply there to keep them alive over the next few days. When their time comes, they're grabbed by long metal pincers around the throat, with their heads forced through the bars as another "operant" swings a wooden bat hard onto their skulls. On one visit, co-worker Annie and I begged the trader to kill the dogs as, one by one, they woke into consciousness again, lifted their heads with blood and saliva pouring from noses and mouths and howled.

Often walking around the markets we've seen terrible sights such as mothers aborting their puppies and new-borns being picked up by heartless traders and tossed to cages of ravenous dogs. Passing by a cage one day I saw two new-born pups on the floor, still alive, and made a promise to the mother that while her fate was sealed, I'd try and save her young. I walked out of the market holding them in a safe and warm place, under my armpit, and we drove like crazy to a local vet we knew in Guangzhou. Tragically, despite the best attempts of Dr John to keep them alive, neither pup made it. They became two more victims of the trade.

In later years, it became too dangerous for me to join our China team on these visits, as the presence of a foreigner could only signal that an investigation was happening, and the traders would be furious with our Chinese colleagues for "betraying their own". Even then, the investigations grew riskier for our brave Cat and Dog Welfare Director Suki and team, and their visits would disguise hidden cameras and audio equipment, ever nervous they'd be exposed.

Sometimes throughout the years of continuing these investigations we would rescue several dogs as our "ambassadors", quickly realising that few of those saved would make the grade as therapists considering their understandable and chronic fear of people.

One dog that did pass the test, just, was Eddie. Excerpts from my blog after he died in 2014 give an overview of his life and the joy that he brought, not to mention that he was the most appalling "ambassador" for his species.

One lick of the hand saved his life. Gail Cochrane, our founding member and then Veterinary Director, and I were in the notorious live animal market in Guangzhou, in the south of China, one memorable day in March 2001 and decided at the end of a horrible few hours of taking photos of caged and terrified "meat dogs" to save just one.

I'd been stroking the muzzle of a black dog who obviously had distemper, with green mucus pouring from her nose. Gail sensibly steered me away from the poor soul that would never have made it through the day, never mind through quarantine, and introduced me to a scruffy terrier-type dog I would fall in love with at first sight.

All around him dogs were barking and crying, sensing their fate, but it seemed that this dog had other ideas and simply lay there quietly and calmly, licked Gail's and my hands whenever we gave him a stroke. After a few minutes of bartering with the trader, the dog was ours for one hundred RMB and was hauled unceremoniously from his cage by the scruff of his neck, before I grabbed him from the man. We walked out of the market, together with the luckiest dog in the world.

The safest place for him while we were arranging for the papers to bring him to Hong Kong was the very first bear sanctuary we had built in the mid-1990s near the ferry port of Pan Yu. Arriving in the car at the sanctuary, we were met by some visitors who had come to see the bears and who crowded around in their enthusiasm to see a dog who had escaped the cooking pot and made it alive from the market. A supporter called Ruth was absolutely lovely, but had a terrible sense of humor which emerged in all its glory when she said I should simply name the dog Eddie as in edible. Despite the black humor, the name suited him, and after miles of red tape and months of quarantine in Hong Kong, I was delighted to welcome Eddie home with the family at last.

Eddie quickly settled in and, despite his diminutive size, quickly became the pack leader with everything on his terms. We used to roll our eyes in mock exasperation whenever Eddie was up to one of his tricks. One of his favourites was to simply bark at nothing which set off the other eight dogs that would bark loudly in unison while Eddie happily wandered off, satisfied with all the chaos he'd caused. His best friend then was Big, a rescued Newfoundland about six times his size. The two of them were inseparable, and Big would obediently wait his turn until Eddie had finished scrounging all the treats, never once minding that his small pal with the big attitude had stolen everyone's share.

Because of his market background and featuring in our "Friends...or Food" campaign, Eddie quickly became our Dr Dog Ambassador, though in truth he was the worst canine doctor in the world. Every hospital visit saw him either relieving himself against potted plants or stubbornly sitting on the floor and refusing to budge and offer the unique animal therapy we'd promised the bemused hospital staff. A master of escape, too, he could put Houdini to shame as he wriggled out of the tightest collar or harness, before heading off towards the doors when he'd decided that he'd had enough adoration for one day. Such was his disdain for behaving like our other very wonderful Dr Dog therapists, Eddie was given the nickname "King Eddie" by Marnie, Cassy and our very tolerant Dr Dog team.

One memorable day he was taken to a school by Anneleise, who proudly took to the stage to present a real live four-legged ambassador to a rapt young audience of about 1,000 kids, who were clamouring to hear all about our programmes to help Asia's dogs and cats. Predictably, Eddie had other ideas. Instead of behaving and endearing himself to a captive audience of potential animal advocates, Eddie went out in spectacular style by parking what could only be described as a large brown pancake on the stage, to the excruciating embarrassment of Anneleise, and the morbid delight of the kids who were already wrinkling up their noses and yelling out "gross". According to Anneleise, they later told their teachers that it was the best presentation they had ever seen.

Eddie lived on for another thirteen years, joining me at Dr Dog events where he would suffer a multitude of pats and strokes in return for anything edible he could sniff out from people's bags. Increasingly rotund as the years went on, Eddie was eventually referred to as "square" and likened to a coffee table. No matter the diet, the walks, the scolding for eating the cat food (and cat poo litter), Eddie's shape never changed, and I was resigned to owning a chubby and very opinionated dog.

But, oh, how I loved him. Every trip home would be greeted by Eddie bowling up to the gate and keeping my other dogs away (including in the most recent years, two huge, rescued Great Pyrenees), as he commandeered attention for at least the next couple of hours. I can never descend the stairs again without seeing him there and acknowledging that his mission in life was surely to see me trip and plunge to the bottom, as he devoted his days to running just inches in front and heading me off at each step.

Then suddenly, Eddie went off his food. It was as simple and as quick as that, with alarm bells ringing that I knew predicted something critical as I took him to the vet. There was Gail, still my vet today, together with her wonderful colleagues, Dr Seems and Dr Tiger, who relayed the news that Eddie had multiple problems and was clearly losing the fight for life.

Dr Seems was there at the end and, with friends Melody, Henry and I holding him in our arms and a hundred kisses duly delivered from my niece Nicole, Eddie slipped peacefully away.

The gap on the floor and in my heart is wider than I can ever describe. Eddie and I have been through a lifetime of pain and happiness together, and he's had more tears cried into his soft beige fur than I care to admit.

Eddie, I miss you and simply want to end this blog offering the most profound thank you for the years of joy and friendship and, in your unique and individual way, helping to pioneer and support a movement here in Asia that so unconditionally and so perfectly shows why dogs are our friends... not food.

That movement has continued to grow to this day, and I like to think the building blocks Animals Asia has meticulously been piecing together in China for decades finally helped lead to the ground-breaking decision in May 2020 by the authorities to remove dogs (and by default cats) from the official Livestock List. We saw one of our founding goals achieved, making it illegal now to sell dogs and cats for food.

While enforcement is critical as the industry "pushes back", the legal mechanism is there, as are the programmes that Animals Asia has been developing for years. Annual conferences are held for governmental and non-governmental groups to discuss key issues such as rabies, responsible dog management, shelter improvement, and so on. They demonstrate to the government that now-illegal dog theft is both responsible for social disharmony within the community and is the perfect vector for the countrywide transmission of rabies and other disease.

No government wants to see harmony disrupted or its people's lives put at risk in a country with the world's second highest incidence of rabies. Our years of investigations and proving the illegal components of the "black industry" finally provided the authorities with the evidence that would help them to make such a landmark decision countrywide.

This, together with our programmes of collaboration with over 200 non-governmental organisations we help across China, has seen their capacity-building strong and many of their shelters improving in day-to-day operation and funding, all prerequisites for showcasing their facilities to the public in both adoption and animal awareness. With Dr Dogs and Professor Paws, plus a multitude of local celebrity supporters flying the companion animal banner, now finally dogs and cats are more often recognised by the public at large as companions rather than lunch.

While this essay focuses on companion animal welfare, it would be remiss of me not to mention another of our founding programmes, ending bear bile farming in Asia, after a visit to a bile farm catapulted me from a life almost normal to one that changed overnight.

April 1993 and, after a call with a horrified journalist who had just returned from witnessing bile extracted from caged bears for use in traditional medicine, I grabbed friends Anna and Kylie and we joined a tour group in Zhuhai, to check out this practice for ourselves.

As we broke away from the tour group on the farm and walked downstairs into a basement where the bile bears were kept, we saw row upon row of Asiatic black bears (or moon bears after the lemon crescent of fur on their chest) who had been imprisoned for decades in coffin-sized cages, declawed, de-toothed and surgically mutilated for the precious bile their gall bladders contained. Tubes were surgically inserted into their gallbladders to make milking them easy.

Within each cage, I saw hopelessness and suffering that shocked me to my core. This dimly lit basement held 32 moon bears in cages that crippled their bodies and destroyed their minds. As they weaved repetitively to and fro in their "cage crazy" world, I could hear the thud, thud, thud of their heads against the bars of each cage, and the smell of blood, infection and feces made it hard not gag.

Reeling with shock at the sight of these "broken bears", I backed too closely to one of the cages and felt something suddenly touch my shoulder. As I turned around in fright, I saw a moon bear with her paw pushing through the bar of the cage, with her claws outstretched as if she was asking for me to take her paw. Stupidly I reached over and took her warm pad in my hand and, rather than hurting me as she had every right to do in that moment of fear and misery, she simply squeezed my fingers and held my tearful gaze with her soft brown eyes.

Several minutes later as I walked out of the farm I knew that I would never see her again, but I knew too that everything about my life had changed.

That one bear, I named Hong (bear in Cantonese), was responsible for Animals Asia being founded five years later in Hong Kong in 1998 together with my then-husband John, friends Gail, Boris and Winnie, and with encouragement from my great friend and mentor, actress and Born Free Founder Virginia McKenna. Our core remit was to both end bear-bile farming and the consumption of dogs and cats in China and Vietnam.

Today the industry of bear farming sees more than 10,000 moon bears, plus brown bears and sun bears, caged and mutilated for their bile used in traditional medicine across Asia, and sold illegally abroad.

For those sceptical about its usage, bear bile cannot be written off as a quack medicine but as something recognised by doctors for millennia for its curative effects as a "cold" medicine to treat "heat"- related disease. Bear bile contains an essential bile acid, ursodeoxycholic acid, or UDCA that helps with high fevers, red and sore eyes and chronic liver complaints in traditional medicine terms. But there are herbal alternatives with the same effect and they have been sold on the international market by the ton in Western medicine to cure liver and gall bladder problems, among other illnesses, for the past seventy years.

In short, no one is going to die for the lack of bear bile and, by working with traditional medicine practitioners, as we do in Vietnam, we can celebrate their belief today that the herbal alternatives are just as effective, and celebrate their promise too on behalf of an organisation 60,000 strong that they will never use or prescribe bile from farmed bears again.

Vietnam isn't stopping there and today the forestry government has joined with Animals Asia in signing a memorandum of understanding, pledging to end bear bile farming completely from 2022. With two award-winning sanctuaries in China and Vietnam, our challenge is to build a third sanctuary, now in Vietnam, to help the remaining 400 or so bears and commit to our promise of ending bear bile farming sensitively, with neither the government nor the farmers embarrassed or losing face.

Our Kindness in Action campaign cements our belief that ending a practice such as this with thoughtfulness, as much geared to the stakeholders as to the bears, will allow us to demonstrate more widely to other bear bile-farming countries in Asia that solutions can be found for all those invested in this trade.

Meanwhile, the sanctuaries themselves stand as beacons of kindness too. Having rescued more than 630 bears in both

Vietnam and China, we celebrate their lives of enjoying football pitch-sized grassy enclosures, complete with climbing frames, platforms and pools that see able bodied and disabled bears enjoying their choices and their days in the sun. Bears like Oliver who spent thirty years in a cage with no free access to food, water or the vital medication he required, was finally able to sleep in the clover or swim in his beloved swimming pool, free of physical and psychological pain and completely unware that grown men would be sobbing as they looked down at his strange disabled form from the roof of his house.

The many bears we've had the privilege of helping have seen visitors overwhelmed with the stoic nature and forgiveness of these bears, as "clowns" like Jasper photobombed every journalist's attempt to feature another hero bear and deliberately walked into the frame. Jasper had survived being flattened to the bars of a "crush cage" for 15 years of his life. Dear three-legged Andrew, with his front limb missing from having been illegally caught in the wild, gently tolerates the younger bears leaping all over his frame, oblivious to the fact that the female bears adored this Brad Pitt of the bear world. Or sweet Zebedee with his joyous love of life, but his strangely disfigured face, after living in a dark kitchen in Vietnam and suffering a wooden plank being smashed over his head.

Every bear tells a story, and every one a hero who inspires the end of the industry, while showing the world that the only cure... is kindness.

Desperation and Deliverance

Stuart McDouall

Just after 1:00 a.m. on 17 March 2006, an off-duty police constable, Tsui Po-ko, attacked two uniformed police constables who were on beat patrol. In the ensuing gunfight Tsui was shot dead but not before he had killed Constable Tsang Kwok-hang and seriously wounded Constable Sin Ka-keung, using a stolen and rusty police issue .38 revolver.

Earlier, at around 2300 hrs on March 16, Constable Sin Ka-keung, 30, with twelve years in the force, had reported for night duty (mid-night to 0800 hrs) at Tsim Sha Tsui police station. In the barracks assigned to his patrol unit he changed into his washed and pressed police uniform, buckling on his webbing belt with water bottle, torch and short baton. He joined the queue outside the station armoury to sign out his equipment, a revolver and twelve rounds of pepper spray, handcuffs and beat radio. After that he took a seat in the briefing room with his colleagues. Shortly after 2330 briefing, Sin (pronounced "seen") was assigned 33-year-old Constable Tsang Kwok-hang as his patrol partner and they were given their beat number.

Tsang, three years older and with three more years of service than Sin, was a newcomer to Yau-Tsim District. Sin, therefore, was told to plan their beat patrol routing. Once on beat, he was talking Tsang through the locality they were in, pointing out matters of policing interest, the night life going on around them and relating incidents that he had previously encountered.

At 0114 hrs, Sin led the way down a well-lighted pedestrian underpass near the YMCA. He thought it was deserted until he spotted a man standing against a corner, suspiciously. Sin and Tsang decided to question him. As they had been trained, Tsang dropped a couple of paces behind Sin, ready to cover his approach. From just a couple of feet away, Sin asked the man to identify himself. In Hong Kong, it is the law that every citizen must have an identity card and should carry it when away from home. Sin watched the man put his left hand into the bag hanging from his shoulder, assuming that he was going to fish out his ID card. He watched him grip something and then, in a sudden motion, the man drew a gun and, aiming directly at Sin's face, almost at point-blank range, fired. Sin lived.

The sequence of events from that point is unclear. There was no CCTV coverage of the pedestrian underpass and Sin is the only living witness as to how the drama unfolded: who fired, when and at whom? Sin's recollection after that first shot is, understandably, confused and vague. However, a reasonable reconstruction has it that, having shot Sin, the assailant turned his gun on Tsang and fired again, hitting him twice, in the neck and leg. In that second Sin managed to grasp the man's gunhand. A violent struggle ensued with a shot fired, hitting Sin in his left foot. Sin disengaged, taking out his own revolver. The assailant tried to wrest Sin's gun off him, and two bullets were fired. At that moment Tsang, mortally wounded, was able to return fire, shooting the assailant dead with five rounds in quick succession. Sin reached for his beat radio and pressed the alarm button, the last thing he did before losing consciousness.

Police emergency crews quickly secured the location, administered first aid and assisted the ambulance men in getting the injured to hospital. Tsang died of his wounds and Sin spent the next seventy-one days in hospital, undergoing several operations. That first bullet entered his head beside his nose and exited through his right ear causing extensive injuries to his ear, his right eye and his teeth. The nerves were so badly damaged that surgeons thought his face would be permanently paralysed but, in the end, they saved him virtually intact. The wounds in his left foot have healed too, but Sin still feels pain. Tsang posthumously and Sin were awarded the police medal for bravery.

The newspapers, TV and radio channels were full of the atrocity and, as the police investigation went on, snippets were released to the press, most significantly that the assailant, identified as one Tsui Po-ko, was a serving police officer who, off duty, had used a stolen police-issue Colt .38 revolver in attacking constables Sin and Tsang. On 7 April 2006, a senior police officer was required to appear before the Legislative Council Security Panel. He said, "Were Constable Tsui Po-ko still alive, there is sufficient evidence to charge him with three fatal shootings." He was referring to (1) the killing of a constable and the theft of his police revolver on 14 March 2001 (2) a bank robbery and killing of a civilian guard in January 2002 and (3) the shoot-out on 17 March 2006. Nothing was said about a possible motive for the atrocities. Rumours began to circulate as to what might lie behind these killings and other seemingly associated crimes.

Some of these rumours were wild, way off the mark, and there was nothing forthcoming from the police to scotch them. So journalist Niall Fraser did some patient research work and, in a feature article, published in the Sunday Post in February 2007, linked a chain of events that began on 14 March 2001, with the theft of a police revolver from a uniformed constable in a pre-meditated ambush, and continuing all the way to the shoot-out on 17 March 2006. Enmeshed in the story were allegations of bribery and corruption, illegal soccer gambling in police stations and internal police feuding,

In the case of the stolen revolver, a complaint of "public disturbance" was made by a man using an untraceable mobile phone just after mid-day on 14 March 2001, to the police station in Lei Muk Shu Division, New Territories. An instruction was passed to 24-year-old, and soon to be married, beat Constable Leung Shing-yan, on foot patrol, to go to an address in a nearby housing estate and investigate. On arrival he sent his last radio message at 12.25 hrs that no one was at the address. Moments later he was ambushed and beaten to the ground. His gun was snatched from him and used by the culprit to shoot him dead, two bullets to the head and three in his back. Taking his victim's gun, his speed-loader and spare ammunition, a total of twelve rounds, the assassin disappeared. The police have never discovered anything more than weak circumstantial evidence that the assassin was Tsui Po-ko.

The next time the gun in question surfaced was in January 2002 at the scene of a bank robbery in a small branch of the Hang Seng Bank in a housing estate. A hooded, lone criminal, brandishing the revolver, forced his way into the teller's space and pocketed $500,000 in cash. As he was making his getaway, the security guard, Zafar Iqbal Khan, blocked him, whereupon the robber shot him dead, jumped over the body and disappeared on foot. Again, the police have not found any evidence that it was Tsui Po-ko who pulled the trigger. While Tsui was apparently not short of money at the time, it may be noted that in 2002 the monthly salary of a constable, at entry, was approximately $20,000 and, at the top end $30,000. This haul of half-a-million bucks amounted to two years' salary.

And then came the final shooting on 17 March 2006.

From 2000, the Police Internal Investigations Bureau was tackling what turned out to be an outbreak of illegal soccer gambling in police stations across Hong Kong. Rumours of bribery and corruption surrounding it were rife. Triad involvement from outside was suspected. In 2005 alone, three police officers died in shootings under questionable circumstances. A fourth committed suicide while facing allegations of bribery. In none of these, however, was any evidence of police criminality unearthed. But the rumour mill kept on churning. A persistent rumour as to the reasons behind the TST shoot-out on 17 March 2006, was that Tsui Po-ko was waiting in the pedestrian underpass, keeping a rendezvous with fellow policemen and/or triad gang members involved in illegal gambling and indebtedness of police officers.

Six months later, in September 2006, Constable Wong Siu-pang was shot in the thigh by a fellow officer during a scuffle. This arose out of an incident where Wong, who had been to hospital for treatment of mental issues, was returning home by taxi. He evaded payment by fleeing on foot but was caught by two patrolling constables. On the face of it, there was no connection with any other illegality. He was recovering well from his wounds when, less than a month later, he died suddenly, while out exercising. The rumours continued unabated.

Nearly a year after the TST shoot-out, the formal inquest was held into the deaths of Constables Tsang Kwok-hang and Tsui Po-ko. As well as those two deaths, Coroner Michael Chan Pik-kiu was asked to look at events surrounding the two killings of March 2001 and January 2002, where the same firearm had been used. Thirty-seven days of hearings were held, one of the longest inquests ever and, Michael Chan said, the most complex he had presided over. Evidence was heard from police officers attending the crime scenes, detectives, government pathologist Dr Pang Chi-ming, hospital doctors and dozens of experts ranging from firearms technicians to psychologists.

Tsui Po-ko was born in mainland China. In 1978 his parents

brought him, aged eight, with his baby brother to Hong Kong. He was a high-achieving student at school and was accepted into the police force in 1991. In his basic training at Police Training School in Aberdeen, he came top of his intake and was awarded the coveted silver whistle. No mean feat. He was also a top-scoring marksman and ambidextrous in that skill. In his initial first three years in the force his annual reports depicted a dedicated and diligent policeman. In the thirteen years to the date of his death he was always well reported on. The evidence aired about Constable Tsui Po-ko's career in the force revealed that, far from being the "Devil Cop" as the press had branded him, he was actually a model policeman. So much so that he was featured in the Hong Kong Police news sheet Off Beat, back in 2000, as the perfect family man with wife and young daughter, an avid sportsman, paraglider and martial arts fighter, completing the 100km Oxfam Trail-walker. He and his wife achieved minor celebrity status when they entered a popular TV knock-out quiz competition for couples and won a $60,000 prize.

Contrariwise, police evidence was that on thirteen occasions, Tsui had not been recommended for promotion on grounds of "character defect". He was a bit stubborn and had inadequate communication skills apparently. A psychiatrist in the witness box, who had never seen Tsui, opined that such career setbacks could alter a person's mental equilibrium. But there were also rumours, cited in the press, of a darker side: heavy gambling, especially on soccer, and visits to Shenzhen, to karaoke bars, massage parlours and prostitutes. There being no direct evidence, however, this wasn't mentioned. But there was circumstantial evidence of something amiss found by police investigators: assets worth $2,977,513 in seven personal and twelve investment accounts in his name but using a friend's address and not his own. His wife knew nothing about these. In addition, he had purchased a property on Lantao Island costing around $2 million, settling the ten-year mortgage in less than half that time. These assets were many times over both Tsui's and his social worker wife's earnings.

At the conclusion of the inquest, the five-person jury returned a finding that the deceased Tsui Po-ko was responsible for the shootings on 17 March 2006. They also concluded that Tsui was the only suspect in the killing of Constable Leung and the taking of his revolver in March 2001, and the killing of Zafar Iqbal Khan with the same gun in January 2002. The jury returned a verdict of lawful killing of Tsui Po-ko by Constable Tsang Kwok-hang.

The next day, the press had a field-day with lawyers complaining that the verdict was out of order. By law, the purpose of a coroner's inquest is to determine when, where and how a person or persons died, and their identities. The one thing an inquest does not do is apportion the blame for deaths. That is the prerogative of the criminal courts. However, since there was no one left to charge for those crimes, the finding was allowed to stand, alongside Tsui's assumed but untried guilt for the first two murders, as well as his unequivocal guilt for the third.

It was noted, too, that legal aid for the inquest hearing was denied to Madam Cheung Wai-mei, Tsui's mother, because she was judged over the threshold of financial entitlement. But the fact is she could not afford a lawyer and it was only at the last moment that the legal aid office relented and a solicitor and barrister were briefed, too late to properly prepare their case.

Meanwhile Sin Ka-Keung continued his recuperation from gunshot wounds, on sick leave for eighteen months before he was sufficiently recovered to return to duty. But even then, there were challenges he had to meet. There were unwelcome phone calls from journalists and other strangers to his parent's home where he lived. He needed his own place and received scant help from his superiors. Eventually a flat next to a police station was found for him. He needed police transport to help him get to medical appointments. This was granted at HQ level but those at the other end, tasked with its implementation, were grudging.

Back in the station barracks there was sarcasm. Sin was said to be exaggerating his trauma. Unkind jokes were made about his leg injuries and time off for foot massage, plus criticism of his not preventing the death of his patrol partner. Depression set in. He wasn't sleeping well, plagued by nightmares. He had few friends and was regarded as being self-centered and attention-seeking, his temper deteriorated, and he started drowning his sorrows in alcohol. His police psychologist eventually referred him to a psychiatrist who diagnosed him as suffering from post-traumatic stress disorder. That was a full two years after the violence. He was returned to sick leave and, despondent, he was thinking of resigning until his senior officers counselled him that he was much better off in government service than he would be on his own in the private sector.

It seems fairly clear that, within a short space of time after the calamitous events of 17 March 2006, Sin was suffering from PTSD, a condition first recognized in the late '70s after the Vietnam War, symptoms being flashbacks, loss of concentration, sleeplessness, anxiety and aggression.

In 2008 Sin had an impromptu meeting with his regional commander, an assistant commissioner, who lent him a sympathetic ear. This quickly led to a supportive policeman-to-policeman relationship that had eluded Sin all this time. It was the start of a complete turn-around for him, more than all the experts he had consulted over the years had achieved.

Sin's "significant other", as he took to calling the senior officer lending him a helping hand, was further promoted to the top echelon of the force, yet continued to maintain the trusting relationship between them. In 2012 Sin's alter ego encouraged him to embark on a public speaking programme, sharing his experiences, both within the force training environment and outside, building up his self-confidence as he went. But it was a shaky start, his first "performance" bringing back the still vivid, traumatic experience, forcing him to face his nemesis again. He retreated to his flat, a last resort comfort zone, and thoughts of suicide. He resorted to the bottle again. In his desperation he telephoned the Samaritan's hotline in the sleepless middle of the night.

Sin's psychiatrist wanted to admit him to the psychiatric hospital. Initially Sin refused but, after negotiations, he saw the sense of it and acquiesced.

A month later he was out again, his alcohol dependency cured as well. But it still wasn't the end of his difficulties. Now the normal vicissitudes of life bedevilled him, one of his brothers getting the family into debt through irresponsible behavior. Sin borrowed money from one of his few friends who, unbeknown to him, had terminal cancer and succumbed before Sin paid the money back. Then his father became seriously ill with heart failure. Once again Sin's demons, plus a certain amount of self-pity, one suspects, landed him, for the third time, back on the psychiatric ward.

Having regained mental stability and confidence Sin got in touch with his "significant other" who had retired in 2013. Together they compiled a journal covering his fight with PTSD and a publisher found it sufficiently compelling that he turned it into a slim book with a print-run of 1,500 copies. It was a sell-out in just two months. Then people started getting in touch with him. First a headmaster asking him to give a talk to sixth-form pupils. Word got around and there were more invitations to talk to this school or that society. The hidden hand of Sin's "significant other" was at work. The police force asked him to run sessions on their training courses and promotion/command courses. These were an unqualified success and Sin began to feel that, finally, after a life-changing hiatus of nine years, he was normal again.

At last, he decided to take up the challenge of university studies in a distance-learning programme with an overseas university that the police force was partnered with.

In 2018, he graduated from Teesside University with a BSc (Hons) in Crime Investigation.

SHATTERING THE GLASS CEILING
Evelyn Lam Man-sai

When I saw on the news in 2016, Hillary Clinton at the US Democrat convention, telling a wildly cheering crowd that she was going to shatter the glass ceiling, to be the first female President of the US, I willed her on, thinking I've been shattering glass ceilings all my working life. Of course, they were nowhere near as high as was the presidential hopeful's ceiling.

In putting together this chapter, I am conscious that I'm blowing my own trumpet but those who know me will forgive me. I'm not the shy and retiring type!

I was born in 1961, the last in a family of five children, two boys, three girls, in Kowloon. Our 200square-foot flat on the fourth floor of a crowded 1930s tenement block, comprised a single room with kitchen and toilet partitioned off at the balcony end. There was no garden to play in, just the busy street outside. There was no television, just a plastic radio.

I have little memory of my father, just a few black-and-white family photographs, for he left us to work overseas. My mother scraped together a living, working long hours every day in a nearby factory, often returning home after our bedtime, when she would wash and iron our school clothes, do some cleaning and hum a folk tune as she worked. I remember there was much fun and laughter in our family. Sometimes Mum would bring home a treat for us, a steaming bowl of beef noodles, and we'd all crowd round the table, chopsticks at the ready. At festival times,

Christmas and New Year, we'd buy roasted chicken wings, ten cents for one, and think how lucky we were.

We children did our best to help out in the house, keeping the flat tidy, making our beds and doing chores. There were rats and cockroaches in the old building and we took this for granted.

We all went to the same school in our locality and made friends with our neighbors. My sisters and I looked for ways to earn some money after school and on the holidays. When I was eleven years old, Mum let me take up full-time holiday jobs in small, family-run factories soldering wires in radios, gluing hair for wigs, cutting cloth to make jeans, assembling parts for plastic toys and flowers all primary industries with products "Made in Hong Kong" in the '60s and '70s.

The pay was low for the gruelling work and occasionally there were injuries. I remember dropping a soldering iron in my lap, leaving a burn scar that I have to this day. I was crying and two of my workmates each gave me a dollar and took me out for a simple buffet lunch, which really meant a lot to me considering their monthly salary was $320.00. I have never forgotten that kindness and, there and then, resolved to emulate it. All of us were from the same sort of background, and I was happy, slowly saving up my precious dollars, enough to buy my schoolbooks and stationery. Although the teaching was free, we had to provide our own books and equipment.

I continued working my school holidays into my teens, in a variety of jobs, which was fun, but for the first time, I witnessed harassment and bullying in the work place, the girls employed in factories being treated badly, even molested. With my limited means I tried to help some who had been reduced to tears. These experiences reinforced my altruistic commitment.

I was sixteen when I left school. My mum took me to a festival banquet for Chiu Chau people in Guangdong at which every guest was given a lucky number. And my lucky number won the first prize, which was a state-of-the-art $3,000 color television set. Given that the monthly salary of a factory worker was $400, this was wealth beyond my dreams, and I lost no time in realizing the cash value of it, sufficient to enroll myself in a UK college for O- and A-level studies, even paying for the airfare. I went there in 1978 for two years during which I paid my way with part-time work for a Chinese restaurateur. My hours were long, from 16.00 to 02.00 hrs. My boss was good to me, even allowing me to accompany him after work to his regular casino where he gambled, and I ate my fill of free steak and chips.

My academic grades were good enough to get me into Essex University where I embarked on a three-year bachelor's degree course in policy making and public administration. I took out a student loan and augmented that with part-time work in Chinese restaurants. In the long summer vacations, I flew to New York on the cheap "red-eye" where I made comparatively good money working for jewelery stores on Mott Street. I graduated from Uni with a 1st class in one subject and an overall 2-1.

Upon graduation, I headed back to Hong Kong after an absence of five years and the homecoming was ecstatic, as you may imagine. My mother was still working in the factory and my older brother and sister had both left home and got married.

Never one for letting the grass grow under my feet, I immediately set about looking for employment, wanting to pay off my student loan as soon as possible. I answered an advertisement for a managerial post with an advertising company and they took me on. It was a 9-to-5 job, which left me free to take on evening work teaching English and banking. I lived with my mum, paying my way. Out of my monthly wage of $1,800, I gave my mum $600.00 and started paying off my student loan at $300 per month. That left me enough for lunches and a cinema ticket.

Looking around me, I could see that working for the government, "the golden rice bowl", was better paid, with more attractive conditions of service such as housing, than anything I was likely to get in the private sector. I prepared my first curriculum vitae and began applying for government service. I received positive replies to my first few applications and one was from the Royal Hong Kong Police. As an Inspector, I stood to earn four times as much as my day and evening jobs combined.

On September 10, 1984, I began my basic training at the Aberdeen Police Training School as a member of a Probationary Inspector squad that included ten men and me. At that time the women police, less than ten percent of the RHKP, were not doing all the duties of male officers. We wore police uniforms, had a similar rank structure to our male counterparts and equal pay, but that is where the similarities ended. Although we had been trained in all police duties, in practice the duties of female officers were restricted to handling women's and juvenile's inquiries, dealing with missing-persons cases, domestic abuse and assisting crime investigations where women were involved. We did not carry arms and we had no role in anti-riot duties.

I found the basic training tough. In my squad there were men who had been promoted through the ranks to probationary inspector and already had a lot of policing experience. I struggled with the physical training and strict discipline. There were times when I thought I couldn't go on; I'd be one of the few who didn't make it through. But I did. I passed my Standard I professional exams and, on completion of basic training, I passed out with a shiny new pip (military star) on each shoulder.

My first posting was to Tai Po police station, starting out in my career where I was eventually to end up, although I didn't know that then. In my first year I was a patrol subunit commander in charge of fifty policemen. I had three station sergeants who were my deputies, each highly experienced who became mentors to me. In my new role, I was eager to learn, never shying away from responsibility. While I have many happy memories, there were also unpleasant duties when I had to attend the scene of every dead body found, be it a violent or natural death. On a few occasions, I had to check two or even three bodies, mostly elderly folk, in one eight-hour shift.

In the summer of '86 I was seconded to divisional CID in Tai Po when a vacancy for a detective inspector arose in one of the investigation teams. By this time, I had passed my Standard II exams and was looking forward to my confirmation in the rank of Inspector. Each team worked a shift, rotating through morning, evening and night, taking every crime report that occurred during that duty time. I remember that the crime situation was particularly busy then. Criminal triad activity was rampant: intimidation and blackmail, assaults and wounding. My team and I were called to robberies, gang fights and choppings (beef knives and meat choppers were the weapons of choice), rapes and murders. The latter two categories of crime were passed to district crime squads who were better equipped for lengthy and complicated investigations.

A robbery we were called out to one morning, in the early hours, was my first big success as a DI. The criminals had tied up and gagged the watchman of a factory and got away with $6 million in electronic goods. When we interviewed the watchman, he was able to describe the getaway vehicle and recall part of the registration plate number. Armed with that information, we spent hours trawling through vehicle records, ending up with a short list of possibilities, which we immediately acted on. One of the leads I followed was a residential address where a woman told me that her husband, a delivery driver, had gone to work at

2:00 a.m. that morning. We set up a fabricated delivery job to our local hospital and laid an ambush. Our target walked right into it, and in his vehicle, we found part of the loot we were after. Under questioning, the driver admitted his part in the robbery and gave us the identities of his two accomplices. We arrested them in short order and recovered all of the stolen property. For that I was awarded my first commanding officer's commendation. A rarity for a CID rookie and, even more so, for a woman DI.

In '87, having been advanced early to senior inspector after passing my Standard III professional exams, I was transferred to Sham Shui Po Divisional police station, heading up one of their CID investigation teams, the same duties as in Tai Po. But the nature of our work was different in that the local crime scene was heavily influenced by a sprawling and crowded Vietnamese refugee camp housed in a former British army barracks. There were all sorts of crime going on in and around that camp, and the pool of Vietnamese language interpreters called on by the police was making a good living. Then, in early '88, it was off to CID training school for me.

My first real break came later the same year when I received a phone call, out of the blue, from CID Headquarters, Narcotics Bureau, asking if I would like to join the newly created Financial Investigation Group. I could hardly believe my ears, the elite CID NB looking for me! The superintendent, Stuart McDouall, had seen my record of service and marked me as a likely candidate.

We were a small, tightly knit group with one superintendent, two chief inspectors and four investigation teams, each headed by inspectors. Our offices were hived off from the headquarters block and we embarked upon highly specialized training. It was impressed upon us that we were professionals, dealing with lawyers and bankers on a daily basis, and must look the part. Suits and ties for the men, smart dress for the ladies.

It wasn't long before our first and biggest case investigation in those two years came along. K.M. Law was a long-time target of CID NB operations group, a major Hong Kong-born drug trafficker on the international scene, with a vast stable of couriers and a global financial network. Law, the chief executive as-it-were, was adept at escaping the clutches of the law and so it was decided to tackle him through his finances. CID HQ employed two forensic accountants to work with us full time.

Alongside that investigation each of our teams were running small-scale cases against other drug traffickers, chasing their money trails, linking them to the criminals, then prosecuting them under the new drug money laundering laws. We were spectacularly successful in those early years, catching many of our suspects completely off guard.

I was fortunate enough to be leading the team, under Detective Chief Inspector Kenny Ip, in the hunt for the assets of K.M. Law and his partners in crime. At times it was nerve-wracking work, knowing contracts could be put out on us as vast sums of money were at stake. Often, we worked late into the night with our civilian accountants, piecing together the web of transactions to complete the evidence against our targets. Then came the arrests, charging and the High Court case. Our two masterminds were sentenced to ten and twelve years apiece and about $412 million in drug trafficking assets were confiscated. Confiscation orders for similarly large sums of money were executed in Australia and the US. For that success, I was the first woman police officer to receive the Governor of Hong Kong's commendation. *Nota bene:* To this date no single case in Hong Kong has netted so much in confiscated proceeds of crime.

In '93 my boss, Superintendent McDouall, put my name forward in the periodic selection process for the post of Assistant Aide de Camp to the Governor of Hong Kong. At the final interview, chaired by the Governor himself, I was selected. Another first for a woman police officer. It was a part-time post to be carried out when required, in addition to my day-to-day duties elsewhere. The first weekend after my selection, I was invited to an evening pool-side barbecue at the Governor's residence in Fanling, hosted by the permanent ADC to the Governor, Superintendent Lance Brown. I had bought a fine dress especially for the occasion. So you may imagine my chagrin when the ADC unceremoniously picked me up bodily and jumped into the pool, which was the signal for the other twelve Assistant ADCs present to jump in as well, all of us fully clothed. That was my initiation! In the end, I held that post for five years during which time I was privileged to escort many dignitaries including visiting ministers of state and royalty.

In 1993 I was promoted to chief inspector, still in CID NB but in '95, I found myself back in operational districts where I was put in charge of a CID team tasked with serious crime investigations. This was very different work, investigating the full gamut of serious crime. And it was full on: on call 24/7 and more often than not, working hours not conducive to a social life. I had three teams under me and took personal charge of the serious and complicated investigations.

I remember one challenging case where a human leg was found hidden in undergrowth. Forensic examination revealed a small leaf stuck to the leg, vegetation out of character with the surrounding flora. The pathologist also told us the murder victim, whom we needed to identify, was a middle-aged lady. Painstaking inquiries into people reported missing came up with an address which, when we searched it, resulted in the discovery of a pot plant with the same variety of leaf found stuck to the amputated leg. So we had the location of the murder and it didn't take us long to identify our suspect who, at that moment, was heading for the China border. We caught up with him at the border crossing point and found in his possession jewelery stolen from his victim.

In '96, just a year into this job, the Assistant District Commander, Crime, was transferred out and, for want of an immediate replacement for such an important role, I was made acting Superintendent for Crime in his place. I was the first woman police officer in that post.

In 1997, the year of the Handover, I was promoted to superintendent. With my CID background, I was posted to the New Territories Border District as the Assistant District Commander for Operations and Crime. This turned out to be another first for a woman police officer. It wasn't difficult to see why because of the physical challenges of working in an inhospitable environment. The thorn-covered hills were home to mosquitoes and venomous reptiles. I was required to liaise with my police counterparts on the Chinese side when cross-border crime such as smuggling and illegal immigration were concerned. I was keen to keep them on side and our meetings usually culminated in a meal when the Chinese wine flowed in toast after toast to our friendship. Fortunately I had learned to hold my liquor in social events, and, I like to think, I represented the Hong Kong Police Force with aplomb.

In 1999, it was time for a change to new pastures, still in the New Territories, and I was given command of a company in the Police Tactical Unit. Another triumph for women police. The PTU is Hong Kong's riot deterrent, its line of last resort. This bastion of male superiority had rarely seen a woman in its ranks, never mind a commander of comparatively small stature. But strong character, self-confidence and no-nonsense discipline carried me through. We were voted best company under training. Mind you, I had some jolly good officers working for me and it was a great team effort.

That posting was for a year, and we were involved in a few difficult situations where law and order had completely broken down. There was a serious riot in Hei Ling Chau Prison on an outlying island, where the inmates overran the officers and guards. I planned an all-out assault but, fortunately, the rioters saw sense, negotiations succeeded, and we were able to stand down without firing a shot. One of the more sensitive issues we dealt with was a clearance operation against illegal squatters that had bogged down in threats of violence and suicide if the government didn't back off. I took the initiative and parleyed with their leader who was overawed by a petite lady, in full riot gear, sweet-talking him into submission. He caved in without a murmur, diffusing a tense situation.

At the turn of the Millennium, I was offered the post of staff officer (superintendent) in charge of training for the PTU. I took it and, in doing so, was the first woman officer in that role. It was at that time that the PTU were undergoing a wholesale revamp of its tactics, and I engaged with some of the world's leading authorities in this arena.

I was taken away from that post in 2002, at the outset of the SARS epidemic, to take up an immediate responsibility with the Health Bureau. I set up a command and control center for them, linking up the police and other government departments, in a coordinated effort to contain and mitigate the epidemic. I flew to Atlanta to study the systems at the Centers for Disease Control and Prevention. Back in Hong Kong, I sat in committee with department heads and was able to draw up the Infectious Diseases Contingency Plan for Hong Kong, which included periodic exercises involving some twenty government departments. It is still in place. It has been used in controlling the 2002 Avian Flu H5N1 epidemic and also in the Covid-19 pandemic, resulting in plaudits from the WHO. A spin-off was upgrading of the police command and control centers.

In 2004 I was promoted to senior superintendent and went back to headquarters, this time as deputy head of the Police Operations Bureau. This was just in time to plan policing of the 2005 World Trade Organization conference to be held in Hong Kong for the first time. It was in the middle of violent anti-globalization protests happening across the world. The threat assessment was high, and a working group of senior officers was set up to manage it. I was the only woman officer in that group. My remit was to set up and run the command center. For technical support I was able to link in road traffic cameras, helicopter communications and establish the first e-log recording system for all police and emergency units, including fire and ambulance—over 7,000 links on the ground. During the WTO conference there were violent skirmishes, but control was maintained at all times. I received the Commissioner's commendation for that one, the first woman officer to bag both the Governor's and the Commissioner's plaudits.

After all that excitement it was back to CID NB, the first love in my career, this time as the deputy head. And yes, you've guessed, the first woman officer to hold down that job. By this time, in 2006, the old Financial Investigation Group had morphed into the much bigger, better equipped and, by now, renowned CID Headquarters financial investigation hub. This was allied with the newly formed world Financial Action Task Force based in Paris. I was able to renew some of my old contacts in the Chinese police force, quite like old times as we discussed cross-border drug trafficking and joint investigations.

When I was promoted out of that post in 2007, the head of China's drug enforcement agency came down from the capital to host a dinner for me, more toasts with Chinese wine, this time leaving me a little the worse for wear, age catching up on me.

Now a chief superintendent, I had a short spell in Personnel Wing before going back into uniform as the boss of Wanchai District. Police Headquarters was on my patch, and I was not only the first woman officer in charge but was also well aware that quite a few former Commissioners had been in command of Wanchai before me. I knew better than to think about such a possibility for myself, one glass ceiling too high, but I am certain it will eventually be shattered, just not by me.

Wanchai is regarded as being the most testing of district commands, hardly a month going by without a mass march or demonstration, some of world-news importance. I also looked after the Hong Kong Convention and Exhibition Center where national celebrations are held and international commercial events and performances by famous artists are staged. Major security issues.

I was in Wanchai for three years when in 2010, the Complaints and Internal Investigations Bureau in police headquarters needed a new head. When I was asked to take up the challenge it was a bit of a wrench as C&IIB was definitely not a glamorous or popular posting, lots of contentious issues as you might imagine, and interminable wrangling with the civilian Police Complaints Commission, which had oversight of the bureau. I think the gods must have deliberately sought me out in order to see how the first woman chief would tackle that command.

Of all the complaints that came across my desk, an odd one sticks out. A woman chief inspector lodged a complaint against a fellow officer for sexually harassing her at a social occasion. That brought back an old memory of something similar happening to me when I was a youngish superintendent. That was at a dinner-dance, and a police officer, who had asked me for a dance, nipped my ear with his teeth. I remonstrated with him at the time but did nothing further about it, knowing, in those days, that my character would be brought into contention if I made such a complaint. Anyway, it turned out that the offender happened to be on my staff as one of the superintendents in charge of complaints for a police region. What a coincidence! I called him in with his senior superintendent and, sure enough, it was the same ear-biter. It was a "Me too" moment. Needless to say, his feet hardly touched the ground as he was rushed out of the door. He left the force soon after.

In 2014, in my last years before reaching retirement age, I was transferred back to my first stomping ground in Shatin District. A lot of water had flowed under the bridge in those thirty years between times.

In 1974, Shatin was a sleepy farming village of about a hundred people surrounded by paddy fields and duck farms. Upon my return in 2004, it was a fast-growing population of more than 600,000. Shatin town was a shining new metropolis with a dozen high-rise (average sixty storey) housing estates, umpteen schools, classy hotels, a business park, shopping malls, a big hospital and green parks. And, of course, all the usual law and order issues that go with such a conurbation. Yes, I was the first woman to take charge there. My district police station was one of our more modern ones, and I had about 700 officers under my command, plus all the civilian back-up. Hugely important was our relationship with the townsfolk; I chaired numerous committees and sat on various boards for this and that. Almost of equal importance was all the socializing I had to do, taking up a lot of my weekends. But I like a good party. In addition to those duties, I found time to inaugurate a few community initiatives of my own, mainly for youth and under-privileged families.

In Shatin, shortly before my retirement in 2016, I received a surprise. I thought it was a joke at first. The Federation of

Women in Hong Kong, a government-funded organization, nominated me for Hong Kong's "Most Distinguished Woman", an award that takes place every five years. Normally this goes to famous socialites on the charity scene, or the CEO of a bank. But a little old police officer: was I chuffed? Of course! Headlines in the newspapers, "First Woman Police Officer Crowned." On the stage with me were seven other ladies, philanthropists, politicians of note and high-flying business women.

My next posting was retirement and, as I said earlier, I wasn't going to let the grass grow under my feet. A job opportunity came my way, vice president of global security for American Express. And that is where I am now. It's no sinecure, I can tell you! In charge of thirteen Asia Pacific markets.

Have I been I lucky, piggy-backing on the equal-rights-for-women movement or did I succeed on my own? A bit of luck perhaps, being in the right place at the right time.

At the start of my career the emancipation of women was nascent. In the early 1990s it was gaining traction in male-dominated institutions. By 2010, equal rights was becoming a feminist war-cry and employers were listening.

By then, my career with the Hong Kong police had almost run its course and I like to think that I helped shape those societal changes. I did it my way! And despite my senior years now, I'm still going strong.

St John's Cathedral: Doing Ordinary Things with Extraordinary Love

Stuart McDouall

The Cathedral church of St John the Evangelist stands in Garden Road, Central, surrounded by tall buildings and just a stone's throw from Government House on the hillside. At the time of writing it is 174 years old and has been continuously in the service of God except for the five-year duration of the Japanese occupation of Hong Kong

In 1846 the government provided the Church of England with what is the only freehold land in the territory, No.4 Garden Road. The building of the first permanent Christian place of worship began almost immediately and, in 1849, just eight years after the British flag was raised over Hong Kong, the inaugural church service was held in the "Hong Kong Colonial Chapel."

Plans for the aggrandizement of this preliminary structure were expedited and, coinciding with the completion of the cathedral in 1852, the first Bishop of Hong Kong and Macau, the Rt Rev George Smith, took up his appointment. His first task was to consecrate the Gothic-styled building henceforth known as St John's Cathedral. Work was done on a forty-two foot extension to the East end of the structure, creating space for a high altar and choir. This was completed in 1869, in time for the first royal visit to Hong Kong by Prince Alfred, second son of Queen Victoria and the Duke of Edinburgh. On 16 November, he laid the foundation stone, which is still in place for all to see. At that time, the cathedral, with its sixty-five-foot battlemented bell tower, was the tallest building in Central, a visible landmark around the harbor.

Initially the cathedral was largely frequented by the better well-heeled of the expatriate community, the British military garrison and senior civil servants. The first governor, Sir John Davis, was a regular worshipper. Of the local population there were few, if any, Christians and not even local dignitaries with government connections attended. This exclusive composition of the congregation continued until the turn of the 20th Century. But by then Christian missionary societies, both Roman Catholic and Church of England, had established successful schools and their alumni were creating a new western-educated Chinese middle class, some entering into the life of the cathedral. More churches were springing up across the territory.

In 1910 the cathedral was the focal point in Hong Kong's celebrations of the coronation of King George V. There are sepia photographs showing the nave completely swathed in flags and canopies, with punkahs swinging from the rafters to cool the summer air.

Between the world wars, the Cathedral collaborated with other Anglican churches, extending their outreach, building ever-larger congregations and assuming a charitable role among the poor and needy. In 1932 the fourth bishop of HK and Macau was the Rt Rev Ronald Owen Hall. A decorated World War I veteran who could read and write Chinese and speak Putonghua and Cantonese, Bishop Hall was an influential and pioneering spirit.

In 1941 he provoked controversy by ordaining a Cantonese lady, Miss Florence Li Tim-oi, as a priest, the first in the world-wide Anglican Communion. Once peace had been restored at the end of World War II, the Archbishop of Canterbury admonished Bishop Hall for disturbing the good order of the church in disobeying ecclesiastic regulations. Bishop Hall, who was expected to resign his position in the face of such criticism, not only declined to do so but robustly defended his action. However, the Rev Li handed in her licence, being fearful of the conflict stirred up on her account. But within the next few years Bishop Hall's precedent was followed by other Anglican bishops, firstly in New Zealand and then in other British territories. Unfortunately, the post-war Governor of HK, Sir Alexander Grantham, was not in amity with Bishop Hall or his social activities, thinking him a communist sympathiser because of his friendship with Chinese Christians on the Mainland. A burr under Grantham's saddle, Bishop Hall made himself the conscience of the colonial government, constantly forcing their hand in housing for the poor, medical facilities for the halt and lame, institution of the first welfare laws and more.

On Christmas Day 1941, Hong Kong was beaten into surrendering to the Japanese forces. The usual church services were held that morning and there wasn't a spare pew left for latecomers. In the ensuing three years the cathedral was maintained by clergy from non-aligned or neutral countries, particularly Norway, but services were irregular at best with minimal attendance. But in 1944, the Japanese evicted the small coterie of clerics, local and foreign, and turned the cathedral into a Japanese social club and public meeting hall. All the religious furnishings and fittings were removed or destroyed.

After the enemy capitulation in 1945, work was begun on restoration of the cathedral. The main building remaining largely intact except for a shell hole through the tower. But the innards of the church, all the memorials and monuments, the carved wood partitions in the chapels and the choir, the stained glass windows, the vestibules and the sacristy had been ransacked by the occupation forces.

One of the first pieces of war memorabilia erected during restoration in St Michael's chapel was the altar piece or reredos retrieved from the Stanley POW camp. It had been fashioned from wooden packing cases by POWs in the shape of a Gothic window arch and a small tin tray tacked on the ledge below for candles to be placed on. It is still in use today. Also in St Michael's Chapel are the memorial books to all those who died in the defence of Hong Kong in WWII, a new page being turned every day under the locked glass cases. Around the architraves of the chapel hang the disintegrating military colours of regiments long since disbanded. Recently the flags or colours of naval, RAF and other disciplined services, including the Royal Hong Kong Police, have been laid up in memory of those who served under them. One eminent member, not understanding the traditions of St Michael's Chapel, has had his old school pennant hung up in pride of place, supplanting the RHKP flag that was blessed and laid up, in memory of all those officers who passed through the cathedral's portals, by the Rev John Chynchen, Cathedral Chaplain, after the handover in 1997 when the RHKP title reverted to the original HKP.

There have been few more poignant occasions in the Cathedral's history than the funeral of Governor Sir Edward Youde, GCMG, GCVO, the only one of twenty-eight governors of Hong Kong to die in office. He served from May 1982 to his death on 5 December 1986, from a heart attack when in Beijing for talks following the signing of the Sino-British joint declaration. Youde, a Foreign Office diplomat and notable sinologist, fluent in Mandarin and written Chinese, was highly respected for his determined advocacy, on behalf of the Hong Kong people, for their civil rights and privileges. Such was the public grief, following news of his passing, that between two and three million (no one ever made a definitive count) residents signed the condolence books, initially in the City Hall, Central, but then in Kowloon and the New Territories where more books of condolence were hastily opened, so great was the demand.

Edward Youde's body was flown to Hong Kong where the British military garrison laid on a state funeral, the cortege accompanied by soldiers, sailors and airmen marching to the traditional muffled drum beat, passed through Central, the normally chaotic roads and pavements thronged by silent mourners, a deafening hush all the way to St John's Cathedral. A seventeen-gun salute was fired across the harbor from HMS Tamar, the crashing roar reverberating around those ancient shorelines. The great and the good filled the cathedral in solemn array. Afterwards, his body was driven to Cape Collinson for cremation and, a week later, Lady Pamela Youde took the ashes of her husband back to England where the urn was interred at Canterbury Cathedral.

The annual Michaelmas Fair

With the exception of the war years, the cathedral has hosted a Michaelmas Fair annually. It's an all-day event mustering the congregation-at-large in a common effort to raise money for charity. In the past, some forty fair stalls were constructed out of lengths of angle-iron, ranging from the basic "square-with-counter-and-canvas-roof" model to a covered alley and iron stands for the coconut shy. All this equipment was stored throughout the year in the bell tower. A day before the fair the heavy trapdoor in the tower is opened; a large wooden ship's pulley, rigged up under the bells, and all the iron spars are lowered in bundles to waiting hands below. For over twenty years, the good Captain David Wright, wearing his trademark bowler hat, masterminded the building and dismantling of the fair, assisted by hangers-on like me. Nowadays modern gazebo tents have replaced those old stalls.

The Fair has always been a favourite in Hong Kong's social calendar, attracting not just the congregation but the expatriate and local community from across the territory. The variety of stalls, from the popular White Elephant, the books and second-hand clothing, the Punch & Judy show, the Filipino "Lumpia" stall and the Scout's hot dogs, not to mention the bar, where old China hands have supped, one or two school bands and dance troupes, Judy the baggy, red-nosed clown, the stocks where fair-goers threw soaked sponges at the clergy, and, the last event, the drawing of the raffle with the top prize being, sometimes, first-class flights to holiday destinations donated by Cathay Pacific. Then the building teams get together again, dismantling the fair ground and hauling it all up into the bell tower before nightfall.

St John's Cathedral also hosts the popular, English-speaking, 36th Scout Group comprising a Cub Pack and a Scout Troop. Once a year, they are the stars in a Scouting Sunday service, parading their flags. Another busy part of the Cathedral is the counseling service, open to the public.

It was Mother Theresa who once said, 'Do ordinary things with extraordinary love.' That's what St John's Cathedral, those who worship there and many Hong Kongers do.

Anti-Darkness Group Versus Triads

Stuart McDouall

In January 1976, I was posted to Triad Society Bureau, in CID Headquarters on the Island, where I took over an operational investigation team. In charge of the bureau was Detective Chief Superintendent U Tat-ming aka Teddy U. Under him was a deputy, a senior superintendent, then two superintendents, one of whom was in charge of the Ops teams. We occupied two whole floors in the CID tower block. My team comprised Detective Sergeant Toby Lau Kin-shing and four detective constables.

Our charter was to investigate and prosecute the illegal activities of triad societies. In the Cantonese dialect the popular pseudonym for TSB was Faan-Haak-Jo, literally Anti-Darkness Group. My induction was a day of meetings and briefings. I was given reading matter to bone-up on, principally a book, *Triad Societies in Hong Kong*, by Police Sub-Inspector WP Morgan. I was surprised, and intrigued, to see an acknowledgement in the flyleaf to a paternal uncle of mine, JC McDouall, Hon Secretary for Chinese Affairs in 1960. It states that the early history, part 1 of the book, was "largely his work". To understand the part played by triads throughout Hong Kong's history, it is worth looking at their origins.

The first English settlers quickly established law and order and in 1843, just three years after the raising of the Union Flag over Hong Kong, the first ordinance against unlawful societies was promulgated. It was the English law draftsman who coined the term "triad" to describe the ancient symbol used to identify society members, the Chinese character "Hung" centered in a triangle. It symbolizes the union of heaven, earth and man, hence, another pseudonym for the triads: the Heaven and Earth Society. The Chinese character "Hung" is derived from the regnal name of the first Ming emperor, Hung Wu, who reigned from 1368 to 1397. That same character is used in the romanized words "Hung Mun", the Chinese name for "Triad Society".

The Manchu invasion of China in 1644 supplanted the Ming with the Qing Dynasty and it is roughly from that time that the triads began to materialize, first among Buddhist and Taoist monks, the educated class. Their temples were used as bases for recruiting patriots operating with the mantra, "Overthrow the Qing, Restore the Ming." A Manchu prince was proclaimed the first emperor of the foreign Manchu Dynasty with the regnal title Shun Chih. The Ming General Wu San-kuei, withdrawing his army guarding the Great Wall, threw his lot in with the conquering Manchus and served Emperor Shun Chih by hunting down Ming loyalists.

A succession of pretenders, self-styled Ming Emperors, attempted to regain the imperial throne, relying on support from influential Buddhist and Taoist monasteries, but to no avail. Thus the patriotic movement was forced underground, forming highly secretive cliques with signs and passwords, operating mainly from temples across all of China. They employed guerrilla tactics in their patriotic pursuit. It was in Fukien that the original Shao Lin Temple of triad legend was said to have existed, opposite Taiwan, noted for its strong Ming sympathies. The subsequent fame of this temple is entirely mythical, based on imagined stories of daring-do by its monks, all martial arts devotees, and exaggerated by film stars and their movies, Bruce Lee being one.

Triads have operated in Hong Kong since the first year of the colony.

Thus it was that Ordinance No 1 of 1845 "...for the suppression of the Triad and other secret societies" came into being. In 1843 there were perhaps a thousand indigenous inhabitants in Hong Kong Island. By 1845 the island was the main storage center for the difficult but profitable China trade. Military depots had been established and the population was 15,000 strong and growing rapidly. In October 1845, the first arrest of triad members was reported. It mentions a police raid "...upon a secret Association of Triad which had exercised evil influence over the Chinese...a body of police captured seventeen members of the society, who made desperate efforts to get away." Such was the threat of triads to social stability that, in January 1846, the penalty for membership was increased from one to three years imprisonment plus branding on the left cheek and deportation. Apparently, these draconian measures did not have the desired effect. The police force, officered largely by British soldiers and sailors, was inefficient in those days and triads based in Hong Kong were increasing their influence throughout the territory and across a vast swathe of southern China. Around 1857, the Taiping rebellion, the last great putsch against the Qing in the north of China, was on the back foot, and the monks were fleeing back to their monastic lives. But the remaining secularized triads, growing used to their parasitic lifestyle, discarded their flimsy mantle of respectability, the altruistic movement giving succour to the poor and adopted their morally corrupt, parasitic persona and rapacious criminal activities.

By 1886, the triads had grown so powerful it is estimated they controlled the entire labor market in Hong Kong and southern China. They had long since split into factions, largely along village or dialect lines, Hakka, Cantonese, Hoklo, Chiu Chau, and so on. Two of the earlier triad societies, the San Yee On and the Fuk Yee Hing, were still extant in the 1980s. They had their roots in the Man On Society founded in Hong Kong in 1886 by natives of Chiu Chau, Hoklo and Hakka from the southern provinces of China.

In 1895 the Republican Party, under Dr Sun Yat-sen, raised a revolt in Canton, spearheaded by triads. The Chinese government quickly and ruthlessly crushed it. Thousands of Republicans and triad supporters fled, many into British Hong Kong, including Sun Yat-sen. The colonial authorities, knowing of his triad connections, immediately issued an order of banishment against him and he left, making his way to London. Not welcome there either, he traveled to Japan and, from there, again sought settlement in Hong Kong. J.H. Stewart Lockhart, Colonial Secretary, answered his application with an emphatic, "No", couched in these terms:

> Colonial Secretary's Office,
> Hong Kong.
> 4th October, 1897.
> Sir,
> In reply to your letter, undated, I am directed to inform you that this government has no intention of allowing the British Colony of Hong Kong to be used as an
> asylum for persons engaged in plots and dangerous conspiracies against a friendly neighboring empire, and that in view of the part taken by you in such transactions, which you euphemistically term in your letter, "Emancipating your miserable countrymen from the cruel Tartar yoke", you will be arrested if you land in this colony under an order of banishment against you in 1896.
> I have &
> Sd. J.H. Stewart Lockhart.

Colonial Secretary

Lockhart appears to have penned this missive in high dudgeon at the brazen temerity of Dr Sun.

Operating from Japan, with forays into South China, Sun's Republican Party suffered little from the Hong Kong rebuff and his emissaries whipped up support among triads in Hong Kong. This resulted in the formation of the first home-grown Hong Kong triad society, the Chung Wo Tong. Its purpose was to co-ordinate support from all local triads. After Sun Yat-sen established the Republic of China in 1911, sweeping away the Qing dynasty, the Chung Wo Tong turned its attention to the local scene and, from it, emerged the Wo group of societies, wielding the most power in the territory well into the '50s. There were smaller triad groups expanding as well, the Tung, Chuen, Shing, Yee On and Luen.

Without a shred of patriotism left, the Wo group were totally self-centered on their pursuit of riches by any means. They corruptly influenced all levels of society, were aggressive in territorial expansion and ruled with an iron fist. Inevitably splits and internecine warfare erupted. At this point, there was a meeting of minds in which spheres of influence were decided among the top seven groups. By 1912 the population of Hong Kong had reached 600,000. Population concentrations were on the waterfront of the island and in Yaumati, Mongkok and Sham Shui Po. Each had different ethnic characteristics, including dialect, and were under the "protection" of triad groups with similar ethnicities.

We now fast-forward to the 1970s when the major triad players are the Wo Shing Wo and Wo On Lok of the Wo group, the Fuk Yee Hing, 14K and the San Yee On. There were also increasing numbers of gangs simply borrowing triad nomenclature to instill fear in their victims. In 1970 TSB intelligence could name 195 illegal societies, more than half operating under the guise of triads. Some were muscling in on the territory of the established triads, causing friction. Triad culture was endemic in all levels of society. There was no genuine patriotic aim or lawful means of making a living among them although some attempted to legitimize their existence under cover of legally registered societies, sports clubs and business fronts. CID/TSB were becoming more successful in garnering information from informers, resulting in a bank of detailed knowledge, a who's who of triads.

One such intelligence gathering foray for CID/TSB was the annual Pak Tai Festival, more popularly known as the Bun Festival, on Cheung Chau Island. In May '76, I took my team, with two other teams led by experienced, local inspectors, to the island in the early morning. There were already crowds of tourists, local and expatriate, milling about in the narrow streets, just a few feet wide, in the old fishing village. In the square in front of the temple to Pak Tai, the most important deity for the island, three rocket-shaped sixty-foot towers, built with bamboo scaffolding and wrapped with sheets of paper, had been erected. They were covered with thousands of white buns, each with a red spot, glued to the paper.

The festival has its origin in the 18th Century when the fishing village was ravaged by a deadly pestilence. The villagers prayed to Pak Tai, the deity for calm waters and healthy lives. The survivors passed down the tradition of parading the image of Pak Tai round the village, warding off evil spirits. Lion dances accompany the procession with much clanging of cymbals and banging of drums. Martial arts groups on the island have for years played a major part in these ceremonials and many of the players were known triads. One could always tell the triad lions by their color, not the usual red and gold but black with white trimming. Such was the spectacle that many senior triad members attended. A few of our detectives operated undercover, using hidden cameras to record and identify these men.

The climax of the festival came in the late afternoon. Teams of barechested, mostly tattooed, swarthy young men, wearing plimsolls, baggy black trousers tucked into socks and red headbands stand opposite each tower. A local dignitary gives the signal and, amid wild shouting and cheers, the teams, ten- or twelve-strong, dash into the bases of the bun towers, clawing their way up the dark interiors to the top. Just seconds later a fist can be seen, then another, and another, punched through the paper top, bursting out and grabbing the prized buns.

In 1978, disaster struck. The bun tower scramble ended in the toppling of a weak and overloaded tower. It fell across the crowd and more than 100 people were injured, some so seriously they were airlifted to hospital. Among them were two uniformed policemen. Fortunately there were no fatalities. Since then only one person has been allowed to be "in the race" up each tower.

In April 1978, information of top-level meetings between 14K factions was received. Of about thirty-six such factions, five were organizing the meetings. The spur for this summit was the opening of the Jockey Club's new Shatin Racecourse and, hence, the opportunity for illegal bookmaking. Such a large scale operation would require unifying 14K factions to maximize profit and minimize exposure to police enforcement. A secondary aim was to prevent further disintegration of the 14K into rudderless gangs.

A decision was made in October '78 to form a central committee headed by Mr Kot Chi-hung, son and successor to General Kot Siu-wong. Five faction leaders, alongside Kot and his treasurer plus three more officials, were elected and one of those leaders, Mr Leung Chi-sang, a solicitor's clerk by day, offered the Mongkok premises of his martial arts school as the headquarters. The senior partner of the solicitors' firm registered a new name for it, the Hung Fat Gymnasium, incorporating the "Hung" character as in Triad.

The parceling out of power by just five of the thirty-six 14K factions proved disagreeable to the majority which organized their own summit, electing a committee in direct opposition to the first. The duplicitous Mr Kot Chi-hung was also their elected chairman. Strife ensued and, using the strategy of divide and conquer, the police succeeded in eliminating triad bookmaking at Shatin Racecourse.

In 1977, the TSB set up an undercover operation to infiltrate the San Yee On Triad Society which had its power-base in Tsim Sha Tsui. The San Yee On was formed by Mr Heung Chin, an officer in the KMT spy section who fled to Hong Kong in 1949. He gathered former KMT personnel around him and took advantage of the comparatively lawless situation that existed in East Kowloon at the time. He prospered and by 1956, had four wives and thirteen acknowledged children. In 1960 Heung was arrested, convicted of unlawful society offenses and deported. He went to live in Taiwan. The first three of his wives remained in Hong Kong with their children. Like father, like son, three of his sons, Heung Wah-yim, Heung Wah-shing and Heung Wah-keung, became leaders in the San Yee On Triad. Wah-yim, the eldest by his father's first wife, inherited his father's "business interests" and status as head of the San Yee On. Wah-shing, son of the second wife, and Wah-keung, son of the third wife, had no inheritance. Wah-keung, a sickly child bullied at school, lived in Kowloon City with his poor mother. In 1970 Wah-keung, twenty, traveled to Taiwan with his older brother Wah-shing, to meet their father and seek financial support. Their mission was unsuccessful but, while in Taiwan, Wah-keung landed a job with a film agent and he made in-roads into the martial arts film industry popularized by Bruce Lee.

After Wah-keung returned to Hong Kong he and Wah-shing spent the next five years or so pouring their energies into the film industry, using triad coercion for their nefarious activities. In 1973, Bruce Lee died at age thirty-three of an accidental overdose of barbiturates in the bed of a well-endowed film actress, Betty Ting-pie. He left a widow with two small children. There was considerable public hostility towards Betty and it was Wah-keung, already friends with her through the film industry, who took her under his wing. In '76 Wah-keung married her but the marriage was short-lived when Betty became a strict Buddhist.

Now wealthy, Wah-keung turned his hand to film directing. Simultaneously he and Wah-shing were recruiting the best actors in town, "protecting" them from other film companies. His first two movies were box-office flops and his capital was all but wiped out. However, in '78, Wah-keung pulled off a scoop, recruiting the legendary beauty Chan Ming-ying, the most popular model in Taiwan with a following in Hong Kong. He married her and she helped him stay afloat with her fashion business while he and Wah-shing recouped their losses through crime, building up their triad influence in the San Yee On. Wah-keung's wife turned actress and their third movie proved a success. He set up his own film company, Wing Shing. In 1982 Wah-keung scored a second coup, recruiting the rising star, Miss Cheung Man. She went on to marry Wah-shing.

In 1992, a famous Kung Fu actor, Jet Lee, was with Golden Harvest films and Wah-keung tried to poach him for his own film company. Jet Lee's agent handled settlement talks between the two companies and Wah-keung lost out. The very next day, the agent was killed in a drive-by shooting. Jet Lee's brother-in-law took over negotiations which, again, didn't go well. A week later he died in a car crash.

The same year one of Hong Kong's most famous pop singers, Anita Mui, insulted a 14K triad boss, Wong Long-wai. Wong very publicly slapped her. The story goes that Anita then put in a phone call to Wah-keung. Within a week Wong Long-wai was the victim of a vicious triad attack, the muscles and sinews of his shoulders and legs severed with a beef knife. This attack was carried out by an infamous San Yee On fighter known as the Tiger of Wanchai. In 1993 the Tiger, himself, was the victim of a 14K triad assassination. These are examples of the extreme measures triad societies resorted to in protecting their interests.

A Hong Kong Standard story on June 17, 1981, recounts the trial in Tsuen Wan District Court of 17 defendants, all in the film industry and all members of the Sun Yee On Triad Society. They were convicted of kidnapping kung fu film star Wong Yu, conspiracy to commit criminal intimidation, being office bearers of the San Yee On triad, unlawful assembly and taking part in a triad ceremony.

The investigation began in November 1977 with the infiltration by three undercover police officers into the San Yee On. On 9 May 1978, they, with four civilian recruits, were put through an initiation ceremony. Two office bearers of the San Yee On assisted the initiates as their guarantors, one of them taking a leading role in the ceremony. One of the undercover officers testified:

"...He and the new members first knelt down and then Chan Kai (senior triad office bearer) made them read out some poems. After this Chan patted their shoulders with a knife indicating how traitors to the society would die. Chan then used a pin to prick the middle finger of each of the new members until they bled, telling them to lick their fingers clean of blood. Next, Chan produced three 'ghost' papers and wrote Chinese characters on each of them. Placing them on the floor he asked the new members to step on them. Chan explained that these papers represented the three rocks 'Tin', 'Hoi' and 'Pau' and that whenever a person wanted to join the 'Hung Mun' he has to pass those three rocks.

"After stepping over the 'ghost' papers, the initiates knelt down again while Chan, holding a strip of red paper, moved it around their heads. Putting it down, he took a hen's egg, drew some figures on it and placed it on the floor in front of them. He then asked them to all hold onto the handle of the knife, telling them to chop the egg in pieces together. He explained that this demonstrates how traitors are treated.

"Chan picked up another piece of red paper which had some figures on it. He then proceeded to write the new members' names on the paper. Having done so he gave each of them a number to remember, telling them that these are peculiar to the San Yee On. That marked the end of the ceremony."

The ceremony described above is a farcical parody of the original, bearing little resemblance to the theatrical and more meaningful ceremony of the '50s described by W.P. Morgan in his book.

The trial evidence continued:

"On October 4, 1978, two of the undercover policemen were part of an ambush set at a construction site in Tsim Sha Tsui to which Tai Huen Chai (Big Circle Gang from China) members had been lured on false pretences. They didn't show up.

"On June 18, 1979, two of the undercover officers were ordered to a restaurant in Caernarvon Road, Tsim Sha Tsui. Outside they were met by another two members of the San Yee On who went into a tailor's shop. They were soon followed by three others, one of whom signaled the undercover officers to follow them. There the witness saw Heung Wah-shing with another senior member. Moments later they all went down the road to Lo Wei's film company.

"On arrival, Lo Wei himself opened the door to them. Once inside Lo Wei, Heung Wah-shing and two other senior members of the San Yee On went into a separate office. Later one of them came out and telephoned a restaurant, asking for Chan Cheung.

"Afterwards the undercover policemen, with two other members, were told to find David Chan Cheung and tell him to leave Tsim Sha Tsui, with the message that if he was ever seen there again, they (the triads) wouldn't be so kind to him. The four were also instructed that, if they found the actor Wong Yu with David Chan they were to assault him, threatening him not to interfere. One of the four asked a senior member why they had to assault Wong Yu and the reply was he had invited another Kung Fu actor, Shing Lung, to dinner, telling him not to work for Lo Wei Film Company. The four located David Chan but Wong Yu was not there. Under dire threat, David Chan agreed to quit Tsim Sha Tsui.

"Upon reporting back to the Lo Wei film studio, Heung Wah-shing and his entourage, including the two undercover policemen, left for the New World Night Club, situated in a shopping mall complex on the Tsim Sha Tsui waterfront. This was Wah-shing's territory. Sometime later a senior member told the four to come with him to the Fu Yiu restaurant where they would abduct the actor Wong Yu. This place was also a haunt of Heung Wah-keung and it was Wah-shing who told them that, if they saw him there, they were to ignore him."

It is clear that the principal triad societies were in large scale, organized crime syndicates, operating through the '70s and into the '80s. But it was the fact that all semblance of traditional triad activity had long since been discarded that led, on March 15, 1978, to a police headquarters decision to disband CID/TSB and integrate it with the Organized Crime and Triad Bureau. I was posted to the Criminal Intelligence Bureau thereafter and one of my first assignments was to research and draft the CID/ CIB intelligence brief on the 14K Triad. This was published in January 1979, the document I referred to earlier.

At the beginning of this chapter, I mentioned Chief Superintendent Teddy U Tat-ming and Detective Sergeant Toby Lau Kin-shing. Toby was a hard-working and skilled detective, demonstrating initiative. He was a triad expert, thorough and reliable. When he was arrested in early 1978, one of 119 police officers taken in one big purge by the Independent Commission against Corruption, I was surprised.

It turned out the evidence against him was the name "KS Lau" in a notebook found in the possession of a Yau Ma Tei market fruit vendor, dating back several years. It listed bribes to Urban Services Department, Customs and Excise staff and policemen. Toby Lau was not identified in a subsequent ID parade or fingered in the witness statements obtained by ICAC. He told me he was innocent of the charge. I believed him.

A few days after the ICAC arrests, demoralized and angry rank and file officers tried to see Commissioner Brian Slevin. He refused to come out and face them. He slipped out of a back gate in the HQ compound (since then known as Traitor's Gate), going to see the Governor. About 300 thwarted policemen then made an unplanned march, which could and should have been forestalled by Slevin, heading for Government House. Detective inspectors, including me, were hurriedly detailed to attack the ICAC offices. There was much shouting and one ICAC officer suffered minor injuries but otherwise there was little damage, one broken glass door after a flowerpot went through it.

As a result of Slevin's meeting with the Governor it was agreed in the Executive Council that there had to be an amnesty for junior police officers and their pay and conditions should be improved significantly. Toby Lau, alongside most of the other 118 arrestees, was eventually released without charge. But a policy decision was made, in view of the public mood, that they would all be ordered to resign. What we now call constructive dismissal. As for Toby, I was able to find him a clerical job with a reputable solicitors' firm whose partners I knew well from my days as a court prosecutor. Toby remains a good friend of mine.

These days, when Toby and I meet on my holidays back in Hong Kong, we reminisce about the good old days and our more memorable exploits as a team. There is one, from my first year in TSB, that sticks in my mind because it exemplified the public respect and absolute awe in which TSB was generally held in the '70s and '80s.

One of my local colleagues learned of a large-scale "settlement" meeting of Yee On triad factions, disguised as a birthday celebration for one official, to be held in a basement nightclub of Tsim Sha Tsui's infamous Chung King Mansion. The building was a thirty-storey apartment block built in the late '30s. Over the years tenants had turned it into a maze of small, illegal businesses, often tampering with the internal structure and breaching fire regulations. The ground floor was a shopping arcade and the basement one huge nightclub and ballroom. The building still exists but in 2010 it was practically gutted from the inside out and re-built. The basement nightclub disappeared.

Knowing there was a possibility of confrontation and violence, the decision was made to raid the establishment and disrupt the proceedings. Given the expected numbers attending, five operational teams were mobilized. A few hours before the "party" all the teams unobtrusively entered the building, avoiding detection by lookouts outside. We estimated there were as many as 360 "guests" seated at thirty round tables. After the first banquet course had been served, it was decided to mount the raid with teams entering the ballroom simultaneously from every entrance. It was D/Sgt Toby Lau who jumped atop one of the tables and silenced everyone with his shouted announcement that Faan Haak Jo was here. He told everyone to squat down on the floor with their hands on their heads, as the raiding teams quickly spread round the tables. There was no resistance whatsoever.

Women and children were released. Every suspect was searched and their identities checked. Many suspects surreptitiously discarded incriminating evidence, including weapons, illicit drugs and triad-related documents, name lists and so forth. Everything was seized as exhibits and taken to CID Headquarters with sixty-four arrested persons. Several were wanted by police for other crimes and all were interrogated.

Teddy U, the boss of TSB, was a true gentleman of the old style, not at all suave, just a plain gentleman, coming from a well-to-do Chinese family and well educated. He was a thoughtful leader, fair and honest. He had a few foibles — don't we all? — and one of these was Chinese superstition, a belief in geomancy or *feng shui*.

His big office was in one corner of the twenty-storey CID Headquarters, known as May House after the first Commissioner of Police, Captain May. His office door opened into one end of a sixty-foot corridor. A traditional Chinese belief is that evil travels in straight lines. To counter this bad luck, Teddy U had a hardboard screen, dubbed the *feng shui* board, mounted in the middle of the corridor, almost next to my office, with only enough room for a man to squeeze past it, sideways.

One day it was found to have a big hole kicked in it by someone's frustrated boot. Feathers ruffled, Teddy walked into my office wanting to know who the culprit was. Naturally (and honestly) I denied all knowledge but it didn't take long to ascertain who it was, Superintendent Ted Perkins who had been grumbling the loudest over the obstruction. Apparently he had torn his trouser-front on a screw of the metal frame as he edged past the panel. The hole in the board was immediately covered with paper and cello tape until a permanent repair was made.

In his retirement, Teddy U indulges in his favorite pursuit of horse racing. Not only is he a member of the Hong Kong Jockey Club, he is steward as well. A racehorse owner, he is seen at the races at every opportunity. Another favorite pastime is attending lunches with former colleagues. I usually meet up with him when I'm back in Hong Kong.

I was a bit of an athlete in my day taking part in cross-country orienteering races. One teamed up with another runner and, equipped with map and compass, ran to a list of map references, collecting a colored tab at each target. During one race, while charging down a scrub-covered slope, I broke a couple of metatarsals in my left foot. The hospital doctor wrapped my leg up to the knee in plaster-of-paris. In mid-summer, this plaster boot was most uncomfortable. A few days later Teddy U, noting my discomfort, asked if I would trust Chinese dit-da medicine. "If so," he said, "I know just the man to mend your foot without all this Western medicine stuff," looking disdainfully at my heavy plaster cast.

Chinese dit-da medicine practice goes back as far as time, based on herbal remedies plus dried bits of animals, fish and reptiles. In the Northern Sung Dynasty the term used for a practitioner's clinic was jing-gwat-foh meaning "bone-setting-office", hence, a common pseudonym "bone-setter" for those early medics. Dit-da, a Cantonese expression, is the shortened form of dit-da-seung-foh meaning, literally, "falling-down-injury-office".

I accepted Teddy U's suggestion. We took his car into the back streets of Western, the oldest part of town. We parked outside a sixty- or seventy-year-old stone-built tenement block. The wooden name board above the slatted front doors was painted black with the name of the dit-da shop in gold lettering. Teddy U, evidently well-known there, introduced me to "Master" Chiu Shing-lam, a stocky, muscular man in his late 50s with a full head of black hair, rugged features and a kind smile. Teddy U didn't mention anything about being a triad and I didn't ask. I was shown a seat, a carved teak-wood bench, and given a cup of black tea.

The dit-da clinic's once cream-painted walls were stained brown, rising to black at the ceiling, especially above the elaborately carved wooden altar to Kwan Dai, the red-faced, stern general, armed with a halberd, who lived in the Eastern Han Dynasty. The old war lord is worshipped by policemen and triads alike for his loyalty, forbearance and courage. Incense was burning before him all day, hence the smoke-blackened ceiling.

Patients were treated in two alcoves, each with green chintz curtains screening the teak-wood divans. Around the walls were shelves of glass bottles, wooden boxes and weighing scales, pestle and mortar. There were dusty photographs, mostly of martial arts groups clad in black, and one or two ancient portraits of ancestors. I recognized a younger Chiu Shing-lam occupying pride-of-place in two of the pictures. He was evidently a prominent martial arts expert in his time. I wasn't surprised as it was common for

exponents of martial arts to apprentice themselves to a "bone setter" so, at the end of their sporting days, they had a well-paid profession.

I waited my turn. A middle-aged man walked out of one of the "operating theaters," his torso completely bandaged, looking like an Egyptian mummy.

Chiu Shing-lam pulled up a stool and started cutting away my plaster boot with tailor's scissors, exposing whitened, damp-looking skin. Taking my injured foot in his lap he kneaded it, feeling the toe bones with his fingers. I was expecting pain but there was none. After a few minutes he explained, in simple Cantonese, for he had no English, that two bones were broken. He proposed an herbal poultice. I would have to return to his clinic every day for a week for the medicine to be renewed.

I watched him prepare the poultice. He spread a sheet of polythene, then white cotton and, opening a jar, ladled out a steaming gray-green mix. He wrapped that in the cotton sheeting, picked up the polythene sheet and folded it round my foot. Then came the bandaging to hold it all in place. The whole session lasted about ten minutes.

I dutifully attended his clinic as appointed and, on the last day, Chiu Shing-lam felt around my foot, smiled and said the bones were healed but that I shouldn't go running just yet. Another week passed and it was time for me to attend the government (Western medicine) hospital for my check-up. The doctor took one look at me, as I walked in to his surgery, and said, "I know where you got your cure."

Cue Chaos

Steve Reels

Half a lifetime ago, I ran a pool hall at the top of Old Bailey Street. It was 1978, I was twenty-one and had responded to a newspaper ad for a manager of one of a chain of pool halls being developed across some of the seedier stretches of Hong Kong. I had no real experience in sports management, or indeed management of any kind, but I could speak Cantonese and had organised cross-country races through my athletics club. I got the job.

I saw it as an opportunity to get away from English tutoring, which I hated, and to try something new, but I could not have imagined how utterly unlike my erstwhile job it would be, a jolting immersion into the gritty underbelly of Hong Kong.

I was sent to the Hung Hom branch of the pool-hall chain as assistant manager for two weeks of training. But if I was expecting a structured fortnight of managerial enlightenment I could not have been more wrong. I walked into a crowded, dimly lit hall with twenty-four pool tables and an equal number of pinball machines lining the walls. Tattooed Chinese youths and young men like roosters with layered Rod Stewart haircuts strutted the floor, cues held like weapons, while their mini-skirted women sat on the edges of pool tables showing off the tattoos on their bosoms and thighs at a time when tattooing was very much the domain of the underworld. Debby Boone's *You Light Up My Life* poured from the jukebox while scuffles and confrontations erupted periodically. And there I was, supposed to keep order, a white boy in short-sleeved shirt and red tie, a sore thumb, a sitting duck.

My fortnight in Hung Hom was a nightmare. I had no idea how to deal even with my own staff, never mind the delinquent clientele. I stumbled through the fourteen days in a haze of inexperience and ineptitude, floundering comically with my naive attempts at authority. Misbehaviour was endemic. The moment I turned my back the mischief would start again, the table-sitting, the cue-bashing, the swearing and the shoving. In my clumsy attempts to run the show I managed to alienate the cashier, the mechanics, the cleaners and the coaches. By the time the fortnight was over, my stock, I felt, was zero. I was a joke, a busted flush. I was ready to quit.

Then everything changed. I was posted to what was known in the company as "Central", the property at the top of Old Bailey Street where it meets Caine Road. This was a smaller branch with just sixteen tables and pinball machines. Hung Hom was already a receding Hadean torment when I stepped through the saloon-style swing doors of Central to find a pleasant, brightly lighted, almost homely leisure parlor. I was told by the boss that I was being given sole charge of the joint. As my breast swelled, he added that it was a smaller branch than the others so there would be no assistant manager.

What this meant was that I would be working fifteen hours a day seven days a week, a proposition that ought to have seemed preposterous but one that seemed to me somehow enticing, a compelling challenge. I loved the Central branch at first sight, the expansive windows, the antique neighborhood, the white-uniformed kids who swarmed the place, the cooperative cashier. It seemed idyllic, and I felt blessed.

Things went well from the start. I had the advantage of two weeks of Hung Hom humiliations in my back pocket, mistakes

I had no intention of making again, although I would make different mistakes. Light thronged the Old Bailey Street windows and from day one I seemed to cruise between genial banter with the regulars and constructive relations with the staff. Customers by and large obeyed house rules and when they didn't the staff were smartly on the job. I set to work with the mechanics building a workshop and came into my element organizing regular pool tournaments with the coaches, establishing rules, designing posters, ordering trophies. All this had to be cleared by head office, but the word was that the boss was impressed with my work.

I was still on a probationary wage but had been promised a substantial increase after six months. I couldn't afford to rent a flat so I took a room in a Sham Shui Po tenement, a six-storey mid-century building on Nam Cheong Street. My shared unit was on the fifth floor (no lift) and consisted of a large front room with a multi-paned window, which was my room, then a corridor running to the back of the premises where the communal toilet and kitchen were located, smelling of excreta and wet concrete. The area between was subdivided into one-room units leading off the corridor by wooden partitions that didn't quite reach the ceiling. There were no windows other than mine, and the rest of the place was dark and dank with little privacy. My neighbors, mainly single men, kept themselves to themselves, with one notable exception when we all gathered in the kitchen for a boozy dog-meat dinner. There were rats.

After my double shift at the pool hall I would lock up late in the evening and rush to catch the Star Ferry to Kowloon then the bus to Sham Shui Po. I would grab some street food at the daipaidongs that flourished in the area, crawl into my tenement bed and leave early in the morning to open the shop for the cleaners. In those pre-MTR days this insane itinerary was starting to take its toll. Other branches had two managers who operated a shift system. I was young and strong but not indestructible. I decided to make my bed at work. But how to avoid attracting attention?

My solution was to use a pool table as a bed. This not only kept me off the floor and its unsavoury fauna, but also meant I only needed to store a pillow and sheet in my office rather than a less explicable bedding roll. After everybody had left I would knock on the door of the mom-and-pop shop over the road, buy a couple of bottles of San Miguel, turn off the lights, pull down the blinds and avail myself of free games of pinball while playing the jukebox, also free. As the Bee Gees, Chic and Donna Summer beat out a disco soundtrack the pinball machines winked a unique light show in the darkened hall. I became quite the Pinball Wizard.

One day I saw a fellow burst through the doors out to the street as if running for his life. But nobody was chasing him. Then I noticed a film crew on Old Bailey Street, camera trained on the center. The company name and logo were emblazoned all over the exterior and I was immediately suspicious. Had they been filming in the center? Had they filmed a pool-hall brawl in-studio, and were now photographing the outside of my center to make it look as if the ruckus was on my turf? Part of my job was to improve the image of pool by presenting a squeaky-clean image of a respectable leisure center that parents would trust their kids to patronize, or even pop along too themselves. This just would not do.

Out I marched to confront the man who seemed to be the director, a short, chubby chap with jowls, who proceeded to ignore my queries. Imperiously. It was as if I wasn't there. My inquiry grew more strident until the director assigned a minion to deal with me. No, they didn't have permission to shoot the outside of the premises, and why should they? No, they hadn't been inside. No, he didn't know if they would film a pool hall scene. They packed up and left. One-nil to the film crew.

I later realized the director was Samo Hung, one of Hong Kong's top martial arts practitioners and directors, almost on a par with Bruce Lee and Jacky Chan. I never did catch the movie.

By its very nature, a pool hall attracts characters who inhabit that shady world lying on the edge of, or within, the bounds of criminality, drug abuse, extortion and violence, and despite its sunny appearance, my pool hall was no exception. The seamier side of Central was slow to reveal itself. I started noticing customers who had a discernibly menacing manner, older men with an air of entitlement. People would move aside for them between tables. It wasn't just that they expected the deference due to age. There was something callous and cruel in their demeanor, and while they never caused any trouble I kept a wary eye out and tried not to engage with them.

One in particular I recall with dread, a short, stocky figure with a low fringe and white skin that looked leached of blood. His eyes had a deep-sunken thousand-yard stare suggesting unplumbable depths and at the same time a coldness that was pure menace. I had never seen such dead eyes. The eyes of a killer.

For all I knew these guys were low-down hoodlums, crack desperados, back-alley muggers, hired guns, but they never gave me any trouble, probably because, in an unspoken alliance of expediency, we avoided each other. Face was not to be lost. In fact, the only persistent bother I had to deal with was the comical feud between Unkie and Sunday.

Unkie was a low-life sleaze ball, tall, gangly and pimply with the sunken visage of the addict. His whining voice was strangulated in the way of adolescents or perhaps he was much younger than he looked. Sunday, on the other hand, was a chubby Filipino drunk who would from time to time produce a brown paper bag from his pocket, the contents of which he would swig furtively. They hated each other.

Typically, a ruckus would erupt heralded by Unkie's wheedling, outraged tones, exactly like somebody imitating a bawling child. The next stage, if we didn't get there quickly enough, would be a full-handbag cue fight, which Sunday always had the better of. I would ban them for a period but they always came back. I had a soft spot for both of them, perhaps because they were so entertaining.

Another lad I liked was CC, short for Chi-choi or perhaps Chi-chung. He was mischievous with a ready smile, an impossibly handsome face and a mop of unruly hair straight from a Japanese manga character. An impish, hyperactive lad of sixteen or seventeen, he had a gang of followers or worshippers in front of whom he would strut and cavort shamelessly, potting balls, stripping off his singlet and striking hero poses with his cue. It was impossible not to like him.

Only once did we have a confrontation, after a display of cue-banging on the table. I manhandled him out of the door as his face flushed and his eyes betrayed anger and confusion. It was a huge loss of face. It was also the last time I saw him.

Two days later I learned that CC had been hacked to death in a gang fight in Wanchai.

As time went by I was befriended by an amiable group of regulars, The Sinn twins, Edward Kwok the hunchback, a bear-like lad my age called Hung whom I employed as a coach, less for his skill with the cue than for his ability to wrap troublemakers in a bear hug and eject them. I started to accompany them and others on late-night visits to daipaidongs for a bowl of noodles. Sometimes these would turn into beery midnight rambles through the back alleys of Sheung Wan, at that time still a squalid warren of tumbledown pre-war shop houses and tenements with wooden staircases and hidden terraces. I loved these roamings and the company of this unlikely gang of misfits and miscreants.

But was my growing familiarity with these denizens of the backstreets becoming a problem? Would familiarity breed contempt? The demise of CC should have been a red flag to my further immersion in this alien pond. Perhaps there was a hidden recess in my brain that knew I was running too close to the cusp for comfort, because I was shortly to resign, ostensibly over money.

The rationale behind the company's business plan had only revealed itself to me after arriving at Central, where I was in charge of accounts. Most of the floor area was given over to coin-operated pool tables where the majority of customers congregated. But it was the pinball machines, also coin operated, that brought in most of the income. So why bother with pool tables at all? Why not fill the space with ranks of pinball machines? The answer lay in the laws governing licences. You needed some sort of non-electronic game before you could obtain a licence for an electronic one so, sixteen mechanical pool tables and sixteen electronic pinball machines.

The company's founder, a bushy-eyed Canadian, was a formidable businessman from whom I learned a lot. I appreciated that he wanted to promote pool through competition, and indeed we organized Hong Kong's first pool championship at the Central venue, but the boss always had his eye on the bottom line.

During the championship I'd cordoned off a competition area comprising two pool tables. This area was also home to two or three pinball machines, which were to be switched off during the tournament. This "crucible" area was the most visible part of the center affording the best views of play for the dozens of spectators. But when the boss got wind of my plans, just before the event started, he decreed that the competition area be shifted to a less accessible part of the center. One with no pinball machines. I was not happy.

It all came to a head when he and I took a stroll along Caine Road, at his suggestion, just before my promised pay rise was due.

I'd previously had a run-in with him over the accounts, which he inspected every month, going through my hand-written ledger and its paper receipts in excruciating detail. There had been a discrepancy of 10 cents between expenditure recorded in the ledger and the sum of the amounts shown on the receipts, and he insisted on finding the missing 10 cents while I sat there fuming, impatient to get back to my job, which of course was much more important than a piddling 10 cents. He kept me there for hours. "It's only ten cents, Boss!" "No Steve," he replied in his honeyed voice. "It's not 'only' ten cents. We've got to get your mind right."

It was this mantra he now dealt my way again as we walked along Caine Road. "You've got a big future with us, Steve, but we've got to get your mind right." He went on to explain that I was too young to be getting the salary I'd been promised, and he wanted me to do another three months "in development". In the meantime, I'd get a ten percent rise. Suddenly it all welled up, the long hours, the low pay, the amount of effort I'd put in only to be diddled out of my rightful wage by this pernicious profiteer and his velvet voice. I didn't want to play this game anymore.

The next day I handed in my resignation, refusing all overtures to change my mind. I helped settle the new manager, whose appointment marked a reversal in company policy in that he was a local Chinese. Months later, I learned that the new man had quickly lost control of the center. The boys had started to ask for tea money and the situation had got out of hand. Hong Kong's finest were called in, a sting operation with plainclothes cops had been mounted and the new manager had been issued a bulletproof vest. At this distance from those events I can't remember the outcome. Perhaps I don't want to.

I was there for just seven months, half a lifetime ago. And I never did get my mind right.

Drunk as a Royal Skunk in Solitary First-Class Splendor

Mark Esterhuizen

This true, unembellished tale of drunkenness and debauchery happened in the Middle East, in a country that will remain anonymous and a main character who will also remain unnamed. The company I worked for until very recently, Cathay Pacific, empowered aircraft commanders with absolute authority, as required by law. However, this sometimes is diluted by "commercial" considerations. Typically, certain dispensations are made for VIPs and royalty, the very well-heeled and recognizable figures the airline frequently has as guests.

When we were to carry notable persons, we would be advised by our flight operations director or line operations manager, both senior and pivotal post holders in the organization.

On this occasion, I hadn't received any prior notification of an eminent person being carried, so when I was advised on arrival in this city that we would be carrying a Royal and his entourage from the city back to Hong Kong, I was a little dubious as some Middle Eastern countries have north of 15, "princes", some of whom are rather interesting characters, to put it mildly.

The company manager (a national of the country we were departing from) also told me that I would, meaning must, delay the departure until HRH and his entourage were on board. I make no apologies for this being somewhat of a red flag to me for a number of reasons: no one tells the captain how to manage his flight. No one, not the country manager, not the director of flight operations nor an HRH. The fundamental principle of the captain being in charge holds true for any aircraft commander, whether of a Boeing 747-400 or a Cessna 172. The ultimate authority and responsibility for the safe and efficient conduct of the flight rests solely with the captain.

There is no love lost between me and certain countries in the Middle East. My mother (still very much alive) is a Holocaust survivor who, through the incredible work of Catholic nuns in Romania and the International Red Cross, managed to survive World War II and was moved to (what was at the time) Palestine. A few years after my mother's arrival in Palestine, the 1948 Arab-Israeli war broke out and my mother, being of eligible age, was drafted to serve in the Israeli Army. To put it very mildly, a concerted effort was mounted by certain nationalities to remove her from the census. To add to the insult, until very recently, this particular country refused to acknowledge the existence of Israel.

As a result, being instructed to wait was not a good move by anyone. Perhaps I heard it incorrectly, or "misinterpreted" the "request", but my response was simple and to the point,

"Please inform HRH that my (emphasis on 'my') aircraft will depart on time, whether he and his entourage are on board or not." The gauntlet had been thrown down.

Aircraft movements are a carefully choreographed sequence of events. Everything runs to a tight schedule, literally to the minute. In some jurisdictions, airlines are penalized financially for late departures, so On Time Performance (OTP) is extremely important. On the evening of our departure, things were running smoothly. The crew arrived at the aircraft at STD minus 50 (fifty minutes prior to scheduled time of departure); freight loading commenced at STD minus 45; fuel uplift at STD - 4; passenger boarding at STD minus 30 and completed at STD minus 20. Our final fuel (finely calculated for the exact amount needed for the planned flight route, anticipated winds and aircraft mass) was ordered at STD minus 20 and ATC (Air Traffic Control) clearance obtained at STD minus 10.

There was no sign of HRH at STD minus 10, the cut off for late boarding and things started looking somewhat ominous. I would have to make good on my threat uttered (possibly in haste) the night before. Then, to my relief, a rather long convoy of large, black American-built (bullet proof?) SUVs appeared on the far side of the apron, speeding towards us with only one set of boarding stairs attached to the front left door.

Dramatically, the vehicles' doors opened in unison, there was flurry of bodyguards, and HRH, resplendent in his white robes, gold glittering in the floodlights, brilliant white gutra flowing like a superhero's cape over the bisht and thawb. He was closely followed by his substantial group of camp followers who in an almost choreographed show, bounded up the stairs and into the aircraft. The stairs were removed, the door closed with a satisfying thump, clearance to start was given and we were on our way.

I neglected to mention that this was all taking place during Ramadhan, the holy of holies. Among other activities, the consumption of alcohol is strictly prohibited. In this specific country, alcohol is so despised that if you as an expat, choose to imbibe, a letter declaring oneself an alcoholic needs to be produced at government-controlled outlets.

Now to the interesting part of this little saga. Shortly after take-off, the ISM (inflight service manager) came into the cockpit to inform me that her sole passenger in first class (HRH had booked all six seats to ensure privacy) had requested, and "chugged" a whole bottle of Chivas, twenty-five-year-old. All 750ml. Neat.

The ISM asked me what she should do as she'd never

encountered behavior like that before. As an ex-Air Force pilot and Hash House Harrier, I can say with confidence that I am fairly experienced in the matter of overconsumption of alcoholic beverages and alcohol poisoning, and I proceeded to give her a briefing on what was about to unfold.

"HRH is going to projectile vomit and likely pass out, followed by more vomiting." With visions of a headline in the SCMP or The New York Times declaring "Prince dies on flight to Hong Kong" and "Captain declared persona non grata in every Middle East country," I then told her to ready a bucket for the first deluge and when HRH passed out to make sure he was on his side lest he did a Jimi Hendrix or Janis Joplin by inhaling and choking on his own vomit. HRH had made the wise move of changing into a tracksuit (luxury brand and embroidered) after he boarded the flight and before the binge began. This made manoeuvring him around in his passed-out state later much easier, and he did follow normal human physiology by vomiting violently and passing out.

The noises behind the cockpit armoured door in flight were, to be frank, disturbing. The ISM handled the situation well and on my advice proceeded to feed HRH in his passed-out state everything that we had in the galley, most of which came back up again. It had the effect of purging his body and he slowly regained consciousness as the flight neared our destination.

To our relief, he was lucid and behaving somewhat normally as we began our descent into Hong Kong. HRH cleaned himself up, changed back into his royal garb and to our utter astonishment walked himself off the aircraft as if absolutely nothing was amiss. Legend. There are a couple of corollaries, almost epiphanies that came from this little escapade.

We are all human. Alcohol is no respecter of rank or royalty. HRH must have been or is a candidate for any Air Force as a pilot. On time performance is a great motivator.

The captain's word does mean something. A vomit-encrusted seat cleans up well. Before all the punters had disembarked, there were new covers on the affected seats (the splash had travelled quite a distance). Despite a positive pressure differential between the cockpit and the cabin, some smells do penetrate. A somewhat fouled red velour Balenciaga tracksuit cleaned up well and made a nice souvenir.

Insurance Man-cum-Preacher Builds Family of God

John Snelgrove

This is a Hong Kong story with a difference from someone who has spent over half of his life on the "Barren Rock", who deeply loves the place and calls it "home". Simply put, it is the tale of an insurance man-turned-preacher.

When confronted with the apparent strangeness of this combo, I always explain that the two businesses are in fact the same. Both are "insurances", but my current product is superior—it goes on forever.

On to the story of the Barren Rock:

In 1987, I was asked to consider taking my family (my wife Sandra, my two sons Paul and Matt, and my sheepdog Bella) to Hong Kong for three years (yeah, right!) to start an investment services company for National Mutual.

Our only previous visit to HK was in 1981: I had brought a group of London insurance brokers and financial planners to Hong Kong for a sales convention. We stayed at the newly opened Regent Hotel in TST. My first sight of Hong Kong after an arduous flight was of the iconic harbor through the Regent's monumental windows. It was blazingly sunshine and there were junks, dhows, call them whatever, gleaming in it. However, my wife Sandra took one look down busy Nathan Road and boldly exclaimed, "I could never live here in a million years." (Moral: never say never.)

On to 1987, we even missed our flight from London Gatwick. Thinking it was leaving at 11:00 p.m., we were astonished to find the flight was not on the destination board—until we realized it had left at 11:00 a.m. This story was leaked to Lai See at the SCMP and we were famous before we arrived—for the wrong reason.

Talking of wrong reasons…

My arrival was swiftly followed by the famous stock market crash of 1987 (Black Monday) and I ended up "trying to sell ice cream to Eskimos" here. The toughest period of my business life. Humbling.

I wish I could tell you the whole story but suffice to say, in that time, God gave me a love for Hong Kong and a vision for His church and thirty-five years later, I am still here!

But I nearly never got past the first six months. Hong Kong is a place of feast or famine. The investment market was a prime example: the bull market of 1985-1987 had been replaced by fear. The taxi drivers and amahs who had started to invest were joined on the sidelines by the more serious investors. It was said the only difference between fund managers and pigeons was that pigeons could still put a deposit on a Mercedes.

Sensing my hopelessness, my UK office had kindly tabled a fairly attractive offer of a job back there. Was this a convenient time to wave a premature farewell to the Barren Rock, in favor of the more familiar? This came at a time when the top rate of UK income tax had been slashed by the Tories from 60 percent to 40 percent, adding to the argument.

But though I was a businessman, I was first and foremost a Christian businessman. In the early '80s, I was a successful sales manager of a UK insurance company, a subsidiary of a merchant bank, when, in my late twenties, I realized I had got practically everything the world could throw at me in a material sense—

yet I had a chasm in my heart. I first saw this in other people who clearly had found something I didn't have and was looking for. And so I recommitted my life, manifested by taking adult confirmation classes in my suburban Anglican church in the UK.

The workplace became my mission field from Day 1, as everybody was curious about what had happened to me. Although I was the company's leading sales manager, my lifestyle had been decidedly self-absorbed. To be honest... I was a foul-mouthed, driven workaholic.

But now I had a new Boss, and was willing to follow Him to the ends of the earth.

Hong Kong was exactly that.

It was Chinese New Year in 1988 that we had our first trip away from the 852. To Bali in Indonesia. Away from the lights of Hong Kong Island and its frightening pace of life, I had a chance to reflect. And it was in the Sanur Beach Hilton that I first felt that renewed sense of calling to Hong Kong and we came back to Kai Tak with the sense that we would finish what we had started, rejecting the kind offer from Blighty in the process. It was ironic that to get a vision for the Barren Rock I had to travel to a destination boasting barren volcanic hillsides and lush rice terraces. Bali (pre-Covid-19) has remained a home away from home for us since.

But how does the claimed vision and call to ministry stack up alongside my comfortable general manager's office in Wanchai, and the perks that go along with it?

The simple answer: my pulpit was my office. Words are not always necessary for preaching any sort of gospel. My door was always open and a succession of colleagues from the tea lady to senior executives would take advantage of prayer, counsel or just plain friendship. I reached more people in an insurance office that I ever have in a church.

Through lunchtime business groups and the famous HSBC Breakfast (on the top floor of The Bank once a month), plus a host of other opportunities, I discovered that I was not alone. Hong Kong had not embraced the post-modern values of the West and is generally receptive to Christians and their teaching, possibly something to do with the amazing work during the colonial period that Christians had done in establishing schools, hospitals and a myriad of social care agencies.

Now that I am a pastor, I am often asked, "How long have you been in full-time ministry here?" My answer is that I have always been in full-time ministry here.

Whether you are a preacher or people call you a super-apostle – or you are a bank manager, school teacher or a full-time mum. Whether you minister to drug addicts and street sleepers – or you wash dishes in a cha chaan teng… You are called!

At the risk of repeating myself, when people ask, "When ere you called to the ministry?" I say I always have been. I do not see my "transfer" from my office at AXA in Wanchai to my office at the Vine in Lan Kwai Fong (yes!) as a flash of lightning in the sky, a spiritual awakening, but rather a working out of the calling that was already there.

I'll go further… I believe we not only have a general calling, we each have a specific calling. Even when I became a pastor, God gave me a specific call to church unity and raising up the next generation, which I hold to this day.

I need to return to 1990, the end of my three-year contract. My UK parent company was looking to find a "pig in a haystack", a suitable job for me. But our family did not want to leave Hong Kong. We had come to regard it as home. Having gone through the crash of 1987 and Tiananmen Square in 1989, we were starting to identify ourselves as Hong Kong people.

A famous preacher, Dr RT Kendall from Westminster Chapel,

had come to Hong Kong in March 1990. We were on the National Mutual boat (I know, decadence!) off Deep Water Bay when he said, "I see that you as a family feel called to stay in Hong Kong," and at 3:40 p.m. on 10 March 1990, he prayed for our family.

Months later, the feeling grew in us that we were not going anywhere, when suddenly the National Mutual Hong Kong Managing Director, Terry Jenkins, called me in and asked out of the blue, "Do you feel like staying in Hong Kong?" After a long discussion, I was asked to go away and write a job description for a new post of general manager, marketing. This time for the whole insurance company and not just the investment arm.

The three-year "contract" went on to become a sixteen-plus year assignment. Ironically, I never even had a contract but was allowed to remain on the same terms, until my "transfer" to the Vine Church in 2003.

This period marked a highlight of my working career. The marketing role included responsibility for advertising, public and press relations, and for the period 1992-1999, when we were listed on the Hong Kong Stock Exchange, responsibility for investor relations.

We had some considerable challenges in that time, including the resignation of our chief executive plus 1,000 insurance agents in 1994. As the frontline for both press and investors, with a share price that fell more than 30 percent overnight, it was responsible for more than a few gray hairs.

But for a boy from Southeast London to have that experience and the thrill of both stock exchange listing and privatization (not to mention investor meetings across the globe and the rebranding of National Mutual to AXA following the French insurance giant's takeover) was an unbelievable privilege. My last few years were spent developing alternative distribution channels.

Throughout this period, I had remained steadfast in both passionately serving the church in Hong Kong and at the same time thoroughly enjoying my role as an insurance executive. For those who may be puzzled by the apparent mixing of oil and water, let me perhaps explain that I find no basis for a division between what may be described as "secular" and what is considered "sacred".

As part of my recent doctoral studies, I had the privilege to study the "Theology of Work" under visiting professor Paul Stevens from Regent, Vancouver.

He said,

For Christians, the problem is that on one side of a line there are Sunday things: other-worldly things, supernatural things, holy things and spiritual things.

On the other side of the line, there are unspiritual things: human things, natural things, this-worldly things, and the things of everyday life.

The problem is the tragic separation of Sunday, and Monday to Friday.

Church life is separated from ordinary life.

Private life is separated from public life.

Inner life is separated from outer life.

And belief is separated from behavior.

The Apostle Paul in the New Testament never said people go to church to worship. Paul believed that we are worshipping God all the time.

This led me to believe that there's no part-time option for followers of Jesus.

Having said that, there was a growing desire within me that I wanted to serve my God and the people of Hong Kong as a pastor in the church. But how? I was just an insurance man. I wasn't qualified, according to normal criteria, which usually involve seminary study of some sort — rather than insurance and marketing professional qualifications.

This irregular route to the pulpit started in 1995 as our family joined a church called Repulse Bay Baptist Church. One of the prime reasons was that a good friend of ours, Rev Alan Boddy, was the pastor and my best friend, Nick Miller, was an elder and the worship leader.

Actually Repulse Bay Baptist Church was woefully misnamed. It wasn't even in Repulse Bay, and was never an official Baptist Church. This was possibly an ideal background for what was going to happen over the next few years.

Alan resigned as pastor in 1996, and the church was left with about forty members and very little money in the bank. Closure was the most obvious option.

I was more than a little shocked when my friend and elder Tony Read called me that same evening to consider being part of the leadership team. I had to ask for time-out. But within a short time agreed to become part of a team that would discern the best way ahead for the church.

And indeed, it was decided this would not be closure but a commitment to "Build the Family of God."

I joined the leadership (elders') team and was given responsibility for the preaching schedule. I have to give a big shout out here to the Union Church in Kennedy Road, which in 1995 had trusted a certain insurance man to deliver live talks at their burgeoning Alpha Course for those asking questions about the Christian faith — only for me to discover I had both a liking and certain gift for this.

One of my sermons in 1996 was based on John 15, in which Jesus had said, "I am the vine." Within a month, we had voted to discard the embarrassing name of Repulse Bay Baptist (given our geography and lack of denominational ties) in favor of the

Vine Christian Fellowship.

Amazingly, our little church began to grow, it was particularly popular with the young and young at heart — down to a contemporary approach with a rock band rather than an organ. People would joke that we had become a church for the younger generation and a few aging rockers. I guess I fell into that category.

As we grew, we felt a desire to be located closer to the public (and a MTR station) and traded our school assembly hall at South Island School for the ballroom of the Regal Hotel.

The church continued its growth phase, which led to the four elders and our spouses taking time out in 2001 to seek what we now call "The Vine Vision". The four of us all had full jobs: a lawyer, an engineer, a government geologist as well as the insurance man. At this meeting we decided that for this vision to become a reality, we would need a full-time senior pastor.

And so we put the word out and started to interview prospective candidates. But as in interviews, I also felt a deep conviction: God had given this leadership team the vision; maybe He wanted us to carry it out. This feeling would not leave me.

I was not alone. Tony Read, an old friend working at Ove Arup as a structural engineer had been an elder since the early '90s and was feeling something similar.

One Friday night, Tony and his dear wife Drusilla joined Sandra and me for dessert buffet at the Marriott in Admiralty. The upshot: we could do this together.

Now what we were saying was that two untrained (by normal standards) pastors who were an insurance man and an engineer were volunteering to run what was by now a church with a growing reputation.

To be fair, not everyone could see this. And a number would strongly voice their opinions to try to prevent the church doing something stupid.

We were to become joint senior pastors. I would work full time as soon as was practicable and Tony would start part-time, moving to full time as soon as it was right for him and the church.

This posed a dilemma for me.

I had (remember?) no contract—and no idea of how much notice I should give.

I decided to give six months' notice with effect from July 1, 2003. Firstly, to allow AXA to find replacements and secondly, fulfill my desire to "finish well". Indeed, 2003 turned out to be possibly my most successful year at the company, certainly in terms of hitting KPI's.

I had made the decision, at age fifty, to permanently swap mortality tables and the corporate life for a Bible and pulpit.

It was a calling, but no less a calling than being a Christian businessman.

God's specific calling for my life can be summed up in four statements: First, I believe I was called to pastor the church, not a church. Over the years, this has increasingly led me to that citywide perspective and towards a desire for church unity.

Second, I believe that I was called to build a family, and allow God to build His Church. This represents a move away from seeing church as four walls and a service, and there is reason to believe this is relevant to the millennial perception of church. Third, I believe that I am called to the unique gateway nature of Hong Kong as a fully international, fully Chinese city, with impact and influence on China and the international community. Finally, I believe that I was called to raise up future generations.

On 4 January 2004, Tony and I and our wives were commissioned as the founding senior pastors of the Vine. By that evening, Sandra and I were in Toronto (thanks to the international dateline) to attend a month-long leaders school at the Toronto Airport Church. It was a radical change after more than thirty-three years in the insurance industry and set us up for what was to follow. Formal training would have to be done online and more recently, through a doctoral programme here in Hong Kong, at Bethel Seminary.

But we returned from Toronto, ready to continue to build the family of God in Hong Kong. And by God's grace, that continued to happen.

Later that year, as part of the vision to "do church" seven days a week, the Vine moved to Central, to an office in Chinachem Plaza. But we began to outgrow the building and even after taking on some extra floors, realized we would be on the move again.

After seven years in Central, the Vine Center in Wanchai saw its first services. Taking the disused Imperial Cinema, gutting it and renovating it was a labor of love. Raising $70 million for a building on which we only held only on a fifteen-year lease was, for many people, craziness in its extreme.

But, remember, our two senior pastors were an engineer and a finance man. I think God knew what we needed! Tony supervised the construction and I formed the team to raise the money.

But remember my call to raise a future generation? Well in 2013, I handed over the senior pastorship to Andrew Gardener, a uniquely gifted leader and speaker. I had known him since he was twelve years old (he was in my son's year at South Island School).

It was a joy to hand over the reins to him and his beautiful wife Christine and to watch him take the church to even higher levels. Our relationship as a spiritual father and son continues to this day.

But the story isn't finished.

Instrument Guidance System

Hong Kong currently has more than 1,300 Protestant churches, of which almost 95 percent are Chinese-speaking, with the balance deemed "international" churches, such as the Vine— mainly English-speaking, but including other languages, such as Filipino dialects, Korean, Japanese, and those spoken by other ethnic minorities. As the Hong Kong churches developed, typically Chinese speakers would attend local churches, with international churches primarily reserved for expatriates. However, with many overseas Chinese coming to or returning to Hong Kong, and their children receiving secondary or tertiary education overseas, the international churches have started to look more Asian than European. A number of international church pastors have commented that the first language of the majority of their congregation is now Cantonese.

Given my calling to the "one church" and to unity, I started to work alongside a wonderful local church with an excellent reputation, but like many local churches with an aging congregation due to their young people choosing an international congregation. In 2016, I was privileged to partner with Kong Fong Church and began a Saturday night service for all ages in English, and more in keeping with the style of the international churches. I remain an ambassador and strong supporter of Andrew and the team at the Vine.

People talk to me about the "R" word—retirement. Wrong subject. Hong Kong is my home and people of all faiths and ages are looking for hope and a future. I don't have much to offer, but will continue, by God's grace, to offer what I do have.

And I can give testimony to thirty-five years of God's grace and His using this insurance man-turned-pastor to help build something of lasting value here on this Barren Rock.

Farmers' Boys Dream of Future Landings

Colin Dyson

A hot summer's day in June 1979, a light SE moist wind was blowing. Two rather unkempt schoolboys were seated at the back of the classroom of the O-level Biology class. Tin Kwong Road was the location of the well-established King George the V School.

Their gaze was to the northwest, well beyond the dusty blackboard and small square windows. A Boeing 707 was making an approach to Runway 13 (135 degrees magnetic) at Kai Tak International Airport. The inbound course was 088M (magnetic).

The procedure was the IGS (instrument guidance system) with a final right turn over Kowloon city and its washing lines. The schoolboys thought that the aircraft was too high for a safe landing. The crew would have to carry out a missed approach and return for another landing attempt.

They were correct, as the four jet engines accelerated noisily for the maneuver and the landing gear was retracted. Stopwatches were running now as they gambled with each other on the time at which the aircraft would return... normally sixteen to eighteen minutes. It was quite some distance flying between Lei Yue Mun Gap, south of Hong Kong Island, then commencing the approach to the west of Lantau Island.

The aircraft returned, as expected on glideslope this time for a gentle right turn, drifting below the horizon of old dirty low-rise buildings.

The pilots had clearly done a better job this time.

The IGS was an almost standard instrument landing system (ILS) providing accurate guidance to landing at most of the world's major airports. Only today are the approaches progressing towards GPS navigation for guidance both for enroute navigation and for departure and arrival procedures.

The IGS was named differently, to ensure that pilots were fully aware that the approach path was not lined up with the runway. It did, however, point at the checkerboard, a red and white painted rock face, close to today's Morse Park. There was also a distance measuring device (DME) that gave an accurate distance to the runway threshold.

The aircraft aimed to descend on a 3-degree slope or 300 feet per nautical mile. So at 2.0 nautical miles 2 x 3 = 600 feet AAL (above aerodrome level) was a cross check of your actual altitude. Final guidance was assisted by use of PAPI lights (precision approach path indicators) abeam the threshold that provided red and white indications to give guidance to the aircraft's path and rate of descent.

On the haziest days, the lead-in lights, a series of powerful sequenced strobes were switched on.

It was always a challenging approach. Non-local airlines took specific simulator training, before operating into Hong Kong's Kai Tak. VHHH is the ICAO (International Civil Aviation Organization) designation for Kai Tak even today.

Cathay Pacific and Dragonair aircraft were known to fly slightly left of the localizer center line, thus giving more room to align on the final turn.

Local knowledge was a bonus.

The other approaches into Kai Tak were the ILS on runway 31 and a radar PAR (precision approach radar). Runway 13 also had a visual approach procedure past Lamma Island, Green Island and on towards Yau Ma Tei and the checkerboard. Cheung Chau Island had the notoriously inaccurate NDB (non-directional beacon) approach. A needle that pointed everywhere, including towards thunderstorms. Using the identifier of the beacon CC (Charlie Charlie), two opposing teardrop patterns would be flown during the descent.

The terrain around Hong Kong and the varying wind direction changes provided all pilots with a focus. There were incidents and accidents over the years, but it was widely accepted that the safety record was good.

The economy continued to grow and the runway was extended several times to accommodate larger aircraft. It also had a dark past with the brutal forced labor of POWs during the war by the occupying Japanese. The hard labor formed runway 07/25 and runway 13/31.

The airport was closed on the 6th July 6, 1998.

The stories were now etched in history from the early days of the Pan Am Clipper flying boats, to the occasional visit from the SST Concorde. Perhaps the airport should have been named after Harry Abbott who set up a flying school at Kai Tak in 1924.

The boys would both be on track for General Certificate of Education O-levels re-sits and promising aviation careers. They had some big shoes to fill following in their fathers' footsteps.

Gavin's father, Mike Wightman, had started in the RAF, qualifying as a Canberra bomber pilot. He now held a top instructional position at the Hong Kong Auxiliary Air Force. He was recognized as the best in his field.

Colin's father, Pete Dyson, had also operated Canberras in the RAF and was now a check captain on the B707 with Cathay Pacific Airways. Gavin would become the Chief Pilot in the UK of Air Atlantique, flying some of the vintage DC3s, DC6s and

Lockheed Electras that had graced the skies in Hong Kong. He would later check and train on the B737.

1998

There were occasional glimpses of the ground as the Boeing 747-300 Classic continued its approach on the IGS towards runway 13 at Kai Tak. The visibility was marginal with low cloud reported by the tower. A number of preceding aircraft had carried out missed approaches with diversions to Taipei and Kaohsiung.

This was a time of full concentration by the captain, first officer and flight engineer. All team members in a specific role. This would be the captain's approach and landing.

Seven miles to touchdown. Gear down and final landing flap. Steady at 155 knots.

Decision height 675 feet, strobe guidance in sight, continue the approach. Cross check the distance to go, altitude good, descent 800 feet per minute, rolling to the right, follow the strobes. A touch low, add some thrust, leveling the wings, runway in sight, use the precision, crossing the threshold.

Close the thrust, touchdown 1,400 feet in, pull full reverse.

Noise, vibration. Keep straight with rudder, spoilers up, auto brake working. High speed exit approaching, reduce reverse thrust, manual brakes, 80 knots, down to 15 knots, hard left turn, reach up to arm the body gear steering. "Nice job." A wink from the flight engineer. Phew... still buzzing... no errors... a last landing into Kai Tak.

Closure in three weeks.

Colin did some training like Gavin at the HK Aviation Club, and then moved to Texas for his commercial pilot's license.

A spell with two airlines in the UK would provide enough experience to join Cathay Pacific on the Lockheed L1011 Tristar. It would prove to be a challenging and rewarding career operating the B747 -200, 300 and 400. Later the mighty twin B777-200, 300, 300ER.

Colin's eldest daughter Christina is also a commercial pilot and instructor. Those idle school days at KGV gazing at the Instrument Guidance System were in truth not wasted.

Guarding the Border: Nabbing Illegals, Spying on the PRC and Recoiling from Snakes

Mike Sharp

It was 0100 and peak activity time for the Duke of Edinburgh's Royal Regiment. I had joined Second Lieutenant Rose, Sergeant Major McLeod and a lieutenant from the Ulster Defence Regiment on attachment to our Rifle Company to check our platoon positions. The thermal imager mounted on Nam Hang MacIntosh Fort had just detected illegal immigrants, IIs, crossing the Sham Chun River. They had gone to ground on the Hong Kong side presumably to get changed out of their mud-soaked clothes from crossing the filthy river, into cleaner ones, if they had them. That would allow them to melt into the Hong Kong population. We were creeping along the border road guided by the radio commands of the fort team so that we could intercept the IIs as they left the foliage to climb onto the road. The only noise was the croaking frogs and the singing crickets, while the smell of rotting vegetation pervaded the whole area. The ambush team for that area had joined us and had taken point to handle the arrests. All signals were by hand and we waited and listened while the fort provided a commentary on the progress of the IIs. Everyone was sweating in the heat and humidity of an August night. "Go forward ten meters… Stop… They've stopped moving… I see them… move forward five meters… standby… IIs two meters from you… " At this point, we could hear the rustling in the bushes and right next to the ambush party the first II poked his head up. He was immediately grabbed and passed down the line to be handcuffed with plastic cable ties (plasticuffs). Several others emerged and were also manhandled and secured. The last two IIs caught onto what was happening to The quick reaction force turned up in an open-top Land Rover and the IIs were unceremoniously herded into the back and taken away to Man Kam To Base where B Company Headquarters was located. their colleagues and turned to find an alternative route.

The ambush team launched themselves into the undergrowth and following instructions from the fort, homed onto the missing pair. There was a lot of shouting and noise of foliage being trampled then the other two IIs were brought to the road by three panting squaddies to join the four squatting along the roadside. Here they would be searched and debriefed by interpreters from the Hong Kong Military Service Corps before being taken to the police station at Lok Ma Chau. The UDR lieutenant was visibly impressed with the slickness of the operation and said so. The regiment had already spent considerable time on the border and was now highly proficient.

The Duke of Edinburgh's Royal Regiment had arrived in Hong Kong in January 1988 to commence a two-and-a-half year posting at Stanley Fort on the Island. Made up of an amalgamation of regiments, their predecessors had taken part in the First Opium War in 1841 in which under the Treaty of Nanking, Hong Kong was formally ceded to the British. Later, the regiment saw action during the Taiping Rebellion when an Anglo-French force marched on Peking in 1860. In 1988, the regiment was taking over from the 2nd Battalion, Coldstream Guards, who were understandably sorry to leave the territory. As a "light infantry battalion", the regiment had three major responsibilities: the first was to support the police in internal security; the second was to take part in manning the border in rotation with Gurkha battalions plus short stints from the Royal Hong Kong Regiment (Volunteers); third, they were to train for deployment to Malaysia as part of the Five Powers Agreement, a group consisting of UK, Australia, New Zealand, Singapore and Malaysia formed after UK withdrew its forces east of Suez in 1967.

Deployment to the Sino-Hong Kong border took place three times a year for six-week stints and had been this way since 1979 when the army had taken over responsibility from the police. In each stint, three rifle companies plus a battalion headquarters team would deploy to the three areas, Sha Tau Kok, Man Kam To and Sandy Spur with the headquarters at Lo Wu (next to the saddle club). The border was thirty-three miles long running through hills, jungle, villages, wetlands and fish farms, and was easily identified by the high wire fence plus border obstacles, towers and control points. At this time, there were only two official border crossing points located at Lo Wu and Man Kam To. The intriguing foot crossing at Chung Ying Street in Sha Tau Kok did not count and, given the volatile history of the crossing, we were under strict instructions to stay away from it. Dotted along the border at tactical positions that could observe wide areas were MacIntosh Forts constructed between 1949 and 1953, built under instruction of Police Commissioner Duncan MacIntosh. These forts were self-contained with sleeping and cooking facilities so they could remain manned for twenty-four hours. Inside these forts were our platoon headquarters, along with one team observing the People's Liberation Army and People's Armed Police through mega-binos.

At this time, Hong Kong was the only place where the West could observe the People's Republic of China. Observations by border units assisted in putting together the "intelligence picture" at brigade headquarters. There were also ambush teams, whose main aim was to capture IIs, in either towers or camouflaged positions. In Starling Inlet near Sha Tau Kok, there was also a small Marine detachment that policed the inlet and coastline. Nam Hang, our platoon area, was positioned east of the Lo Wu border crossing point. Painted green, it appeared pretty innocuous when you stand on the Mainland side by the Lo Wu shopping mall looking towards Hong Kong. In 1988, it was engaged in surveillance of Chinese units and immigrant activity. We had several aids assisting us to catch IIs. First, there was the fence that had an alarm and built-in microphone. When an II attempted to cut or climb the fence, it would alert the operations room that would switch on the microphone to listen to what was happening. The nearest border tower or ambush team would be contacted by radio and they would mount BMX bikes and quickly cycle to the spot. This was not a fool-proof system as wind and animals could activate the fence. Our guys often had meetings with snakes and civet cats. Second, there were geo-probes, basically a solenoid placed in the ground. When the core moves it generates power and signals the receiver monitored by the troops. Although rugged, they were sensitive, giving us a false alarms. Last, we had the brilliant thermal imager, placed tactically to achieve the best coverage.

Unlike the modern FLIR (forward-looking infrared) systems, the imager required bottles of compressed air to operate, and the soldier using it would temporarily lose normal vision in the eye focused on the screen. Most illegal immigrants were caught at night by teams alerted by the observers.

Life along the border was quite tedious and soldiers could easily get bored if there were no IIs coming to their area. The IR torch, another device, was normally shone across the road to alert the squaddies to approaching Land Rovers, meaning unannounced visits by senior officers or worse... the Padre. Each four-man team normally had a collection of porn and ciggies and these would be hung out in a plastic bag on the Chinese side of the observation tower to avoid detection during snap inspections. The towers consisted of a hut at ground level and a viewing platform on the top. There was no air conditioning and we never slept inside the huts due to lack of ventilation. Instead, we rigged up ponchos on the roof and slept there. When the operations room alerted the tower to suspicious activity, the two on observation reacted while the other two manned the tower. This was the theory. However, due to lack of sleep, the resting pair would often remain where they were, monitoring the radio, while the other two did the check. Most accidents occurred when squaddies were riding BMX bikes. They were lethal. When I took over Nam Hang Fort, I drew a landscape of the view covered by the observation point. I then gridded it with numbers and letters so areas could be referred to as "A9" or "B4" or "bamboo wood", "fishpond" or "swamp". I passed copies to the ambush teams and towers so they could understand directions given by the fort observation post. This became standard procedure helping vector teams to capture IIs attempting to get through the border fence.

Enter the Serpent

It was unusual not to meet venomous snakes while out on patrol. Within one hour of taking over Nam Hang Fort, my men had killed a banded krait, then thirty minutes later, Private Gary Cross (HK international rugby player) had wandered in with a Chinese cobra, to show — so he claimed — then lost it, causing Mr Rose, the platoon commander, and me to jump onto the top bunks shouting "Get that f------ snake out of here!" We also found bamboo snakes wrapped around the border fence where they could grab flying prey, plus the occasional Burmese python would scare us as it crossed the road. Towards the end of a six-week stint, I happened to focus my binos on the ambush team including Gary Cross. I saw sudden blur of movement as a machete came flying down on a hapless rat snake too close to the troops. I watched as Gary gutted the snake and made soup out of it, then giggling, the team took turns trying his concoction.

Most illegal immigrants were economic migrants coming to Hong Kong for a better life. They would be stinking, especially if they attempted to cross the border near the Mai Po marshes, covered head to toe in mud. Some were sorry cases but it was important to remain unmoved and just process them through to the police. The whole experience working on the Sino-Hong Kong Border was interesting, but by the end of our time in Hong Kong we were getting tired of it and people were calmer about their duties. Even the Gurkhas NCOs told us they were bored and longed to get back to jungle training or the UK.

Human migration is the story of Hong Kong and the majority of the Chinese population has roots going back to migration from communism and economic woes in the People's Republic. Across the South China Sea, another race of people was to provide a problem for Hong Kong authorities. My regiment was thrown in the deep end. Vietnamese refugees had been arriving in Hong Kong since 1975, escaping political persecution after the war and later, repression of ethnic Chinese. In 1988, a large invasion occurred. The Government decided new arrivals would not be eligible for automatic resettlement. Instead they would be screened to determine if they were genuine refugees. This meant camps were needed to hold them and rifle companies were tasked to erect tented camps at Shek Kong RAF Base and Tai A Chau Island. Typhoons delayed the work. The Shek Kong camp was never secure and the regiment was ordered to provide security at the base for four-week stints to prevent repeated escapes and thefts. This proved to be a sobering and weird. We were the first European soldiers the Vietnamese had seen and we were essential as the Gurkha married quarters was nearby and the base management didn't fancy the chances of any Vietnamese caught in their housing estate. By 1990, there were 35,000 Vietnamese immigrants being held in camps across Hong Kong.

Is Flying for a Living Dangerous?

David Newbery

It all began when I was a first officer with Cathay Pacific Airways, having arrived in Hong Kong two and a half years earlier after sixteen years as a fighter pilot in the Royal Air Force. My wife was grateful that I was now in a less dangerous job. I was looking forward to operating an Airbus A330 to Colombo in Sri Lanka — a good trip, with a couple of days to explore this fascinating country and meet up with a tourist guide who had become my friend, and to visit an orphanage we were helping. There was a civil war going on at the time, but all had been relatively quiet for a while and I thought no more about the security situation.

The flight was uneventful, and we retired to our hotel, the Colombo Hilton, next to the new World Trade Center. After a good night's sleep, in my comfortable room on the 10th floor, I was awakened just before 7:00 a.m. by some loud bangs. I recognized the noises — firing of AK-47 assault rifles — just outside my window. I got out of bed (naked) and went on hands and knees to look over the windowsill of my room, which was about 50cm high beneath a large plate-glass window. As I looked down onto Lotus Road, the colonial-style Ministry of Finance was on the other side, I could see armed men to the left, who were firing AK-47s and rocket propelled grenades (RPGs) up the street towards a group of military personnel, who were firing back. This went on for about ten minutes, then a truck drove up from the left and smashed through the gates of a car park to the right of the hotel and behind the World Trade Center. There was some more shooting (I later learned four security guards were shot dead) then a couple of men left the truck and ran off back down the road—covered by their friends along the street. A while later, I saw an RPG being lined up and fired towards the truck.

The next thing I was aware of was a huge bang, the plate-glass window I was underneath shattered, and I was covered in glass. I lay still for a few seconds and then, tentatively, began to move my arms and legs. Everything seemed to move OK but there was quite a lot of blood all over the place. I stood up, shedding glass, and removed a large piece of glass, about 5cm square, sticking out of my right ankle and, carefully, in bare feet, walked through the bedroom into the bathroom, where I could have a good look at myself. As I went, I saw the state of the bed—the sheets were shredded by flying glass and there were large chunks of glass embedded in the wooden headboard—I would have been severely injured had I still been in bed when the bomb went off. Looking at myself in the bathroom mirror, I looked a bit of a mess—my face was covered in tiny cuts and abrasions although, thankfully, my eyes were uninjured. My back was covered in cuts and small pieces of glass, which I was able to brush off, but I had to pull out another large piece of glass embedded in my right shoulder. However, when I cleaned myself up and had a shower, I was obviously not in really bad shape, although bleeding a bit.

My next thought was for the state of the rest of the crew—the captain and eleven cabin crew. I rang the skipper's room. The phone was answered by the chief purser, who explained what had happened to them. Apparently, the captain had done the same as I and had gone to the window to look at the gun battle. Meanwhile, several of the cabin crew, hearing the gunfire, went to the captain's room to see what was happening. They knocked on the captain's door and, as he was halfway across the room to answer the door, the bomb went off, hurling him across the room and into the bedroom door. He was knocked out for a few seconds. When he came around, he was a little concussed and confused and wandered up and down the corridor, talking to the cabin crew and "taking charge", his authority a little eroded by the fact that he was stark naked.

I went around the hotel, tracking down crew members, stopping from time to time to empty blood out of my shoe. We all got together in the captain's room – he was quite compos mentis by now. Miraculously, none of the cabin crew was injured, despite severe damage to the hotel, many injuries and at least two hotel staff killed. Four of the crew were outside the captain's room when the blast came, and other crew members were either in their bathrooms or in one of the crew's bedrooms on the far side of the hotel from the blast.

The hotel staff were wonderful, and we were all asked to congregate downstairs in the hotel lobby. The intention was to evacuate the hotel; however, the battle outside was far from over and there was the constant sound of gunfire with the occasional grenade explosion from all around the hotel for several hours. After a while, an armed detachment of Sri Lanka sailors came to the hotel to guard us – not without incident, as one of the sailors accidentally discharged his rifle in the hotel lobby, causing us all to dive for cover, as we thought the terrorists had broken in. We were asked if anybody needed hospital treatment. The skipper and I deferred – we were not seriously injured – and the thought of going to a Colombo hospital dealing with scores of injuries from the blast did not appeal. In the meantime, we had contacted the Cathay country manager in Colombo, assuring her we were all okay and she passed the message on to Cathay Hong Kong. My wife had heard about the blast from the BBC on her car radio, but it was a while before she was told I was okay. The radio was full of news about how many people had been killed but, eventually, Cathay was able to tell her that I was injured but not seriously. It was impossible to get in or out of the hotel while the battle was raging so we had to wait until early evening when the Cathay manager got to us with a doctor to attend to my wounds.

Eventually, we were moved to another hotel for the night and, the following morning, we flew to Bangkok with Thai Airways then on to Hong Kong with Cathay. We were greeted by a supportive deputation of Cathay management and our spouses, then went home.

That should have been the end of the trauma, but not for me. When I got home, my wife went up to the study to tell all our friends and relatives that I was okay. Our helper was getting dinner ready. I got myself a beer and sat down in the lounge with my injured leg up on a stool. We live at Hoi Ha in Sai Kung Country Park, with a wonderful wide open view of Hoi Ha Wan Marine Park. Just as I pulled the ring-tab of my beer, there was an almighty explosion, the glass of the large French windows of the lounge beside me bulged in and I was convinced the glass was about to shatter all over me—again. Luckily, the glass held but my blood pressure must have gone up a bit, as my ankle wound started bleeding profusely again. I called for help, but everybody was busy—my wife was phoning the police and residents were in the village square wondering what had happened—the thought was that a gas cylinder had exploded. Eventually, I persuaded my wife that I needed help and she came down, took one look at me and ran away to get help—she doesn't "do" blood. Luckily, there was a trained nurse in the village, and she came to our house and rebandaged my ankle.

So, what had happened? We had had some recent problems with dynamite fishing in the marine park. People were putting sticks of dynamite in beer bottles and throwing them over the side of boats to stun fish — we had heard several muffled explosions in the previous weeks and there was a lot of glass being washed up on the beaches. Apparently, the police found a small cave on the shore of Hoi Ha Wan, where a cache of dynamite was stored. The police summoned bomb disposal experts who took one look at the poor state of the explosives, decided that it was too dangerous to move them and that they would blow up the stack of dynamite in situ. They hoped that nobody would notice and so did not see fit to tell anybody. The explosion was rather larger than they had anticipated — and the timing was unnerving.

Over the next week or so, we had a procession of senior police and government officials popping in to offer their apologies.

The attack on the Colombo World Trade Center was carried out by six members of the Liberation Tigers of Tamil Elam, part of the Tamil Tigers organization. The bomb was a big one — 350kg — leaving a crater six meters wide and four meters deep; it killed fifteen people and injured 105. All the attackers died as a result of gunfire from security forces, blowing themselves up or taking cyanide pills.

To our knowledge, there have been no more incidents of dynamite fishing in the Hoi Ha Marine Park since the discovery of this cache of dynamite. Commercial and private fishing still takes place although it was another twenty years before commercial fishing was banned in the supposedly protected waters of the marine park.

In the aftermath of the Colombo bombing, the captain was off work for about six months, as head injuries are taken seriously by aviation doctors, but he made a full recovery. We were all given counseling to help us cope with the events. The cabin crew had a few weeks off to recover. I was off work for about six weeks. My wife reckons I was a bit "peculiar" during that period. I was still a bit nervous around plate glass windows so the wife of one of the Mandarin Oriental Hotel's management kindly arranged for us to spend a night there to allow me to get used to hotels and large windows again. Otherwise, I recovered well. However, I didn't get the last tiny piece of glass out of my nose until ten years later and I still have a couple of scars on my back and ankle. So much for civilian flying being less dangerous than military service.

Light Aircraft Flying: Best Fun You Can Have With Your Clothes On

Roger Medcalf

"Call the Tower after you've landed." This blunt command over the Cessna's radio. Was I going to be lambasted by Air Traffic Control or worse, face a criminal charge under air law? Flying solo in the Cessna 172 Uniform Victor, I had found myself and the little aircraft where we were not allowed to be: over densely populated Kowloon with just a single engine keeping us aloft. This had come about because of disorientation in poor visibility. I had banked the Cessna flying in circles in the murk at about 2,000 feet, trying to find a gap in the hills to fly over Tolo Harbor and around Ma On Shan to Sai Kung. In the low visibility, I flew through the wrong gap. As the view over the cowling and beyond the whirling prop cleared, I saw where I was. Masses of gray buildings were below crowded on the Kowloon peninsula. I realized I had better tell ATC where I was. In that area they have you on radar anyway. I did so, calmly. There is no room for panic solo in a light aircraft. And no need. The Cessna was flying happily, key instruments in the green and I could see where we were. ATC directed me to bank left and fly straight to the harbor. Engine failure over the sea is not likely to hurt anyone but the pilot. They instructed me to fly over the harbor through Lei Yue Mun Gap, across the hills to Port Shelter, over Sai Kung, around Ma On Shan, over Tolo Harbor then back through Kadoorie Gap to land at Sek Kong airfield. All of this was uneventful.

Uniform Victor hummed along contentedly, squatting down on the runway like a well-trained duck. Back at the Aviation Club base at Sek Kong airfield, I dutifully called ATC. The controller wanted to know why I had found myself flying over densely populated Kowloon in a single-engine aircraft. I explained the disorientation in poor visibility, flight through the wrong gap in the hills and braced for a bollocking. All the controller said to me was, "We're glad you landed safely."

It is said light aircraft flying is the best fun you can have with your clothes on. There are many joyful experiences: flying solo for the first time and walking around like you're ten feet tall for weeks afterwards; gaining your private pilot's licence (PPL) and flying your first passenger, an innocent whose life is in your hands; winging through Hong Kong Harbor with the sun flashing off the skyscrapers and sparkling on the sea. This is at 1,500 feet, the height of the ICC Tower. That's if you're flying west. In the reverse direction, ATC want you at 1,000 feet for separation. It doesn't matter how often you fly through Hong Kong harbor in the middle of this great city. It always seems astonishing and an enormous privilege to be allowed to do this in a single-engine aircraft when you've just a little PPL.

Along with the joy there come mishaps, the human factor. I nearly killed a friend. Clive Knott is a big lad with a fondness for women in boots. I know him through the Hong Kong Hash House Harriers. Clive came flying with me as a passenger in the Slingsby Sierra Bravo, a motorized glider of French design. I loved that aircraft, calling it my No. 5 girlfriend after my wife, daughter and our two dogs. This was in the days when the island of Chek Lap Kok was a vast construction site. For the fun of it I said to Clive in the right seat as we flew around the western end of Lantau, "Let's pretend we are landing on the new runway."

I cut power, lifted the nose, slowing the aircraft, took flap and we glided down towards the island at about 70 knots air speed. As we descended, I made a potentially fatal decision. Take out the flap. A stupid error. All pilots know not to do this. As the flaps are retracted the aircraft loses lift and it will sink. It did. Clive and I would be dead now, but for the fact we had just enough height to power out of there before hitting the sea. That was the worst mistake I have made in thirty years of flying.

It used to be said proudly by pilots of the Hong Kong Aviation Club that we had never had a fatality in a club aircraft, at least in living memory. That was last century. But two tragedies have occurred in recent years. Before telling those sad stories, we recall a club member who killed himself in his private aircraft, a slippery, aerobatic Pitts Special. Tony van de Klee was a gynecologist known as 'Goldfinger'. Kai Tak was still operating in those days and I happened to see Tony take off on his fateful flight from Runway 13 in his red and black, bi-winged Pitts. It was typical Tony. He roared the aircraft along the runway at maximum power and when it had reached flying speed, stood it on its tail. He soared straight up until the aircraft was hanging on its prop, nosed over and raced out East Pass to the waters of Port Shelter. There Tony did a series of aerobatic stunts. A witness said he did loops at low level, so low that at the bottom of loops he was causing waves on the water. Then he over-cooked it, plunging into the sea. And that was the end of Tony. Sadly. This century the Aviation Club's safety record has been shattered by two fatalities. First there was the tragic story of an instructor known as MT. A week or so before his accident he had been failed by an examiner for renewal of his instructor's rating. Friends at the club thought the examiner had been unfair. MT felt under pressure. He decided, ahead of his next test, to practice spinning solo in our new Zlin 242L, a Czech-made aircraft as rugged as a tractor with stubby wings so it would roll quickly during aerobatics. Flying over Plover Cove where aerobatics are permitted at about 3,000 feet, MT radioed to air traffic control asking for permission to climb higher so he would be safer throwing the aircraft around the skies. More recovery height. ATC declined. Commercial traffic was overhead. MT spun the Zlin at around 3,000 feet. With short wings it loses height quickly. MT did not arrest the spin and recover in time. The aircraft plunged into the sea. MT was killed.

Another club pilot died a year or so later. This time in a helicopter, an R22. Flying through Kadoorie Gap back to Sek Kong air field after a sortie around the New Territories, the chopper broke up under him and crashed into hillside trees. It burned to a charred mess.

Those are the sad stories of recent Aviation Club mishaps. Others had happier endings, albeit with red faces. Engine failures are rare. Trainer aircraft are built simply to keep pilots and passengers safe. But they do happen on rare occasion. An instructor called Alex, also a former club president, had an engine failure flying a Cessna 172 over Tolo Harbor. Even in Hong Kong — mostly rocks, water and buildings — engine failures are survivable if the pilot keeps his head. Alex did. With the propeller stopped, he set the Cessna up for best glide, 65 knots, no flap. Look for a landing spot. Alex figured the gliding aircraft would make it to the Garden Farm near Ma On Shan where there are landing areas. He slowed the aircraft down to about 55 knots and took flap. The Cessna ploughed into leafy trees under control at only about 50 knots. It was a relatively soft landing and Alex and his student pilot walked away.

Some astonishingly skilful flying has been pulled off by club pilots after engine failures. Twice our Cessnas have landed on the Plover Cove dam in emergencies, both times piloted by instructors. The dam is short for a landing strip, narrow and has light poles on one side. With amazing skill and refusal to panic, our pilots have put their aircraft down on the dam. Spectators think a movie must be in the making and look around for cameras.

Some incidents, potentially fatal, have turned out to be ironic and funny, sort of. One character, clearly incompetent, lost control of a Cessna on landing at Sek Kong. He had three passengers in the aircraft. In their early training, student pilots are taught that if the landing is going pear-shaped, select full power, which will give you more control, climb out of there and go around the circuit for another attempt at landing. This card with three lives in his hands didn't. The Cessna likely started porpoising, bouncing backwards and forwards, out of control. It may have dug in a wing. The Cessna flipped, landing on its back, skidding to a halt. All four on aboard climbed out with only scratches and bruises. All the passengers were funeral directors.

Is learning to fly scary? At first, yes. During your early flights with an instructor, you are likely to have little understanding of what is going on and will be nervous. Get your head into the textbooks so you quickly learn how to control the aircraft and how it works and your confidence will grow. You need to have a deep, heart-felt love of the beauty of flight. Few people have a go at learning to fly, even fewer succeed. Only about one in ten who try to attain a private pilot's license will have the desire and perseverance to succeed. Many scare themselves in training or during first solo flights and depart never to be seen again. Some quit because it is an expensive game (currently about HK$2,500 an hour to fly with an instructor).

If you persist, that heart-felt love of flight driving you, you will be richly rewarded. After you go solo you will walk around for weeks, saying to yourself, "I'm a pilot; how incredible is that?" Feeling you are superior to grounded people. Perhaps in a small way you are. Here's how going solo for the first time works. Your instructor will have flown with you probably in a Cessna 172 around the circuit dozens of times. Take off, climb into the circuit (800 feet at Sek Kong) fly the downwind leg, do pre-landing checks, take one stage of flap, slow the aircraft down, 80 knots then 75, power back and nose up a little, bank onto final approach, nail the airspeed at 65 knots and descent path (combination of aircraft attitude and power), take another stage of flap, over the fence, easing the air speed back. In the flare a few feet above the runway, pull the control column back in little jerks, raising the nose farther and farther, slowing the airspeed, until the aircraft runs out of lift and settles onto the tarmac—"chirp" go the tyres—keep the Cessna rolling straight with rudder pedals and gently apply the brakes.

Your instructor will fly the circuit with you multiple times at first demonstrating, then letting you do most of the flying, then allowing you to do all the flying—just correcting you when necessary and giving quiet words of advice from the right seat. After many lessons like this, one day you will notice the instructor is doing nothing. He or she is sitting there in the right seat arms folded, just watching as you do take-off and landing, take-off and landing and take-off and landing for several lessons. One day, the instructor will ask you to stop the Cessna at the airfield. He will climb out, saying, "Way you go. On your own."

That's the big day. You are likely to feel elated. Wow, just me and a little aircraft flying together! You will realize the Cessna will fly even better without the instructor's weight. It does, soaring off the runway earlier than usual. You fly the circuit, doing all your checks, setting up the aircraft for landing, which you carry off with aplomb—"chirp"—because you have done it so many times before. Cue huge grin from ear to ear. Texts and calls to family and friends. I did it. And you give them the old joke, "Not long ago I couldn't spell pilot, now I are one."

Gaining your PPL is a license to start learning. There will be many scary experiences when you are first allowed to fly as pilot in command. Imagine you are flying the Cessna Kilo Alpha near East Pass at Kai Tak airport. You're in a holding pattern waiting to land. Required height is 1,200 feet, unfortunately the base of the cloud is also 1,200 feet. You're scudding just below the cloud. It's illegal with VFR (visual flight rules) flying to actually be in the soup. And the radio is giving you trouble. Round and round the circuit. The ATC keeps you there for 45 minutes until there is a gap in the commercial traffic and you are allowed to land on Runway 13. You've got to keep your head. No choice, solo, in a light aircraft.

Approaching one of the world's great international airports from the harbor on your own in a Cessna is a magnificent experience. Imagine the view on a sunny day over the cowling from the little cockpit. If, because of the wind you are told by ATC to land on Runway 31 (the Lei Yue Mun Gap end) you have plenty of room for a sweeping banked turn over the water until lined up on the runway, then setting up the aircraft for final approach. If you're required to land on Runway 13 (the reverse direction) the approach is very tight. You're not allowed to fly over the Kowloon buildings in a single-engine plane. It's a tight, banking turn, with flap, speed back, and losing height quickly to get Kilo Alpha down on the little runway that seems to be left.

ATCs can save your life. Hank Josey was an alternately grouchy and charming American instructor who would fly his private retractable-gear Cessna in the morning then sit at his favorite table in the Aero Bar regaling his friends with aviation stories while sipping whisky. Hank was instrument-rated and he would fly solo in cloud. Then tell everyone listening at the bar, while fingering his collar, a constant mannerism, "On Cathay, it

ROGER MEDCALF & ROD OLSEN

takes three of them to do what I do." One afternoon I was due to
fly, probably Kilo Alpha again, as pilot in command. Hank said
to me, "Don't go. If you go flying, I'll never talk to you again." I
didn't listen—young fool—and taxied Kilo Alpha to the Runway
13 holding point. I sat in the tiny plane waiting for a gap in the
big-jet traffic to be told by ATC, "Kilo Alpha, you are cleared for
take-off, Runway 13. Watch for wake turbulence." But not this
time. Over the radio, "Kilo Alpha, we don't think you should
fly. We think the weather is going to turn bad." I thanked ATC
and turned KA to taxi back to her Club parking spot. About
45 minutes later, WHUMP! The heavens opened. A torrential
downpour. KA and I would almost certainly have crashed if we
had been flying in those conditions. It took a while, but Hank did
talk to me again.

Last century the Aviation Club was graced with a lot of fine
characters. There was Paul Clift, a lantern-jawed, squash-playing
land surveyor who was chief flying instructor for fourteen years.
Paul ran a tight ship and we had nothing worse than a bent wing
during his time as flying boss. Mel "Egg on Legs" Rose was a
portly, entertaining engineer who propped up the Aero Bar in
the 1980s. Mel was famous for taking big aircraft to pieces then
neglecting to put them back together again. There was Mike
Gotfried, a man's man who drank beer and chased women.
He was much admired for starting on light aircraft and rising
to CX Captain. Mike is also credited with being the founder of
the modern HK Aviation Club. Norrie Galbraith was a police
officer with something of a superiority complex, perhaps hiding
psychological problems. A mere light aircraft instructor, Norrie
would lecture Cathay pilots about their 747s. Colin Dyson was
a club instructor when he was young, then joined Cathay and
rose to captain. Colin (one of this book's authors) is the ultimate
gentleman in

his behavior towards others. In the same category is Hogan Loh, a teetotaller who turns up at every party and charms the crowd. Some people gave much of their lives to the Club. For example, John Li, scion of the Li family that controls vast assets including the Bank of East Asia. John could afford to gain every fixed-wing and helicopter rating available and for a time he was president, chief flying instructor (fixed-wings) and chief flying instructor (helicopters) simultaneously. A CX check and training captain, Bob Tandy was the best instructor I ever flew with. He was also the toughest, apparently believing light aircraft pilots should attain the same standard as commercial ones. The only time I was failed after the general flying test the instructor was Bob. He was right. I had gone for the test too rusty, with too little re-training time, in the parachutist-flying Cessna 182. It's a heavy aircraft, like a flying truck, and I never became fully comfortable in it, unlike the 172s and the Slingsby. Captain Gupta, chief flying instructor for many years, was an Indian Air Force officer who had flown in three wars. He would proudly show you the international waypoint named after him. Captain Gupta, an amiable character who would inevitably ask you, "How was your sortie?" was quite lenient with young pilots. He passed me after a general flight test and sent me solo in the Slingsby. I was jittery during that flight. Too rusty.

All private pilots should have aerobatic training. Otherwise, if they are the nervous, common-sense type, they are likely to fly aircraft around the skies straight and level, doing only gentle banks. Aerobatic training will show them what the aircraft are capable of and how to recover from unusual attitudes. Their confidence will grow and they will be better pilots for it. Many, however, including myself, will never have the confidence to do aerobatics solo — it seems you are too close to killing yourself. The only time I took part in an aerobatics competition, CX captain

Bob Scott, was safety pilot. He lay in the Slingsby's right seat as if he was asleep. But I was so glad he was there.

I blotted my copybook something woeful flying with Charles Montgomery, a Dragonair captain who was a captivating raconteur. We did aerobatics in the Slingsby over Plover Cove, including stall turns. You fly the aircraft straight up until it is hanging on the prop, kick the rudder one way or the other, and the aircraft flips, plummeting and going back in the reverse direction. After doing this for about fifteen minutes, I said to Charles, "My stomach is becoming unglued." We stopped aerobatics and flew back to East Pass ready to land at Kai Tak. ATC said go away. There's too much traffic. Flying outside East Pass at about 2,000 feet, I said to Charles, "What shall we do while we wait? How about an aileron roll?" He said okay. Nose down, build up the airspeed, and then whack! Shove the control column to the left and you are in an aileron roll. I knew immediately this was a dumb idea. My stomach revolted. All over the instrument panel. Charles took control and landed at Kai Tak. After taxiing into the club's forecourt and climbing out, he simply said in his gruff way, "Clean it up."

A group of Hong Kong Aviation Club members decided it might be fun to go to Africa and tour the southern countries in light aircraft. Young fools. We nearly killed ourselves. At the marvelously named Wonderboom airfield south of Johannesburg, we hired six little aircraft, Cessna 172s and a Piper. Sensibly, we took South African instructors with us. It was notable how poor some of them seemed. Shoes falling apart.

Our group included the (late) Professor Tony Hedley, head of epidemiology at the University of Hong Kong. Square-jawed, tousle-headed Tony spent hours lecturing us on the dangers of mosquito-borne diseases in southern Africa. During the entire trip of about two weeks Tony was so heavily dressed he looked like a beekeeper. We never saw a mosquito.

Flying not in formation but within sight of each other, the little aircraft headed to Kruger Game Park, up to Botswana and onto Victoria Falls. Over Victoria Falls I'm sitting in the back. I see both pilots in the front are damn near hanging out of their windows taking photographs. I'm yelling from the back, "Who's flying this thing?" We literally landed on truck tracks in the bush, notably at the Okavango Delta. We slept next to our little aircraft in tents. One night memorably I shared a tent with Tony, a wonderful man, modest despite his eminence. We lost him to cancer some years ago.

It was on the way to Victoria Falls that we nearly killed ourselves. Tony was in the back seat. I was in the front left pilot's seat and a young South African was beside me in the right front seat. Because of a technical problem, we took off late flying north, intending to land at Victoria Falls. The Cessna had a dicky electrical system. It began to get dark, soon we were in black African night. Still we're flying north to an airfield none of us had ever flown to before, including the South African. My yellow streak or was it common sense? showed. "Let's turn back to Bulawayo airport," I harped on, the others agreed. The young South African was not yet an instructor, but he did have navigation and instrument flying experience. He got jittery. The situation was clearly dangerous. A precautionary landing in the bush during a black night was out of the question in an aircraft with fading electrics. Tony, to his credit, sat quietly in the back. At the time he was the least experienced pilot on board. Fortunately, Instructor Hank Josey had taught me the rudiments of basic instrument flying. Keep the wings level, no more than 15 degrees angle of bank, scan the instruments — the artificial horizon is God — but keep checking it against the other instruments. Our South African friend did the navigation and I flew the aircraft and between us we nursed it back hours later to flood-lit Bulawayo airfield. What a gorgeous sight. That's the closest I've come to killing myself — and Tony as well as the young African.

Do you have that hankering in your heart to fly? For me it began at an air show when I was eight years of age and I saw a Vulcan bomber flying along the runway at Napier, New Zealand, about fifty feet off the deck. The pilot suddenly stood the aircraft on its tail, lit the afterburners and the delta-winged jet soared into the vast amphitheater of a New Zealand sky before disappearing from view. I had never seen anything so thrilling. If you do have that heart-felt desire to fly, get along to the HK Aviation Club and ask to take off with an instructor.

Persist, overcome the initial scary stuff, and you will find flying light aircraft really is the best fun you can have with your clothes on.

A MURDERER WITH A DOUBLE LIFE

Guy Sanderson Shirra

On 10 January 1997, I attended my final interview at Police Headquarters with the Commissioner of Police, my former boss in the Emergency Unit Kowloon West, the late Eddie Hui Ki-on CBE, (a fine man and arguably the best local Commissioner Hong Kong ever had). He gave me my eight-page valedictory retirement letter. On page five it reads:

"In October 1984, you returned to mainstream UB (unarmed) duties as Assistant District Commander Administration, Yaumati. It is worthy of note that in this post, you identified an individual wanted for and subsequently convicted of the murder of two police officers and a young secretary and for a number of armed robberies."

This letter recorded my contribution to the sentencing of triple murderer and robber Lam Ho-yee to death (later commuted to life by the Governor), following belated official recognition by Eddie's predecessor in February 1991, six years after my identification role had been overlooked or forgotten by the Criminal Investigation Department Headquarters. So, what was all this about?

On 16 January 1984, after nine knife robberies of women and girl students in the Upper Levels area of Hong Kong Island and the formation of a combined plainclothes CID and uniformed task-force, Detective Station Sergeant Tse Chan and Sergeant Ma Chik-lau were on an anti-robbery patrol in the area.

When a suspicious Ma stopped Lam for a search, the suspect stabbed Ma to death and took his revolver. On encountering Tse lower down the hill, a brief exchange of gunfire ensued and Tse, close to retirement, was also killed, shot in the head. The suspect was seen escaping on a minibus by pursuing police and an Identikit picture of him was published on January 19 with a $100,000 reward following on February 4.

The suspect evaded a colony-wide manhunt led by the Organised and Serious Crime Bureau. On 21 November 1984, 26-year-old secretary Ms Chan Po-king bravely pushed an alarm bell in a lift in the Great Eagle Center in Wanchai, while the occupants were being robbed at knife point. She was savagely stabbed and died of her wounds two days later. I was struck by the unusual ferocity of this crime, which reminded me of the terrible police murders ten months earlier.

Again, on 23 January 1985, an Identikit picture of this murder suspect was published in a wanted notice and I was struck by the similarities between the two. I called my friend Paul Roger who was second in command of the Criminal Intelligence Bureau at the time (he was later head-hunted to lead a similar unit in Queensland's Justice Commission). He agreed they appeared to be of the same suspect and passed this view to Serious Crime Bureau. The wanted notice was followed by a reward of $50,000.

By now I was posted after command of a Police Tactical Unit company to be ADC Yaumati in the winter of 1984/85. I became aware during daily "morning prayers" of a series of lift knife robberies on women in the Canton Road area of Tsim Sha Tsui. On 7 January 1985, another brave young female victim of a previous robbery, Ms Leung Mei-po, recognized her robber in Canton Road and told the civilian Kowloon Wharf Police. They grabbed the man and, luckily, managed to subdue him and disarm him of a sheath knife before the prompt arrival of a EUKW car.

CID TST identified the man as Lam Ho-yee and charged him with eleven robberies and circulated two detailed teleprinter messages containing his description and his modus operandi force wide. Lam was sent to Lai Chi Kok Remand Center to stand trial on these robberies.

On 28 January 1985, the officer in charge of the case, unable to find either his divisional commander or CID boss, came to me with his file purely to get my signature as a superintendent to submit the file for legal advice. On reading the teleprinter messages for the first time, I asked the detective inspector whether he realized that Lam's description, his modus operandi and his knife matched the description of the man wanted for triple murder and robbery. He looked glum and I immediately picked up the phone and called Detective Chief Inspector Norrie MacKillop, the officer in command of the case at the Serious Crime Bureau. I told Norrie I believed Lam to be his man and he told me that he would take a team to interview Lam in Lai Chi Kok straight away, which he did. I told the detective inspector to keep his mouth shut and minuted his file to the senior crown counsel, recommending a High Court trial for the robberies.

After interviewing Lam, the bureau were also convinced he was their man and began a thorough investigation to prove it. On 19 February 1985, Norrie invited me to attend their Bai Kwan Dai ceremony in PHQ after they had charged Lam with three counts of murder and eleven counts of robbery; many were surprised to see a uniformed superintendent there and wondered what I was doing in their company.

Lam was convicted in the High Court on 20 November 1985, of all charges. He was sentenced to death for the three murders and twelve years for the robberies by Mr Justice Bewley. Norrie and Ip Pau-fuk each received CP's Commendations and Charlie Wink, forensics officers and others received Commanding

Officer's Commendations, all well deserved. Miss Leung Mei-po and two Kowloon Wharf Police officers, Chan Ming-on and Li Kai-yan, received Good Citizen Awards for their bravery.

I believe that if Lam had continued to keep his mouth shut before, during and after his trial for robbery, and if the CID file had never crossed my desk, Lam would most likely have gone to gaol, unidentified, served his time and become free to rob and murder again after a few years. As it is, I trust that he is still banged up in Stanley Prison, now in his seventies, and that life in his case means life.

One Spare

Chris Emmett

Josh Delany was a happy policeman. He was the chief inspector in charge of Kowloon Courts and as far as he was concerned, it was a grand job: plainclothes, nine-to-five, weekends and public holidays off. It needed a bit of brainpower but on the whole, the work was pretty leisurely. But not always. Last Friday had been a bugger of a day. On the Thursday, there had been a roundup of illegal street hawkers and the station duty officer had bailed them all to appear in North Kowloon court on the following day. That was why last Friday had been the worst day in Josh Delany's life.

The day had started well enough. The weather was fine, there were no domestic crises and the morning traffic had been light. Delany eased his car into his usual parking space, then the noise struck him like a sonic wrecking ball. It was as if a football crowd had invaded his normally tranquil courthouse.

Inside, illegal hawkers jammed the lower and upper floor lobbies. The main staircase was impassable. The marble and concrete atrium amplified the din of more than a hundred shouted conversations. Delany pressed his hands against his ears and took the back stairs leading from the cells to the Number 1 court prisoners' dock. At the counsel's table, the prosecutor peered at him over a wall of case papers.

The court sergeant squared his shoulders, flung open the courtroom door and, in his best parade ground voice, bellowed.

"Sau seng la!" Silence.

In an instant, there was silence.

The court interpreter was shaking his head and wringing his hands. "We will be here all day," he groaned. "All day and into the evening".

"No, we won't," Delany answered. "Trust me, we'll clear this lot by lunch."

The interpreter gave Delany a look that said, would you bet a month's pay on that?

"Follow me and learn," Delany said. Together, he and the interpreter stepped into the lobby.

"Listen up," Delany called.

'Gok wai, teng jue," the interpreter translated.

Delany set about explaining the rules of the day. Everyone was to form an orderly line, step forward when called, plead guilty and accept a HK$50 fine. If they did this, they would be back on their illegal hawker spots by the afternoon.

"Never mind whose name the clerk calls," he said. "If you're first in line, just step up, plead guilty, and accept the fine and go."

There were smiles and nods. Street hawkers are a pragmatic bunch.

And so it went, an orderly line of hardworking but unlicensed street hawkers filed into court.

"Wong Ming," the court clerk called.

"Ngoh hai." That's me, Mister Chan Woo answered.

"Maai siu fan." Street hawking, the clerk intoned.

"Sing ying." Guilty, the hawker answered.

"Faat ng saap man." Fined fifty dollars.

That was it. Mister Wong Ming, or perhaps it was Chan Woo, paid his fine, went back to work and put it all down to business expenses.

Within minutes, the court clerk hit his stride and proceedings moved along at a fair clip.

"Maai siu fan. Faat ng saap man."

It was starting to sound like a rapid-fire poetry reading.

"Maai siu fan. Faat ng saap man."

As soon as the prosecutor scribbled the result on the case papers, another hawker was up before the bench.

"Maai siu fan. Faat ng saap man."

The defendants were moving through the court like a happy conga line.

"Maai siu fan. Faat ng saap man."

"Maai siu fan. Faat ng saap man."

And then there was no more. It was as if a human tsunami had swept through the court and departed without causing any damage. The prosecutor slumped into his seat and massaged the back of his neck. The magistrate's voice cut across his repose. "Next case, Mister Prosecutor.'

"Ah ...yes. Indeed, Your Worship." That morning three new cases had come in. The prosecutor took a moment to skim through the case papers: a blackmail and two theft cases. The blackmailer was out on bail, which in itself was unusual. There was more surprise when he pleaded guilty.

The interpreter rattled through facts. "Tung yi on ching?" he asked. Do you agree? "Tung yi." Agreed, the defendant answered. The magistrate sentenced him to two years. The courtroom constable bustled him into the dock and through the door leading down to the cells.

The remaining two defendants pleaded not guilty and the magistrate remanded them for trial. As the last defendant left the court the magistrate glanced at his watch. "Well, well," he said. "That was quite a morning. Time for lunch, I think."

The court officials rose and bowed to the magistrate. The magistrate rose and bowed to the court officials. As the door to

His Worship's chambers banged shut, the prosecutor sighed and mopped his brow. The court interpreter was silent and seemed content he had not followed up on his bet.

Delany spent the afternoon clearing up overdue paperwork. Finally, he checked his watch. Quarter-to-five, nearly home time. He picked up his phone and punched in the number for the court cells. The earpiece chirped a few times, then a voice answered.

"Sah-jin luk ling baat yee," Sergeant 6082. Funny, Delany thought, the sergeant usually was as sharp as the military creases in his uniform but today there was a catch to his voice.

"Has the escort team collected the jailed prisoners?" Delany asked.

"Er ... Yes, sir."

The sergeant's hesitation troubled Delany.

"So, the prisoners have all gone, right?"

"Yes sir. Nearly."

"What do you mean, nearly?' Delany's voice took on an edge.

"Nearly all gone, sir. Not quite all gone."

A thought flashed through Delany's mind—oh bugger. Courthouse chief inspectors were darned near fireproof. Nothing could dislodge a court CI from his post, nothing that is except problems with case exhibits, problems with prisoners' property, or problems with missing or injured prisoners. "I'm on my way down," he snapped and dropped the phone onto its cradle.

As he half-ran down the stairs, worst case possibilities flashed before him. Suicide, escape, both. Jesus, don't let it be either. He pounded on the cell block door and a nervous constable let him in.

The cell block was a long rectangle with a line of barred cells running the full length of one wall. The decor was an indistinct shade of off-white and the floor was smooth concrete.

Neon strip-lights made it stark and hard.

The sergeant rose from his desk. He held his hands before him, palms facing out. "Don't be worry, Ah Sir," he said. "No problems, I think." He jerked his thumb at one of the cells and there, seated on a low stone bench, was a solitary prisoner. He wore a grubby singlet, faded cotton shorts and rubber sandals.

"You said they'd gone," Delany fumed.

The sergeant shrugged. "They have."

"Then who's he?"

The sergeant's mouth worked as though it was trying to form unknown words. "He's... he's..." he shrugged again. "He's spare."

"Spare?" Delany demanded. "Bloody SPARE? How can he be spare?"

"Loaded all prisoners onto the prison van," the sergeant said. "Check, double-check. All counted twice." He nodded to the prisoner. "One left over. One spare."

Delany's rolled his eyes. "Ask him what he's in for."

The sergeant spoke to the prisoner in hushed Cantonese. The prisoner stepped up to the bars and answered.

"He say he is arrested for illegal hawking," the sergeant said.

"Then what's he doing in the bloody cells?"

There was another exchange. "He say he sentenced to two years."

Delany was ready to explode. "Two years? TWO YEARS for hawking?"

The sergeant spoke to the prisoner again and shook his head. They spoke once more. The sergeant turned to Delany. "He say... he say the clerk read out strange charge," he said. "He say clerk read out charge of... read out charge of blackmail."

Delany's head was beginning to reel. This could not be happening. "Blackmail? How did he plead?"

The sergeant pulled a face. "He plead guilty."

The hawker thrust his hands through the bars and gave Delany a thumbs up. His face split in a toothless grin. "Daai bong giu ngoh sing ying," he said. The chief inspector told me to plead guilty. "Si si do hap jok." I always cooperate.

The sergeant put his head close to Delany's. "Maybe we just let him go," he said. He grinned and nodded. His eyes were wide and expectant.

Delany sat on the edge of the sergeant's desk, reached for the phone and dialled the number for the magistrate's chambers. As the phone chirped in his ear, he turned to the sergeant. "Get him out of the cells and give him a cup of... "The magistrate's voice interrupted him. "Ah, Your Worship," Delany said. "I... I don't know how to put this."

And he really didn't.

THE HOKEY-POKEY SQUAD EMPTY BROTHELS

Barry J Smith

It looked great in the recruiting brochures, young police inspectors leading raiding parties up gloomy staircases or aboard police Land Rovers, charging to the scene of major crimes with sirens blaring and blue lights flashing. Do not get me wrong, there was no shortage of that but mostly, the first three years of a one-pip inspector's life in the Royal Hong Kong Police involved a lot of on-the-job training. It started with nine months basic training in law, firearms, physical fitness and the inevitable square bashing. After graduation, there would be a three-month immersive language course and, hopefully, somewhere along the line, there might be a nine months attachment to the Police Tactical Unit, better known as the Blue Berets. Even with the formal training done and dusted, we found ourselves slotted into challenging career development posts. Then, the bosses would stand back and give us chances to shine or, as in some cases, crash and burn. It sounds tough and it was, but for young men new to the Orient, it was the most varied and exciting time of our lives.

Basic training ended with the grandeur that colonial institutions did so well. After the examinations, we togged up in our military-style mess uniforms for a farewell dinner. There was wine, good food, funny speeches and fine comradeship. Finally, there was a graduation parade where, to the accompaniment of the police band, we showed off the precise drills we had been honing for months. Then we loaded our stuff into the back of a police lorry and headed off into the real world.

My posting was as the inspector commanding a patrol subunit in Homantin division, a part of Kowloon City Police District. The patrol subunit is at the heart of city policing. The police constable you see walking the beat is part of such a subunit. On day one, I discovered that a one-pip, probationary inspector was not the stellar rank described in the recruiting brochures. To the seasoned constables and sergeants of Homantin, he was just another *bongban-jai*, a boy inspector. There was no point in fighting it, I could only put my head down and get on with the job. I must have been a fast learner because just a year after graduating from basic training, my mates in Homantin considered me an old sweat. I was just twenty-two years old but in probationary inspector years, I was a veritable Methuselah.

The Royal Hong Kong Police did not let its probationary inspectors stand still. There was training to do and careers to develop. As soon as young inspectors became competent in one job, they moved to another. In a three-year probationary period, they might start by commanding a patrol subunit of thirty or more beat officers or they might be the duty officer in charge of the station report room. The report room was no place for the fainthearted. The duty officer's responsibilities were legion and everywhere it seemed, there was a disaster in waiting. There was a front desk for receiving public reports, a store for found and case property, a safe for bail money and valuable case exhibits; there was the armory and the station cells. There were ledgers, registers, log sheets and all manner of forms, all of which were targets for frequent snap checks by senior officers. The duty officer post was stress in spades. It did not help that when the boss was looking for someone to bollock, the duty officer was the easiest person to find. That is not to say an inspector's life was all ledgers and bollockings. My career path was about to take a more interesting turn. After months commanding a beat patrol subunit, I found myself in charge of a vice squad. Kowloon City had three squads, each led by a probationary, one-pip inspector. There was the drug squad, the anti-gambling squad and then there was mine, the women and juveniles squad. This was the district's anti-prostitution unit, known as the hokey-pokey squad. It was not *Miami Vice* but I got to wear plainclothes, grow my hair, work undercover and carry a concealed firearm. It was honest-to-goodness police work and it beat the hell out being station duty officer.

To be honest, Kowloon City did not have the glitziest vice industry. Tourists and well-heeled locals preferred the fleshpots of Mongkok and Yaumatei. Not that Kowloon City was all was chastity and decorum. There were numerous unlicensed massage parlors that offered more than a rubdown with wintergreen liniment. These places were tucked away in crumbling tenements, marked at street level by a grubby signboard pointing to a gloomy stairwell. Then it was up a narrow staircase leading to an apartment with an illuminated sign above the door hinting at the pleasures within. There would be a small reception area with a battered sofa. The pungent smell of incense would drift from a small shrine fixed to the wall. The lights were so dim it was hard to tell if the girls were still in their flush of youth. A bored overseer would take the fee and a woman would lead the customer along a cramped corridor to a windowless cubicle where the deal would be consummated.

The problem with these places was not so much with the girls or even the operators. The biggest problem was the customers who would knock on random apartment doors, hang around the stairwells, and pass lewd comments to young women going about their daily business. This, together with the parlors' disregard for fire and health regulations, meant the community expected their local police to do something. And of course, like most other areas of syndicated crime, it was all carefully controlled by the triads, so each time a parlor was closed down by police, the local crime bosses took a financial hit. Not something they ever warmed to.

Vice squads had a well-trodden action plan. First, a young constable entered the apartment posing as a customer. Having obtained an offer of some intimate distraction, he paid the fee with marked bank notes then entered the cubicle where, if the timing was right, he would still be when the vice squad burst through the door. He would then calmly produce his warrant and be the main witness in the unlikely event there was a "not guilty" plea. Mostly the managers and girls would simply plead guilty as the triad boss would pay the fine anyway and there was little chance of a custodial sentence. But of course, you could never assume any outcome so the squad would detain everyone, seize the marked banknotes and grab anything else that helped prove the case. This included massage oils, condoms and any pornographic material. It sounds simple enough but getting the right evidence was tricky. There was a constant duel between the vice operators and the undercover police. The operators were wary of offering sexual services to a possible undercover officer and the undercover officers could not ask for sex. If they did, the courts would treat them as agents provocateurs and throw out the case. The easiest way was often to not go after a charge of "operating a vice establishment", which required proof of sexual services and opened up a very murky world to the undercover constable. It was much better to simply go for a massage and leave it at that.

The answer lay in the words, "unlicensed massage

establishment".

In an unlicensed massage establishment, anyone offering even a straightforward massage committed an offence. This should have made the job easier but in practice, no one was about to offer my officers anything. They were too well known. Bringing in new agents did not help; there is something about a policeman that always gives the game away. It might be the way he carries himself, it might be the way he dresses or in the way he talks. No one is sure how they do it, but seasoned vice overseers can spot a policeman in a heartbeat. That is to say, they can spot most policemen.

Known as the auxies, auxiliary police officers were part-time coppers. Most had jobs outside the force but in their spare time, they put on police uniform and worked alongside the regular officers. They were well trained, disciplined and performed the same day-to-day duties as the regulars but there was one key difference. When out of uniform, an auxie looked just like Joe Public.

I spoke to my boss and he had a word with the district's auxiliary superintendent. In short order, there was a long list of auxie constables volunteering for undercover work. It worked perfectly. The auxie went into an unlicensed establishment and paid just enough for a straightforward massage. That was all it took: no massage license; offence complete. There being no need to protect his virtue, the auxie could remain in-house until the squad arrived. Then he identified the operator and helped collect the case exhibits. Sometimes the operator denied having anything to do with the place. A quick chat with the customers would solve that. They could point out the operator or we could pop round to their homes and talk things over with wives and girlfriends. Job done. Well, job almost done.

The last item on the checklist was to get everyone back to

the police station, lay charges, then bail them to appear in court the next morning. And that was where the problem started all over again. Having spent most of their working day dealing with blackmailers, robbers and sundry hoodlums, magistrates did not get agitated about the occasional bit of unlicensed fondling. More often than not, His Worship just rolled his eyes, imposed a small fine and confiscated the meager case exhibits. As far as business overheads went, this was a drop in the bucket. Raid after raid, I was picking up the same people. Another day, another dollar, and the same old people running the same old trade.

This did not sit well with the good people of Kowloon City who were sick of the whole business. Letters were written, elected councilors were lobbied, and the district commander received polite but firm approaches from community leaders. The message filtered down from the lofty floors of district headquarters: get your backside in gear and do something.

I had a problem. I could not control the magistrates and, of course, the massage parlor operators were no help. I gave it some thought and it took me a while to come up with an idea. At first, it seemed crazy but it was to change forever the way the Royal Hong Kong Police handled vice cases. Like any good plan, it was simple: send in an auxie constable, follow up with a raid, detain everyone and finally, seize anything likely to be a case exhibit. Looks like the same old plan, right? And so it was but with a sledgehammer.

I assembled my team and briefed them on the evening's operation. I revealed the target address and everyone relaxed, there was even a yawn or two. I persisted. I nominated an auxie officer to act as a customer then assigned duties to the rest of the raiding party. Finally, I gave special instructions about exhibit handling. The room fell silent. The constables swapped troubled glances. Had they heard right? My sergeant furrowed his brow in a way that said, "Not sure we can do that, Boss."

"Any questions?" I asked.

The sergeant's frown deepened. His brow now said, 'Really, really, not sure we can do that.' A constable smiled. Then another. Seconds later, they were chattering and laughing. The sergeant shrugged and smiled a smile that said, "Okay, but it's your nuts on the chopping block."

In the station compound, a uniformed driver stood by the cab of a ten-ton Bedford truck. We loaded our gear and clambered aboard. In addition to the radios, handcuffs and exhibit bags, there were a couple of crowbars and a massive sledgehammer. Tucked under my arm was a pink file jacket. Written on the cover were the words "Vice Intelligence—Confidential".

The driver slammed shut the tailgate. We were off. The first part of the operation went without a hitch. I gave the auxie a few minutes then the game was on. As I entered the target premises, the overseer sighed, shrugged and waited for the squad to do its worst, which as far as he was concerned was not very much. He smiled when the auxie identified him as the customer. He gave a little chuckle as the squad fanned out and gathered the girls in the reception area. The corners of his mouth turned down at the sight of the crowbars and sledgehammer. His jaw dropped at the splintering crash of iron on wood. He let out a small cry as two constables manhandled a bed through the reception area and out onto the staircase landing. Then there was another bed, and another, then one more until not one bed remained.

"Take that," I ordered, pointing to the reception area's music system.

"Jo mat gwai yeh?" What the hell are you doing? The overseer made two-handed shooing motions at the exhibits constable. His face was ashen.

"Jing mat". Exhibits, I told him. "M'yeh do jing mat."

Everything's an exhibit.

An hour later, the massage parlor was a shell. The squad had stripped the place of beds, music system, cubicle doors, shower doors, sauna doors, tables, reception desk, and sofas. The only thing left was the telephone, which now stood forlornly on the floor. The exhibits constable dropped to one knee and lifted the receiver. I handed him my vice intelligence file, which contained a list of every unlicensed massage parlor in Kowloon City. It had names, addresses and, more important, telephone numbers. The constable grinned and dialed the first name on the list.

A scratchy voice answered in Cantonese. "Wei?"

"Is that Happy Villas?" the constable asked, also in Cantonese.

"Who's that?"

"It's Ah Biu. I work at Gentle Touch Apartments."

"What do you want?"

"Police just raided here."

"So what?"

"I heard them speaking. You're next. They're on their way now."

"Wah. Thank you, Brother. I'll clear the place now. Thank you."

The constable hung up and dialled the next number. I checked my watch. It would be a quiet night in Kowloon City.

The next day, the court prosecutor stood to close his case. "Your Worship, the Crown applies for confiscation of all exhibits," he said.

His Worship had never seen such a long and detailed list of exhibits. He was the very picture of a perplexed magistrate. I was ready for him. Every exhibit, I explained, contributed to the running of a vice establishment: doors for privacy, soft furnishings and music for waiting customers, telephones to call extra girls when needed, beds for, well, we know what the beds are for. The list went on, each seizure perfectly reasonable.

The magistrate hummed and hawed. He scratched his head and consulted his case law but bless him, he came around. He hesitated for a few seconds then announced, "Case exhibits confiscated." Then he gathered his papers and retired to his chambers.

It was a turning point. As the cost of refurbishment soared, Kowloon City's massage parlours moved downmarket. The bed became a mattress on the floor, the reception area became even more shabby, the girls less appealing. One by one, they shut their doors.

Within months, the police station compounds at Mongkok, Yautsim and Shamshuipo became cluttered with furniture and neon signs. Later, every district in the force took up the strategy. To the upmarket vice establishments, it still counted as a business overhead but thanks to the Kowloon City Women and Juveniles Squad, the cost of doing business soared.

I waited for an invitation for tea with the police commissioner and a commendation to hang on my wall. It never came. I had become something of an expert on vice raids and in the Royal Hong Kong Police that meant only one thing.

It was time to move on.

You've Found What?

Barry J. Smith

In a busy district like Kowloon City, there were all kinds of jobs for an old-sweat, one-pipper like me. For example, there was the post of miscellaneous inquiry subunit commander, known as the ME. Sometimes it needed a bit of unofficial overtime but generally, the hours were nine to five with Sundays, public holidays and alternate Saturdays off. The ME was something of a dogsbody outfit. It dealt with licence applications, building site regulations, lost and found property enquiries and all the other odds and ends that no one else wanted to bother with. The ME commander served as the coroner's officer and looked into all non-suspicious deaths. Nasty accident on a construction site? Sudden death at home? If the duty detective was not interested, then the ME took the case. It was all part of a busy station's day-to-day routine. Suicides were different. No matter how hardened a police officer became, there was always something sad about a life gone so desperately wrong that death seemed to be the only solution.

In a district like Kowloon City, with its growing number of high-rise apartments, the suicide method of choice was jumping from a high building. It was messy but quick and irreversible. After the case had been classified as suicide, no suspicious circumstances, the miscellaneous enquiry subunit would take it on board. Among all the statements and reports would be photographs chronicling the last moments of a life gone sour.

Some were horrific but most were simply views of the suicide scene: a suburban street, a tower block and the rooftop or balcony where the deceased spent his or her last moments. And there, beside the balustrade, would be a pair of shoes. They were always neatly placed, as though the jumper had decided to slip quietly into a still pond.

As it turned out, I did not move to the ME immediately, although I would soon find need for the unit's expertise. Instead, I was a victim of my own success. Having closed down all of the massage parlors I was told to take over the district's anti-gambling squad. Given half a chance, Hong Kong folk will bet on two cockroaches going for the same breadcrumb. In Kowloon City, the gambling divans had good escape routes and employed sharp-eyed lookouts. We had to plan well and move fast. Get it right and we netted dozens of players and thousands of dollars. Get it wrong and we found ourselves in an empty room. For all its excitement and frustrations, the anti-gambling squad sharpened our instincts. A police officer equipped with skill, experience and good instincts can handle anything. Generally, some things are straightforward, others less so.

And some are just downright bizarre.

November in Hong Kong is a glorious time. The temperature falls and the humidity drops. In November, there are days when all seems well with the world. It was on such a morning that I arrived at work wearing my gambling squad dress uniform: shorts and t-shirt. My office was on a lower floor at the back of Homantin police station. Actually, it was more a cupboard than an office but at least it had a window and air conditioning. With my team out checking some bookmaking information, I took the chance to catch up on paperwork. Lunchtime came and I wandered up to the officers' mess on the station's top floor. The mess was a pleasant retreat. In one room, there was a canopied bar of dark-stained wood. The bar had been rescued from a Victorian-themed pub that had closed its doors some years earlier. There was also an airy dining room that served a decent lunch. I made my way to the dining room and found myself in genial company. Sandy Boucher and Guy Holland were relatively new and each commanded a patrol subunit. They looked sharp in their khaki bush shirts and slacks. The single pip of a probationary inspector gleamed on their epaulettes.

Lunch passed in a cloud of chatty goodwill until Boucher's radio crackled. He pulled a face and pressed the transmit button. "Subunit commander here. Send message. Over."

A message crackled back. Boucher arched his eyebrows. "Say again. Over.' He held the receiver close to his ear. He turned down the corners of his mouth. "Well, bugger me," he muttered. He pushed back his chair. "Sorry lads. Got to go. He fastened his belt, slipped the cross strap under his epaulette and settled his revolver more comfortably against his hip. "Human leg found," he said and headed for the door.

For a moment, Holland and I gawked at each other then we pushed ourselves back from the table and half-ran after him.

"A found what?" Holland demanded. "A human leg," Boucher answered. He jabbed at the lift button and swore under his breath. Someone was holding the lift on a lower floor.

I must have misheard. "A leg?" I asked. "A human leg?"

"Yes, a leg," Boucher answered. "A human bloody leg."

"You don't hear that every day," Holland said.

The lift arrived, the doors whispered open and we three stepped in. "Do you need a hand?" I asked.

"Why not?" Holland answered. "Somebody's found one of the other bits."

In the station compound, a driver waited in Land Rover, the engine running. Boucher sat in the front and flicked a switch.

Instantly, blue light strobed across the compound walls. The driver gunned the engine and crossed the compound. He paused at the gate, checked the road then stamped his foot on the accelerator. Boucher pressed a button on the Land Rover's Power call console and a high-pitched warble filled the cabin.

There is something about an emergency response that brings out the child in every police officer. To be honest, there was no real need for blue lights and siren; the leg was going nowhere but, dammit, it was fun. The driver accelerated down the Princess Margaret Road clearway. The engine snarled, the radio chattered, the blue lights strobed, the siren wheepwheepwheeped, the smell of hot oil filled the cabin. The driver stood on the brake as a minibus moved into his lane. He dropped into a lower gear and barreled down the inside lane. He swung into a side street, his knuckles white on the steering wheel. On the sidewalks, people stopped and stared. The driver's eyes were hard, his mouth a thin line. Accelerate, brake, turn, brake, and accelerate. He was throwing the heavy Land Rover around like a performance car. I had to grip tight to my seat as the vehicle bounced left, right, up, down, forward, back. All the time I was thinking, what will we find? How will we handle it? Will we get it right? I stole a glance at Holland and Boucher. Both were leaning forward, eyes fixed ahead. Three young men all with the same thought.

The Land Rover entered a middle-class housing complex and the driver slowed. Barclay switched off the blue lights and siren. Ahead, a constable stepped off the kerb and signalled the driver to pull to the roadside. The complex was typical of the new estates cropping up all over Hong Kong. The blocks were slim and elegant, rising twenty floors or more. Each rested on a one-storey podium. At ground level, there were shops and welcoming teahouses. Between the blocks were neat sitting-out areas with stone benches and well-tended flower planters, all shaded by small trees.

A constable was trying his best to control a group of rubbernecking passers-by. Some wore badges marked 'Press'. One had a camera and was trying to take a photograph over the constable's shoulder. A third constable snapped Boucher a salute. He spoke a few words then nodded to an object lying in the plaza next to a tower block. It was an untidy bundle, wrapped in some kind of material.

"That it?" Boucher asked his voice low.

"Buggered if I know," I answered.

"Probably a busted mannequin," Boucher offered.

"Only one way to find out," I answered.

We walked toward the bundle. As we drew closer, we saw its wrapping was a torn trouser leg. A foot protruded from one end. There was a sock, ragged flesh and the white flash of bone.

At this point, Hollywood cops always show their sensitive sides. To the accompaniment of suitable music, the hard-bitten one gives a manly wince while the young one turns away and loses his breakfast. Be they hard-bitten or queasy, both will then look around for a young woman to comfort. Sadly, reality does not measure up to fiction. At some point in their training, Hong Kong Police officers must watch a post-mortem examination. Day-to-day duties put them at the scenes of traffic accidents, knife attacks, mishaps with industrial machinery and all manner of grisly incidents. All this makes for an officer who can remain stoic under any circumstances. That is not to say Hong Kong police officers are uncaring. Under the professional veneer, there is a soul as sensitive as any.

"Those pants must have cost an arm and a leg," Boucher said.

"Hmmm. Perhaps just a leg," Holland answered.

One of the constables looked on with a half-smile on his lips. He was keen to see how three boy inspectors would handle the case.

My instincts told me we were missing something. It was that feeling you get when you momentarily forget the name of a good friend. It should have been obvious. What was it?

We rummaged through the trouser pockets. No wallet, no papers, no identification. Nothing.

"What the hell's happened here?" I asked. "Gang fight"?

"Taken away by the perpetrators?"

"Why leave the leg?"

No answer.

No weapons. No other body parts. No identification. Again, nothing but still, the niggling feeling I had missed something.

"Ideas?"

There were only frowns and silence. Then it hit me. "There should be a shoe," I said. That was it. That was what I had missed. "Why isn't he wearing a shoe?"

We fanned out and searched the litterbins, the concrete flower planters, car-parking bays, doorways, storm drains, bus stops. Nothing. No shoe.

In Hong Kong's high-rise setting, we sometimes ignore what is above us. I do not know what caused me to look up but there, up on the second floor, something caught my eye. From the second floor to the rooftop, a series of small balconies projected from the block's public stairwell. And there, on the second floor balcony was a splash of red.

We hurried to a side door leading to the stairwell. Inside, the staircase was musty and airless. As we climbed, sweat formed on my brow, my t-shirt clung to my back. There was some relief on the second floor landing where a breeze drifted in from the little balcony. We took a few seconds to catch our breath, then stepped forward to investigate. Flies buzzed around our heads. Something red and sticky dripped from the balcony guard wall and puddled the floor. There were splashes of it on the walls and ceiling. I stepped up to the guard wall and put my face close to the stain. It was thick and tacky. Where it had congealed, it was a dark rust color. I peered over the balcony and there, sprawled out on the podium, was the rest of the body. It lay in a spreading pool of blood. The head was pulp. I leaned out over the wall and peered up to the roof, eighteen stories above us. "Poor bugger hit this wall on the way down," I said. "He was traveling at a hell of a speed."

Boucher crowded in beside me. "Jesus," he sighed. "He must have fallen all the way from the roof." Boucher moved away and spoke into his radio transmitter. The radio cracked back. "Roger,'" he said at last. To me he said, "Control room has called out the duty detective but asks that we check the rooftop."

Set in a corner of the stairwell was a service elevator. The doors wheezed open and the elevator grumbled its way up to the top floor where a narrow staircase led to an iron door. I squinted into hard sunlight as I stepped onto the roof. The search did not take long. There, by the balustrade, stood a small stool and beside it were two shoes placed neatly with the toecaps facing the wall.

"Tell control to cancel the detective," I said, nodding to the shoes.

"Right," Boucher answered. "A jumper." He turned away, shaking his head. "Why do they always take their shoes off?" He spoke into his radio. "Control, Inspector Barclay. Over."

"Inspector Boucher, send. Over."

"Reference human leg found. Now classified as person fell from height. Possible suicide. No suspicious circumstances. Repeat, nothing suspicious. Over."

"Roger, Inspector Boucher. Do you require ambulance? Over."

"No. Alert miscellaneous enquiry subunit commander. Over."

"Inform ME. Roger. Out."

For a moment, all was silent then there came an insistent beepbeepbeepbeep. I fished a pager from my pocket. "That'll be my sergeant," I said. "I'm needed back at the station."

"Take the Land Rover,' Boucher said. "Just make sure it comes back for us."

I headed for the stairs, then paused and looked again at the stool and the shoes. "Poor bugger," I said to no one in particular.

Then I stepped through the door and made my way down the stairs.

RISING DAMP

Mike Tinworth

Sailing in the tropics conjures up images of sipping gin and tonic while gently cruising through calm azure seas. This can be done in Hong Kong, but the archetypical tropical environments such as Thailand and the Philippines lie further south. And getting there requires facing conditions as far from tranquil as you can get.

Annual sailing races from Hong Kong to the Philippines have been conducted since the sixties, with the first China Sea Race (to Manila) held in 1962, and the San Fernando Race (unsurprisingly to San Fernando, which is 240 kilometers north of Manila) first held in 1977. Both events became a must-do for anyone interested in competitive sailing, with the San Fernando fleet size regularly reaching upwards of one hundred boats in the eighties.

These races are held around Easter when there is still a strong northeast monsoon wind blowing. This creates an ideal angle for sailing to the Philippines, with the wind generally set at around 90 degrees to the port side of the boat, creating what is known as a "beam reach" point of sail. Consequently, there is no need for constant tacking or sail changes.

However, when the wind speed is Force 6 and the height of the waves over three meters, then one's attention becomes seriously focused. The Beaufort wind scale classifies a Force 6 wind as a "strong breeze" where "large waves begin to form and white foam crests are extensive" and Force 7 is a "near gale". The

Douglas sea scale describes conditions in a wave height of up to four meters as "rough" and up to six meters as "very rough". There is also a bonus condition known as a "confused sea", defined as "a highly disturbed water surface without a single, well-defined direction of wave travel".

All these conditions can be in effect for much of the first two days of the race. Pouring a gin and tonic would be hard enough, and trying to drink one without spilling it near impossible. Not that anyone drinks anything much other than water when conditions are consistently rough. Constant attention is required to control the boat and ensure safety of the crew and rigging at all times.

"The Farr Side" was a 38-foot racing cruiser designed by Bruce Farr, a renowned sailboat designer from New Zealand. It was built in Auckland in 1978, and sailed to the Aberdeen Boat Club in Hong Kong by owner Ashley Wagg. Originally named "Intrigue", she was sailed in many racing successes by subsequent owners, most notably Dr Ian Nicolson, a Hong Kong surgeon.

When technology advances rendered the boat less competitive, a new "Intrigue" was built and the older boat was sold on to two well-known Hong Kong stalwarts, Ian Campbell and Barry Will, and renamed "Auld Intrigue".

Changes of ownership over the years resulted in Doug Castledine acquiring the boat. On his first inspection of the cabin, he was so impressed by the chaos in which the equipment has been strewn around, seemingly at random, that he renamed it *The Farr Side* after the surreal cartoons of Gary Larson.

When Doug decided to spend more time in Australia, he offered up shares in The Farr Side and together with John Berry and Alan Child we formed a consortium to run the boat. The first major adventure would be the 2005 San Fernando Race.

It should perhaps be noted that at this point the boat was twenty-seven years old, so clearly not in pristine condition. However, we took good care of it and the sail racing handicap system still made us competitive in our class.

Preparations for offshore sailing races require that a number of regulations are met, including the ability of the crew to perform emergency first aid at sea and to conduct a rescue in the event of a man overboard. Various courses need to be attended and certifications granted in order for entries to the race to be approved.

Much effort also has to be spent ensuring that race boats meet rigorous operational standards. Our preparations went to plan, but there was some concern when we scraped over a submerged part of Fury Rocks during the Four Peaks race a few months before the San Fernando race. Fortunately, inspections afterwards revealed that no damage had been done.

So everything was good to go when we set off, joined by John Blay, Graeme Brechin, and Sol Leeder, all with plenty of on and offshore sailing experience. Between us we had completed scores of South China Sea passages.

The race starts in the morning in Victoria Harbor and after heading out through the Lyemun Gap and Tathong Channel, you can set a course for the Philippines that won't change much for the next three days. However, for around the first one hundred miles out of Hong Kong, the water depth is relatively shallow, compared to the deeper ocean trench that follows. A number of oil rigs are located on the shelf at the edge of the trench.

In high winds the shallower water causes a constant succession of breaking waves that frequently come right across the boat. The distance between the waves is also shorter than the more extensive surf waves encountered in deeper water. This creates a very choppy (and sometimes confused) sea and consequent heavy bumping as the boat falls off one wave straight into the face of the next one.

The first day and night of the race will therefore generally be extremely uncomfortable, although conditions improve once the deeper water has been reached. Sailing a boat at maximum speed across the surf waves is one of the great experiences in life.

Conditions for this particular journey were as severe as they get, with Force 6 to 7 winds and highly confused seas. However, with two reefs in the mainsail and the headsail furled we were well-balanced and maintaining an optimum speed of eight to nine knots, although we were constantly driving into and falling off four-meter waves.

Sailing requires crew on deck at all times, but it is essential that the crew get sufficient rest to cope with the rigors of the passage. A watch system is implemented so some of the crew is on watch while the rest attempt to sleep. With a crew of six we operated three-hour watches of three people.

Slipping into this pattern is surprisingly easy, and falling asleep after three hours fighting the elements is almost instantaneous, despite the turmoil of the boat motion.

Auto-pilot kicks in when you need to wake up to take over, although this needs to be done at least twenty minutes before the changeover time, as it can take that long to put on all the required kit in turbulent conditions. Warm clothing, wet-weather gear, boots, life-jackets and harnesses all have to be put on in an environment that is somewhat akin to a roller-coaster. The secret is to somehow wedge yourself between parts of the cabin where you won't be thrown around too much and to take a long time between each article of clothing. Thus the first day progressed in severe conditions, but nothing out of the ordinary. There was one slight problem. We appeared to be taking on some water. Nothing exceptional given the amount of water was coming across the boat from the waves. Some water will inevitably seep in through weak links such as the front hatch. There was, however, a distinct sound of sloshing water in the cabin when I went up on deck for the 3:00 a.m. watch.

During the night, things clearly became considerably worse. As the next watch shift was getting ready to take over, a plaintive voice from the cabin was heard to declare, "I think we have a problem." This came from Graeme who had just woken up in the aft starboard bunk with seawater lapping in his face and his trainers floating past his head.

"No shit, Sherlock," came the droll response from Alan, was in a port side bunk and able to look down on the alarming level of water now in the cabin.

We did, indeed, have a problem.

In the morning light we were able to conduct a detailed investigation of the possible causes, having started an ongoing manual baling operation. The bilge pump had stopped functioning, but thankfully no cracks in the hull, keel or steering could be found.

Investigations of the water ingress, examination of the bilge pump, and baling continued for the next hour. This was all done at maximum boat speed with water still swirling round the cabin, and the boat constantly being knocked off the waves. The view from the helm through to the cabin from the cockpit was in fact reminiscent of many *Farr Side* cartoons, although an air of calmness prevailed.

No great progress was being made and we now had to consider contingency options, the most extreme being to evacuate to the life raft. This is an absolute last resort as staying with the boat is always the most advisable option, even in distressed situations.

Turning back is not an easy option, because you will not get to your destination for a well-earned holiday and months of preparation will have gone to waste. However, with San Fernando two days away and no solution in sight, after much deliberation, we reluctantly decided to abandon the race and turn back to Hong Kong.

Turning a boat through 180 degrees in high winds and steep seas is not a simple operation. There is a high chance of getting knocked over if you get it wrong. The engine was turned on and the maneuver was completed without incident.

Heading back towards Hong Kong we contacted race control by SSB radio advising our decision, in accordance with race regulations. The message was, "Yacht *Farr Side* has retired from the race due to rising damp, and is returning to Hong Kong."

We were now sailing on a different tack with the starboard side raised well above the water line. One of the main factors for the rising water level was identified shortly after turning round.

The bilge pump operation had been stopped due to a wood chip or carpentry shaving in the impeller. This had prevented the pump operation, but had not stopped water flowing into the boat through the pump discharge pipe, located at the starboard bow below deck level. With the bow wave constantly at deck level the discharge pipe had been acting as a syphon into the bilge, achieving the opposite effect from its purpose. This problem can be prevented with the use of a non-return valve, which allows water out but not in.

The bilge pump was repaired and the bilge water ejected. With the discharge pipe now out of the water, we blocked it for additional safety – with a wine bottle cork.

It was also evident that the bilge outlets had been blocked by a sodden mass of cardboard from the Australian cask wines stored in the cabin bunk lockers. The boxes had all dissolved, leaving the unlabelled bladders. These were put into plastic bags and hung in the cockpit for a blind wine-tasting session on the return journey.

We had reached approximately the mid-point and could have turned back towards San Fernando. However, we had had more than enough drama and it was prudent to get back to Hong Kong for a boat inspection to ensure there were no other defects.

The sail back turned out to be almost perfect. The wind and seas had abated somewhat, and we surfed back on what had now become a cruise rather than a race. The boat had been provisioned with three days' supply of beer and wine, and we had touched little of it so far due to the rough conditions.

Time slipped away and we succeeded in drinking all the wine before we got back to the Aberdeen Boat Club late in the evening on the day after setting off.

Our arrival back at the club in a very relaxed frame of mind was, however, not entirely appreciated by our spouses who had come to meet us. They had spent the last twenty-four hours in a state of some anxiety, only knowing that we had a problem and had had to turn back. However, their concerns were soon placated by the relief of seeing us back on dry land, the level of which was certainly matched by our own.

We didn't make the Philippines, but we did have an adventure!

Raining Fire in the Sky

Mark Esterhuizen

In Cathay Pacific, the ultra-long-haul point-to-point flying that eluded so many airlines in the '70s and'80s finally became a reality with the development of the A340 into a longer range A340-600 and with Boeing, the phenomenal 777-300ER. Cathay finally could offer nonstop Hong Kong to Chicago, Toronto and New York. Our polar routes from New York, Toronto and Chicago were a kind of "flex" route, very much wind and weather dependent, and occasionally, dependent on radiation modeling.

Under our personal health statistics with Cathay, we could monitor the amount of millisieverts of radiation we were exposed to over thirty, sixty, ninety and 365-day periods. Once it reached a threshold, we were taken off high-latitude trips (North of 65°N) until it dropped below the "unsafe" level. That was the intent, anyway. A bit of background as to what we were experiencing on that particular flight.

So there we were, at 35,000 feet and in the dark over Ellesmere Island, about 80° North latitude, trying to achieve a balance of the optimum route, track a Great Circle (the shorter of two arcs that bisect the globe), a route that would also keep us clear of the predominantly westerly jet streams, clear of Russian airspace (the Russians were notorious for exorbitant navigation charges if you overflew their airspace) and finally, crew health concerns.

We'd been cautioned by our dispatch specialists in JFK that solar flares were expected, with solar storms and high levels of electromagnetic and radiation activity. Communications, even CPDLC (Controller-Pilot Data Link Communication via satellite) in the high North in EMF (electromagnetic storms) is a major concern, so we'd made our mandatory reports with Anchorage and Gander, CPDLC was up and humming, and it was only the first officer and me, up on the super-quiet A340-600 flight deck, looking out at the stars on a gin-clear night, reminiscing about past lives.

At about 2 o'clock, just to the right of straight ahead, a faint blue line appeared, almost like a sunrise, and as we watched, it grew, spreading up and across the horizon edge to edge, to the limit of where we could see above us. Luminous sheets, like veils, dropped from the skies and began dancing around us, first only in blue, then green and pink and white. The shimmering curtains almost felt so close we could touch them and faintly, under the white noise in the cockpit. We could hear hissing as we passed the waves of light. In total radio silence. The hum of the electronics, the air conditioning and the Aurora. It was so bright you could read without the cockpit lights. The Aurora surged and receded like waves on the beach, changing colors and hissing at us, like a beast.

Then, slowly at first, then faster and more frequently, bright streaks were passing overhead at fantastic speed, some petering out like spent Roman candles, and others exploding in a shower of sparks, tens, perhaps hundreds of thousands of feet above us but feeling so close it seemed we could almost touch them. There were thousands of sparks and hundreds of meteorites flashing and exploding all around us mixed up with the Aurora.

It was absolutely breathtaking. The two of us sat in silence, mouths agape at this once-in-a lifetime event, lasting about an hour. It passed too quickly. We tried to take photos but unsuccessfully. We must have sat for hours after the event, not saying anything, but reflecting on the magnificence of it all.

A long time after, I was listening to *Rocky Mountain High* by John Denver, and I understood what he meant when he sang of "seen it raining fire in the sky".

I'll never forget that night.

THE BODY IN THE SACK

Guy Sanderson Shirra

After the Confrontation, the Hong Kong Police Force gradually returned to normal work which, in my case, meant uniformed duty in Causeway Bay as a shift commander, attachment to the HKI District Vice Squad and Police Training Contingent, internal security training at Fanling with deployment in the New Territories and Kowloon. After PTC, I returned to Bayview Division and was posted as a shift commander to Shau Kei Wan Sub-division where I continued my practice of arresting the "wrong people". The force, it seemed, had a laissez-faire attitude to vice law enforcement which, in my naivety, I "failed to properly appreciate".

However, in June 1968 I was to make a genuinely significant arrest.

Annie Yip and I were married in the City Hall with a reception in Eastern Police Officers' Mess followed by a traditional Chinese banquet in the famous Ying King restaurant in Wanchai. I chose to live as close as possible to work in Shau Kei Wan so we must have been the first, and probably the last, married couple to choose the Showboat Hotel (now the Showboat Apartments) as our accommodation, pending allocation of a quarter. This establishment in Quarry Bay had a Chinese restaurant, ballroom, sauna and swimming pool, about ten floors of rooms tastefully decorated with unusual furniture and mirrors and a top floor coffee shop and roof garden.

Great consternation was caused to the other hotel guests by my comings and goings in police uniform but as they never booked in for long anyway, the management were not concerned. I asked my mother to either come for the wedding or wait until we had a married quarter but she chose to join us in the hotel. She was rather puzzled by her room décor but was spoiled rotten by the staff who had never met a proper English lady there before, nor were they ever likely to again.

After a few weeks in Shau Kei Wan, I was called to see the new "God", Frank Kong. To my astonishment, he asked me if I would like to go to the Criminal Investigation Department. This was unheard of for a greenhorn like myself with no previous UK police let alone CID experience. After I recovered, I cautiously told him that I would accept any posting. He said, "Good. You are being transferred to the Commercial Crime Office tomorrow." I had never heard of CCO and left his office in a daze.

CCO shared dilapidated former guest house accommodation in the Li Po Chun Chambers building in Central with a small section set aside from the Anti-Corruption Branch. I arrived there in September 1968 and stayed until my first home leave in the spring of 1970. Naturally, they did not know what to do with me so I was assigned under my former training school instructor, Sammy Cheah, to the fraud section and given one detective to assist me. DPC 4455, A Chan, was a cheerful chap with a bouncy walk who took his new assignment babysitting me with aplomb. Sammy bunged me a few old files to cut my teeth on and I was involved in several interesting cases and was even highly commended by the Commissioner of Police for work on a complicated conspiracy to defraud the HK Telephone Company.

My time in CCO concluded with my membership of a task force of twenty officers headed by Detective Senior Inspector Pat Park of CID HKI comprising officers from CCO and the Narcotics

Bureau with Special Branch officers lurking in the background. This was formed on 4 December 1969 to investigate the murder of a millionaire Chiu Chow businessman and alleged narcotics and jewelery smuggler, Woo Chi-kiu, whose body had been found in a sack floating off Kennedy Town Praya on 29 November. Woo and his wife lived very comfortably in a colonial-style mansion in the Mid-Levels and their children were privately educated in the UK.

The case was quickly dubbed "The Body in the Sack Murder" by the press and it was strongly suspected that Woo was a victim of triad in-fighting connected with his smuggling business. There was concern that his murder would result in full-blown gang warfare. Naturally, the Hong Kong and Bangkok press were all over it and speculation was rife. Pat Park was under considerable pressure to solve the case.

So, while NB task force members concentrated on the smuggling, CCO officers concentrated on the commercial side of things and assisted CID HKI with the triad aspects. I myself joined one of HK's top sleuths of the time, Detective Staff Sergeant Au-Yeung Kwan, investigating the scene of the crime, i.e., the Kennedy Town Praya where his body had been located with his locked Mercedes-Benz sedan parked on a pavement. We both thought it a very odd place for him to park his car and surmised that he must have been murdered in a nearby tenement building during a meeting. But exactly where, by whom and for what purpose?

However, the case was rapidly and unexpectedly solved when it was discovered the two young culprits, Miao Tak-yin and Li Hon-ling, teenage boys with whom Woo was allegedly having homosexual relations, were intent on blackmailing him. Foolishly, they tried to cash a cheque of Woo's at his office. Under interrogation back at the Tai Kwun (CID HQ HKI), they quickly confessed to his murder in a Kennedy Town flat round the corner from where we had found Woo's parked Mercedes—at 7 Belcher Street, to be exact. An argument over money resulted in their beating him to death with an iron bar, robbing him of his belongings, stuffing him in a gunny sack, dragging him downstairs, around the corner, across the praya and into the harbor.

The suspects led us to the Caritas Center in Caine Road where they said they had dumped his clothing. It was left to me as the youngest and fittest to climb two floors down the central light-well to recover a pair of bloody trousers in the trash at the bottom. In a safe deposit box belonging to Woo, we found several photographs of naked young men and other pornography. Traces of heroin were found in the boot of Woo's Mercedes and the victim's blood in the Belcher Street flat.

Later I was joined by Marine Police to drag the harbor below the sea wall in Central to find an iron bar, fountain pen and other items belonging to Woo, which the suspects claimed to have thrown there. This activity attracted a horde of jostling and annoying press photographers. Every pile of disgusting debris we pulled up the ramp revealed nothing so I decided to have some fun with them.

Within the next pile of muck I pretended to find significant evidence in the form of a folded and soggy piece of paper. I spread it out reverently on the ground and dozens of flash bulbs duly popped. When they had finished, I turned to them, asked them if they were happy and then balled up the evidence and threw it in the harbor to the groans and curses of the press. We never found the iron bar murder weapon but the boys were convicted of murder nonetheless and served jail sentences "at Her Majesty's Pleasure". The Supreme Court case was prosecuted by the able and flamboyant Senior Crown Counsel Max Lucas.

Search the internet for this case and those involved and you will now find only one obscure AFP news report. Woo's UK-educated son became and remains an influential member of Hong Kong's elite.

For this case, along with other task force members, I received not one but two Commanding Officer's High Commendations, one from the Director of Criminal Investigation and another from the Assistant Commissioner HKI, both major formation commanders claiming the credit for solving the case.

Which actually solved itself...

The Four Peaks Race and the Naming of Captain Barbecue

Lynn Seymour

This event combines one hundred miles of coastal sailing with the challenge of climbing four of the highest peaks in Hong Kong: Ma On Shan in Sai Kung, Violet Hill in Repulse Bay, Lantau Peak on Lantau Island and Mount Stenhouse on Lamma Island.

The race is usually held in January when the winds are more consistent, but the downside is the very cold temperatures at night, both for the runners and the ones left on the boat trying to keep warm or sleep, if they are lucky. Regulations require a minimum of two persons running a Peak. Usually there are four pairs, i.e., each pair designated one Peak but it has been known for the same pair to run all four Peaks and then been awarded a case of beer. The race begins in Tai Tam Bay when twenty to thirty yachts sail towards Sai Kung, where the runners from each boat go ashore by canoe or dinghy to climb Ma On Shan before returning to the boat and heading off to the other Peaks.

Eighteen years ago, I joined three guys on a recce of Lamma a few weeks prior to the 2003 Four Peaks Race. They wanted to track the quickest route possible to Mt Stenhouse and with the aid of the dinghy and a boat boy, we all launched ourselves onto slippery rocks from an exceedingly rocky dinghy. From there we clambered up the cliff face and into dense scrub and bush where we got torn up and could not see very well. Our leader was convinced there was a path that would lead to Mt Stenhouse, and we split into twos to find it. After a lot of crashing about in the undergrowth and swearing, we heard yelling and on looking up and ahead we saw a lot of black smoke and then flames

Our leader had found the path that, unfortunately for us, was blocked by a large hill fire. He made the suggestion to jump through, which was thoroughly vetoed by the rest of us as the fire was blowing in all directions and vegetation was snapping and cracking and heading our way. As there was no other access to the pathway, obscured by the fire, we stumbled back to the rock face to see if we could see our boat, but it had already motored off to Sok Kwu Wan without a backward glance. We were faced with the horrible thought of becoming char-grilled but, to our amazement, we saw a small dinghy bouncing in the waves and heading towards us. Luckily, we were rescued by a friend who had moored overnight around the bay and was doing his own recce for the race. He had seen the fire from his boat, came to investigate, saw us waving and shouting and went to our rescue. Once delivered safely onto his boat and handed beers all round, we celebrated our delivery from the face of death and renamed our esteemed leader "Captain Barbecue".

As a postscript, the yacht commanded by Captain Barbecue won their class that year and was also awarded the geriatric mug — for the fourth year running.

Here's US$25,000, Now Let's Get Out of Here

Mark Esterhuizen

Parked at gate in Heathrow in a Cathay Pacific 747-400 on a cold and wet late afternoon, ready to go and OTP (on time performance) a really important issue, the load coordinator, the "conductor" of the ground services, came up to the flight deck to advise us that we were missing three first-class passengers. The company policy was (and still is) not to fly with unaccompanied baggage, so a search for the missing passengers' bags was started. This isn't a really complex process. The location of the bags, each with a unique identification, is recorded and tracking the bags and removing them isn't anything but a minor delay, ten minutes at the outside. It's more an inconvenience than anything else.

The load controller was dispatched back onto the ramp with instructions to find and remove the bags. As the process of finding and removing the unaccompanied bags began, the load coordinator advised us that the three "pax" had been found and were on their way. He added that there was an interesting back story, and that he would be up to tell us all about it.

The three pax had been briefly detained in security when the officers had discovered they were carrying a significant amount of cash, all in sterling and well over £1 million. In a paper carry bag, no less.

As this amuse-bouche was being consumed by the four impressed aircrew, the passengers appeared, running down the jet way, brown Harrods shopping bag clearly visible. They boarded without any incident or delay and we proceeded with the engine starts and were on our way.

This curious start to our day was fodder for the flight and we carried on as professionally as ever until the stories began to flow thick and fast after we'd reached our cruising altitude somewhere near Bremen.

The winner for the flight was undoubtedly the captain, a real Old China Hand who had been with Cathay Pacific a long time. He started his career in Hong Kong with Jardines Aviation at a time when inter-racial dating between the British expats and local Chinese was frowned upon. Local Chinese were not allowed to own properties on The Peak.

The captain had flown the earlier model Boeing 707 for Cathay and although it was a long-range range aircraft, it could not fly from Hong Kong to London without a fuel stop.

This is his story:

The 707 under his command had already stopped in Bahrain for fuel and had reached its cruising altitude after take-off from Bahrain enroute to London, the sun starting to light the skies behind the aircraft when two armed Royal Jordanian Air Force fighters—Hawker Hunters--appeared on either side of the Cathay 707. Tensions were running high in the region and fearing for the safety of the occupants and themselves, the captain followed the internationally recognized interception signals for "follow me" and began a mandated descent, landing in Amman, Jordan.

The passengers were duly informed about the diversion and all necessary preparations were made. After landing, the authorities in Amman told the crew that overflight for that flight had been denied, and after a radio call to operations in Hong Kong, it was amicably resolved. The crew were free to continue their flight to London after a landing fee had been paid and fuel uplifted. This was easier said than done as the airport authorities in Amman denied the on-board "fuel carnet", a type of credit card used by airlines to buy fuel. They would, however, accept a wire transfer, which the captain proceeded to arrange through flight operations in Hong Kong. As this was bound to take a few hours, the captain informed the passengers of the issues, the process as well as the time involved.

Once again, the crew settled in the cockpit waiting to hear the SELCAL (Selective Calling on High Frequency Radio, our primary long-distance radio communications), bing when a gentleman appeared at the cockpit door.

Given his clothing, yarmulke (skull cap) and accent, it was clear the gentleman was Jewish.

"Captain," he said, "my name is Katz. I'm not very comfortable with this situation and I heard that you were waiting for a wire transfer from Hong Kong to pay for the fuel. Exactly how much money are we talking about here?"

The captain replied, "About 25,000 US dollars."

"Oh," Mr Katz replied. "Just a moment." Two minutes later he returned with the cash in his hands. "I'll take an IOU. Let's go." So there they were, once again on their way to London, with a relieved passenger holding an IOU, which of course, was honored.

The Nine Lives of a Chinese White Dolphin

Clinton Leeks

It is fair to say that when the Hong Kong Government announced its intention in October 1989 to build a new airport at Chek Lap Kok Island, off north Lantau, after four years of studies that I had been tangentially involved in, I knew nothing at all about the occupants of the area. Well, I knew about some of them. I had visited Chek Lap Kok by helicopter in 1979 to see if the staff manning the lonely weather station there deserved extra pay. I had walked the north Lantau coast from Tung Chung to Tai O many times. But there was another mammal species in the area that would generate far more "interest" for the new Airport Authority trying to build the airport than all the villagers on and around Chek Lap Kok put together... I refer, of course, to Sousa Chinensis, or the Chinese White Dolphin.

I can't say environmentalism as a concept tickled the average Hong Konger's interest much in the 1980s. Yes, people liked the beaches in between the red tides and sewage, and country parks when they weren't setting them alight with fag-ends and ill-extinguished BBQs. But the concept of protecting the environment per se, or even its fragile ecology, was as welcome to a city of developers and budding flat-owners as the proverbial pork chop in Hong Kong's nice old Ohel Leah Synagogue on Robinson Road. Which, rather to make my point, the developers demolished.

So by 1991, we had an airport master plan for its construction at Chek Lap Kok. It had all the stuff Kai Tak had had, plus some nice new additions. Part of the plan lifted from Kai Tak was to supply aviation fuel (known as avgas—not a medical condition) direct from fuel tankers coming up alongside the runway. Then they would offload their precious avgas into a fuel distribution and storage system under the runway and parking apron. The system was to be operated by a consortium that would then supply the avgas to the individual airlines. This mattered. Not just because aircraft running out of fuel did bad things, but also because it was big business. Most countries round Hong Kong charged a lot for refueling, adding on heaps of tax. Hong Kong was cheap, efficient and low-tax. So airlines came into Kai Tak flying on fumes and then filled their boots with as much avgas as possible, to avoid being taken to the cleaners by our Asian neighbors. Interesting to think of some of the world's most expensive real estate being just a glorious gas station for aircraft, but there you are. Good business for the fuel companies, and not bad for the airlines.

But the new airport also had lots of other much newer stuff than Kai Tak—new instrument landing systems, new weather detection systems, new air traffic control wizardry and so on. Unlike Kai Tak, the runway would be bang alongside a very high line of hills on Lantau. Tall hills and runways don't mix well. And then we discovered that the new IT guidance and detection systems we would need to develop for Chek Lap Kok would be confused by large metal vessels maneuvering right beside the runway. Fuel tankers are quite high-sided, slow-moving things, ideal to confuse airport radar. Which does sort of make one wonder why navies don't just creep up to invade well-defended nasty places by using ships disguised as fuel tankers, but I digress.

Environmental studies had been conducted for the new airport as part of the planning studies comparing various site options in from 1986 to 1989, and refining the master plan of 1989-91. But now we'd need to add something... An off-airport fuel system that would receive tankers some distance from the airport platform, store the avgas they offloaded in large onshore tanks, and then pump it in pipelines under the sea to the parking apron where aircraft would be waiting to refuel. So we needed to find a location, preferably uninhabited, not far from the airport (new pipelines cost, so the shorter the better), then do a quick environmental study to satisfy everyone.

Enter the Dolphin

We knew about dolphins, of course. Ocean Park had them, and we'd seen *Flipper* at the cinema. And we knew there were some in the Pearl River delta, near Hong Kong. The massive reclamation the Airport Authority would need to undertake at Chek Lap Kok would, it was confidently assumed, just shift the cunning mammals northwards or sideways, out of the way. Whatever else they were, dolphins were smart (we knew that from seeing them at Ocean Park and in the movies). They got out of the way of slow-moving noisy dredgers. So far, so good sort of—it was still better if you weren't a dolphin.

These were not the Flipper-type of blue bottlenose sea-going dolphins. They liked shallow sandy water, the sort you got in river estuaries. They'd been around for millennia—a Western traveler to the Pearl River in the early 1600s recorded seeing dolphins "milky white as snow". And there's another thing. They weren't always white—like humans, they were gray and spotty in their youth. As they got older, the spots faded to white, and then in maturity changed to pink. But for reasons we can understand, the dolphin's PR managers didn't think a label like "the spotty gray/pink dolphin" had quite the same cachet as "Chinese white dolphin". And it wasn't Chinese. It just liked big river mouths with preferably not too much boat traffic. It inhabited the Yangtze, the Irrawaddy and the Zambesi, among other places. And the last and most annoying thing, and not only for the dolphin, was that it was dying out. Too many people, too many boats, too much disturbance, too little food and too few places to breed. The Yangtze variety was already on its last flippers.

As an extra complication, the dolphin had a little mate, rather the way Winnie the Pooh had Piglet. Alongside the dolphins was an even smaller critter called the finless porpoise? Small, dark, and sort of bobbing along in the ocean, a bit like a discarded rubber tyre. I asked a dolphin expert one day how to spot them and he said assume you're looking out for an old rubber tyre in the ocean swell. I was not expecting something as majestic as an orca, but when it came to the great genetic plan by the Almighty for designing the finless porpoise, one could not but feel Nature played a bit of a mirthless joke.

Water, Water Everywhere
People in the early 1990s were becoming more aware of their Hong Kong surroundings, which was good. It was, after all, one of the reasons why we were moving the airport out of downtown Kowloon where its noise and air pollution blighted the lives of millions. The Maipo marshes were unbelievably popular for bird-watching. Tour operators were now taking groups out hiking and dolphin-watching. People were rightly becoming aware that even busy, chaotic and skyscrapered Hong Kong was a movable home for an unusual, even endangered, creature. Who'd have thought?

Meanwhile, we needed to find a site for a fuel facility. There were several options around Chek Lap Kok. But north Lantau itself would raise too many problems, with so much related development planned. The Brothers Islands east of the runway had been flattened for the same IT reasons that we were now searching for an off-airport fuel site. Lots of new industrial land were being created near Tuen Mun, to the immediate north. It would be ideal but it wasn't ready yet. A consortium with Chinese links offered Guishan Island, in the Pearl River to the west, formerly a quarry site — but having the airport's fuel depot outside Hong Kong waters seemed problematic. As in one of those quiz shows with a spinning arrow on a dial, or a huge roulette wheel, all the pointers were firmly heading one way — to Sha Chau, a little uninhabited group of islands just to the north of Chek Lap Kok, but closer than Tuen Mun — and well away from aircraft flightpaths. We would need the selected site to be approved by the Government, and a land lease, and that meant we had first to do an environmental impact assessment, and get that approved too.

What could be simpler? Sha Chau was boringly simple. Uninhabited, the name meaning in Chinese "sandy island" (a perfect if unimaginative label — I had gone there by boat to swim in the early 1980s), just outside the main shipping channel. We'd need to build a platform for the tankers to offload against, and tanks to store the avgas until it was pumped undersea to the airport. There was one looming problem. As we started building the airport, the dolphins seemed to have done as we'd predicted, i.e., packed their suitcases and moved home northward. But where? Exactly across the shipping channel to the waters round Sha Chau.

Our experts agonized over this. We'd need to pile into the seabed to build the platform. The fuel tankers would need to come in and out of Sha Chau regularly. There might be fuel leaks. The dolphins might get thoroughly peeved by all this stuff and move away again, especially for breeding. But they were running out of places to go. Dolphins were smart, our experts said. When things got annoying they got out of the way, then came back afterwards. They sounded cleverer than many of my work colleagues. But proof was the problem. Interviewing dolphins was hard, and I shrewdly suspected those cute gurgling, screeching and whistling noises they made underwater would make less than compelling testimony on land—even Legco might struggle to understand them.

We had a more immediate practical problem. Our environmental study of Sha Chau concluding, "No Problemo" would need to be approved by a non-notorious committee called the Environmental Impact Assessment Subcommittee of the Advisory Council on the Environment (governments don't go in for snappy labels). Otherwise, no Sha Chau, which meant no fuel, which meant no airport. The dolphin's pretty, fluked little tail would wag the huge shaggy Chek Lap Kok dog.

A Horse Designed by a Committee

This is what Neville Chamberlain said a camel was. Well, equine or not, we needed our dromedary to get approved. The EIA Subcommittee was chaired by an elegant charming University vice-chancellor and comprised about fifteen members representing either Legco or various bodies with an interest in the environment. We had to convince them to tell the main Advisory Council that, even if they didn't trust us an inch, on fine balance, they grudgingly concluded we were not dolphin-killers. Not as easy as you might think.

It took us about a year of meetings with them. We had engineering experts galore, who came along to make lengthy presentations that left one's brain, as Jim Morrison of the Doors once sang, "squirming like a toad". We had environmental experts super-galore, who perfected the art of looking both worried and very humane at key moments.

Above all we had our trump card cetacean noise experts. These are wonderful people. You might think that to be a cetacean (i.e., whale and dolphin) expert would be enough in our crowded world. But no. These guys are experts in how dolphins react, or don't react, to noise. We had two. A lovely man called Bernt who spoke with a strong American-German accent, and was endlessly patient and charming. The more he heard nonsense on his chosen subject, the more he sucked it up, smiled like a cherub, and produced another set of charts to explain once again what we thought the average dolphin heard or didn't hear, and even more wonderfully, what we considered the dolphin actually felt about the whole thing. More human brains squirmed throughout.

We nearly lost lovely Bernt. At one point he went off to Russia and accidentally ate a bucket load of toxic mushrooms. He nearly died. I never found out if the meal was part of research into what sort of noise dolphins made when they ate mushrooms. But the point is that Hallelujah! Like Lazarus, Bernt returned from the edge of the grave and lived to fight and smile again. Bernt 1 Mushrooms 0.

Our other expert, also an American, was an equally lovely guy called Tom, and disconcertingly with the same name as a former US President. He was Bernt's disciple, and wonderfully he stayed on after Bernt went home, continuing to study dolphins in Hong Kong and advise useful people such as those in the Agriculture and Fisheries Department and Ocean Park.

Bernt and Tom were our secret weapons. Whatever people thought they knew about dolphins and noise, The Bernt and Tom Show was there ever so gently and politely to correct and educate them. And they had more tricks up their sleeves than

Houdini and David Copperfield combined. One day, in a heated discussion about noise impacts Bernt smiled the smile of Mother Teresa and said to me quietly, "Mr Leeks, Mr Leeks, scientifically there is no such thing as 'noise'. There is only 'sound'." What a hero.

And there were presentations, endless presentations. We lived in a pre-Powerpoint age, so the chosen means of brutality to unsuspecting stakeholder committees was Death by Flipchart, or, if you were a really high-tech tormentor, Death of a Thousand Overheads. Every time the EIA Subcommittee got truculent, we showed them another presentation, gradually weakening their collective will to survive. It was indeed vicious. But we needed that airport.

And then we had Bill's box. It was a sort of intellectual "chamber of little ease". Bill was an engineer with the Airport Authority, and he helped us with the engineering aspects of the site selection for the fuel system. Bill had a big open box holding dozens of huge reports on the various site options. I made sure he always brought that box to the subcommittee meetings. You could almost hear the collective sotto voce groan as Bill entered the room, manfully struggling to carry his box. For all I knew, it was mostly stuffed with old telephone directories. Whenever a member asked a particularly thorny question Bernt would be sent into bat with his latest presentation and Bill would start rummaging in his huge box. I always prayed he wouldn't accidentally give the game away by bringing out a baseball bat. The innocent inquirer's eyes would gradually widen like golf balls and the question would magically fade away.

So finally we came to a vote by the subcommittee one rainy evening in August 1994 on whether they would recommend to the main Advisory Council that the government should proceed with the statutory processes to deliver sandy Sha Chau unto the

Airport Authority. I'd had a message from Government House that the Governor would not overrule the Council. We had to convince their worthy subcommittee.

I had also been told the Governor's weekly postbag at that time over-flowed with letters from overseas on two main subjects: second by volume was the future of Hong Kong and its people; first was the future of the Chinese White Dolphins. So we had to convince the subcommittee: no lifelines or "phoning a friend" were permitted. We had, meanwhile, come up with some extra mitigations (as environmentalists call measures to reduce adverse impacts) to strengthen our case. First the vessels that brought avgas from Hong Kong's main depot at Tsing Yi would be specially designed, with size and speed restrictions, and double hulls (to prevent leakage should the hull be damaged). It would have special procedures to watch out for and avoid dolphins. Second, during construction, we would lay a "bubble curtain" on the seabed around the site: this would force a rising curtain of air out of a flexible pipeline and thus conceal the underwater noise of piling that might otherwise distress the dolphins outside the site. An endless encompassing circle of marine flatulence. This technique was a "world first" for Hong Kong, and experiments showed it worked. Finally, and more important, the area around Sha Chau would be legally designated a marine park to protect the dolphins. There would be special rules for vessels wishing to enter the area, and set speed limits, all enforced by the government. By a neat coincidence, the marine park area of 1,200 hectares, was identical to the size of the new airport.

We finally came towards a vote. I head-counted the room in my brain and knew it was close. Then one of our alleged allies scampered to the loo. That made numbers too tight, if he did a runner. I followed him into the gents' and stood behind him while he urinated (I'm not sure what I'd have done if he'd gone into a cubicle). He jumped when he realized I was right behind him, and pleaded it was hair-washing night or something. "Oh no you don't," I said. "Your hair looks lovely. Wash your hands and back you come." I then frogmarched him back into the committee room just in time to cast his vote. We won by eight votes to five.

Gathering winter and summer fuel

The rest, as they say, is history. The Sha Chau site was gazetted and granted by lease to the Authority. A franchise was awarded to a fuel consortium to operate the facility. Sha Chau duly supplied the new airport on and after its rather fraught opening on July 6, 1998, and went on doing so, well into the next decade when finally a permanent facility opened on industrial land outside Tuen Mun. Sha Chau was then mothballed and retained as an emergency or standby facility, as had been agreed all those years ago in 1994.

The Sha Chau marine reserve I'm told still flourishes, and has a sister in the waters east of Sai Kung. Most importantly, I really hope Sousa Chinensis does well—the same wish I have for all Hong Kong's residents, transient or otherwise. Interest in the dolphins certainly grew massively in the period before and since airport opening. I knew this because soon after Sha Chau was approved we started getting approaches from Mainland academics pressuring us to employ their students at inordinate airport expense on dubious dolphin-related studies. Always a sign something has changed—it's only a short step from being a pariah to being a fixture. As Mae West so wisely observed, "It's better to be looked over than overlooked." We gently turned them down.

Legco continued to check up on us. Indeed they visited us en masse one day at the airport site as construction neared completion. As they toured around rather aimlessly, one of our environmental team rang me to say a specimen of the finless porpoise (remember them? Discarded rubber tyres floating at sea) had inconsiderately washed up dead on the sea wall. It would be highly inconvenient if the Legco members happened to come across the corpse so the team keeping the seawall clear of marine junk had thoughtfully tried to cremate it, doubtless while singing an appropriate hymn. There was just one problem. First, the corpse was inflammable. Second, like all seawalls the boulders of ours were crammed by debris and flotsam washed up during typhoons. A conflagration duly burst forth like the fires of Hell, and a smoke column could be seen from all over the airport island. It was probably observable from the moon. Decently, our Legco visitors never inquired what the cause of this distant volcanic eruption was, with its Vesuvius-like towering smoke plume at the far end of the runway.

This is not, I hope, a metaphor for the future of the Chinese White Dolphin. Forced to live, feed and breed in ever more crowded, busy shipping lanes around the Pearl River Delta, its long-term future sadly cannot be assured. But I take comfort from the fact that I gather numbers of sightings have increased noticeably during the Covid-19 pandemic. Maybe that is the answer. As one dominant species retreats on Earth, others are only too happy to fill the gap, as they probably did before Man first clambered out of the Primal Ooze. That's only fair, and if the ever-resilient and rather graceful Chinese White Dolphin is able to take our place here and there, well, I for one will salute them.

RAMBLES IN THE ISLANDS WITH BUTTERFLY NETS AND A PODGY MISFIT

G.T. Reels

I had already been working on the Hong Kong University Biodiversity Survey with Michael Lau for a year when, in early 1997, I had to prepare space for a third occupant in our cramped laboratory. David Dudgeon and Richard Corlett, our bosses at HKU, had decided to recruit a field and laboratory assistant for our project.

"We want a new natural sciences graduate on a one-year contract," David had said. "The money won't be great. Do you know anyone who might be daft enough to want to apply?"

As it happened, I did know of someone who, despite living in Hong Kong, had just earned a bachelor's degree in Earth Science from the Open University in the UK. He was out of work and looking for something to do. He was forty, British, hearty and rather podgy, calling himself Hasbian. He famously liked beer. He was not, perhaps, what David had in mind when he spoke of a fresh graduate, but there was no denying that he fit the modest job specifications. Scarcely able to believe what I was saying, I mentioned his name to David and Richard, both of whom happened to be acquainted with him (through me). David gave an incredulous whinnying snort, Richard a despairing groan.

"Well, he qualifies," I found myself saying. "He likes being outdoors, at least," I feebly added.

After some inarticulate moments, David dabbed his eyes."

Okay, tell him to send in an application if he's interested."

I did and he was. Before I knew it I was dazedly introducing Hasbian to the Kadoorie Agricultural Research Center laboratory at Shek Kong in the central New Territories. "So, here is a microscope and here are vials of insect specimens and here are books that will teach you how to identify the insects to the family level."

"This is great!" Hasbian enthused.

"Here are forceps and here is a squeezy bottle of ethanol and here are petri dishes for putting the insects in when you're examining them under the microscope."

"Brillo!"

"Here is the reference collection of identified insects from last year's fieldwork that you can use to help identify the insects in the unsorted vials."

"Fantastic!"

"This is where I sit and this is where Mike sits and he's doing similar work so if I'm not here you can ask him for help."

"Splendid! Right, let's go and have lunch and a beer at the Lion & Rickshaw."

I spent some time training Hasbian in the laboratory side of things before we made our first field excursion of the year to Tai Long on the scenic east coast of the Sai Kung peninsula, in early March. We met up with Michael, who had greeted the news of Hasbian's appointment with good-natured amusement, at the Ma Liu Shui ferry pier near the Chinese University in the early morning on the March 11. A couple of old friends had also come along for the journey and to help carry equipment as it was quite a long hike from Chek Keng at the end of Long Harbor, where we would disembark, to Tai Long, involving climbing up and over a saddle near Sharp Peak. The ferry journey took two hours.

After an hour's walk we reached the top of the saddle, from

which the remote eastern coastline of the peninsula, with its beautiful empty sandy beaches, was visible. To our left was the 1,500-foot pinnacle of Sharp Peak.

We descended to Tai Long and paused at a point where a stream crossed the trail. There was a pooled area attracting some common dragonflies. Ostensibly for the benefit of our two companions, but actually to savor Hasbian's reaction, I pointed out the different dragonfly species, reciting their scientific names.

"That blue one's Orthetrum glaucum, the red one there with the purplish thorax is Orthetrum pruinosum. This damselfly here is Ceriagrion auranticum. That navy blue one is Trithemis festiva, the one that's completely red is Crocothemis servilia. That brilliant pink one is Trithemis aurora."

Our friends made appreciative interested noises. Hasbian's previously cheery and confident demeanor was replaced by an expression of trepidation.

"Shit, these things have names? Wait—am I supposed to know these names?" I grinned viciously. "Well, it might help, I said.

He stared in comic discomfiture as the dragonflies flew around us. Michael, a charitable soul, took pity on him, slapping his shoulder. "Don't worry: that's not really your job when you're in the field with us."

We got to work establishing three survey sites (in a rather boggy abandoned paddy, a feng shui wood and a patch of secondary woodland) and showing Hasbian what his duties actually were: erecting malaise tents, laying out and filling yellow pans, setting up the interception trap, putting out small mammal traps. He perked up considerably.

"Still," he said, as an attractive rare chestnut tiger butterfly flitted through the woods above us, "maybe I can learn the names of some of these things."

"Of course, and you can borrow my old binoculars if you like," I said. Hasbian nodded absently, gazing at the butterfly nets that Michael and I were holding.

"Maybe I could have one of those? They look fun."

I gave him a dubious look. The prospect of Hasbian hurling his imposing bulk through the countryside in clumsy pursuit of every common butterfly he saw was a little troubling.

"Well, let's see how you get on, eh?"

By early April I felt that Hasbian, by now climbing walls in his eagerness to get outside, could be excused laboratory duties for a few days and join Michael and me for a full field survey. We met up at the Ma Liu Shui pier and again took the ferry as far as Chek Keng, but this time instead of going east over the saddle we went west along the coastal trail for half a mile and set up survey sites near the old Chek Keng village, beside which we put up our two tents. Hasbian cheerfully got to work setting out equipment with me and we started exploring, but unfortunately the weather was mainly overcast and drizzly for the duration of our four-day stay and we didn't find a great deal to get excited about.

Anyway, the point is things were waking up for spring. Where should we go to take advantage? Tai Lam Country Park was large and under-explored. We decided to make two consecutive surveys there, starting with Tsing Fai Tong, which is a village enclave, barely inhabited deep within the park. We set our sites in disused paddy, woodland, and the area in between and went through the usual routine, although by now Hasbian was able to perform some tasks (such as laying out yellow pans) unassisted.

It was a good site for larger land mammals, and we had sightings of porcupine, barking deer and a seven-banded civet over the four days. The latter was particularly gratifying. It happened on 23 April late at night after refueling the generator for light-trapping. At about 11:30 p.m., as we drove along the single track road between Tsing Fai Tong and the nearby enclave of Tin Fu Tsai, we caught a sprightly adult in our car headlights. It ran down the road in front of us for fifty yards or so before leaping nimbly up a steep embankment. All three of us were captivated. It was certainly the best view I'd ever had of this lithe, rather feline creature leggier than the masked palm civet, almost like a Chinese leopard cat with an extended snout, the seven dark bands along its tail clearly visible.

Apparently it was the breeding season for feral oxen, if indeed they have such a season. At any rate, the following day, while searching for anything I could find, I almost became embroiled in a joust between two big black bulls with pronounced shoulder humps and stocky horns. They were shoving each other around and heedlessly trampling through the vegetation as they did so. They took no notice of me but they were barging heavily all over the place and I got a sense of how powerful these normally rather docile animals actually are. I prudently put some distance between us.

Later, I bumped into Hasbian. He had continued to plead for a butterfly net and I had reluctantly passed him a spare net head, which he had affixed to the end of a wooden pole. Now armed and dangerous, he was out to test his netting prowess and make new discoveries for the Biodiversity Survey.

"Have you got anything?" I asked.

"Yes. These," he said, pulling a handful of specimen envelopes from his waist pouch.

I examined them doubtfully. Most were very common species that I'd already noted, but there was one that I had not yet recorded at Tsing Fai Tong.

"Okay, this one's a new one for this site. The others are all common nymphalids and whites. You don't really need to collect these species in future. We can let them all go."

He pointed to the one I'd singled out. "What's that one, then?"

"It's Iambrix salsala."

He looked worried.

"Chestnut bob. See, the wings are a chestnut color and it has these nice bright white spots, including that obvious larger one in the center of the hindwing. It's a skipper. A lot of skippers are quite difficult or even impossible to identify in the field and I'd prefer it if you went after them."

He squinted at the chestnut bob before I released it. "They don't look much like normal butterflies."

"No, that's right. They're a bit different, especially in the size and shape of the wings, and the way they perch. Where did you catch it, by the way?"

"They look more like moths," Hasbian ventured. "Maybe. But you see the antennae? Thickened and hooked at the end. That's a distinguishing feature."

He peered closely. "Well, how am I supposed to see that from a distance?"

I sighed. "Skippers are obviously skippers. But if in doubt, catch it."

His face brightened. "Ah. Good."

"So where did you get this one?" I repeated, pencil hovering over notebook.

"Oh. Over there in the old paddy field."

"'Right. Thanks. Have you checked the malaise tents and yellow pans yet?"

"Just about to."

I nodded, and he sloped off, brandishing his net, not particularly in the direction of the yellow pans. Hasbian had tasted the thrill of the hunt. It contrasted favorably with the mundane business of setting out and checking traps.

I groaned inwardly. There'd be no holding him back now.

The following week we set up shop at three habitats around Sheung Tong, a few miles from Tsing Fai Tong. The stream here was very good for dragonflies. It was clean and well-oxygenated, gurgling down from the hills at a moderate pace, with stones and large cobbles in the riffle sections and shoals of sandy gravel at the more sheltered slow-flowing reaches. I quickly found the massive ochre titan damselfly and giant hooktail dragonfly.

On the second day of the survey, Michael and I left Hasbian to move the yellow pans from the plantation forest to the abandoned paddy fields, and explored a low ridge overlooking the site. Presently we reached a point where a gap in the vegetation permitted a clear view down to the paddies. There, two hundred yards away, slowly ambling along, was the unmistakeable figure of Hasbian. I trained my binoculars on him.

Michael chuckled. "What's he up to now?"

"He's putting out the yellow pans, thankfully."

I watched as Hasbian placed a yellow pan on the ground, then filled it from a large plastic demijohn containing the pre-mixed water and detergent solution. He then turned around and walked slowly back to the pile of pans, picking up another one and languidly strolling to a point about ten yards from the first pan. After he had placed this one on the ground, his attention was drawn to a butterfly fluttering around a nearby shrub. I could see, even from where I was standing, that it was a rustic Cupha erymanthis — a very common orange and brown nymphalid that was abundant at the site. He raised my old binoculars to his face and peered at it for a few seconds, before hastening back to the pile of yellow pans and picking up his butterfly net. He approached the butterfly stealthily. I looked on with growing exasperation.

"He's not supposed to be doing that!" I said. Michael chuckled again.

"Well, you gave him the net."

Hasbian swung unsuccessfully at the butterfly, which promptly flew off. He watched it for a few moments before slouching back to the yellow pans and putting down his net. He picked up another yellow pan.

"Good," I commented. "Get on with putting those out."

Almost immediately, he put it down again. He'd seen another butterfly. This time it was a common mormon (Papilio polytes). He picked up his net and ponderously stalked his new quarry.

I lowered my binoculars and shut my eyes in disbelief. "I can't stand it!"

Michael was now merrily laughing, and I grinned at him ruefully.

"You need to teach him the really common species," he said, picking up his bag and resuming the walk.

Later, when we had all met up again, I gave Hasbian some pointers on the common swallowtails, the massive, predominantly black butterflies of which there are several Hong Kong species, most of which were present at Sheung Tong.

"This one that's flying by now, with the white bar across the hindwing, the same as the one you were trying to catch earlier, is Papilio polytes, a common mormon."

"Right."

"Now, some female common mormons look just like the red Helen, Papilio helenus, which has a broad white patch on the hindwing, rather than a band."

"Ah."

"The difference is that in the red Helen the white wing patch reaches the wing margin."

Hasbian nodded sagely.

"Now, Papilio paris, the Paris peacock, has blue wing patches instead of white wing patches."

"I see."

"Sometimes the blue looks more like green, and the wings have a greenish gloss all over. It's a very beautiful species, actually."

"Mm." I was losing him.

"The Chinese peacock, Papilio bianor, on the other hand, has a bluish tinge on the hindwings, but no patch."

Hasbian nodded dumbly.

"Papilio memnon, the great mormon, has very extensive white on the hindwing, much more than the red Helen or the common mormon, while the dark mormon, Papilio protenor, is pretty much entirely black apart from the pinkish markings at the edge of the hindwing, but we don't need to talk about those."

"I'm glad we don't have to talk about those."

"Any questions?"

"Do I have to remember all that?"

I exhaled heavily." No. Just don't bother trying to catch any of them."

It was a few weeks before we set out into the field again. We decided to visit the isolated Hakka village of Lai Chi Wo located in a cove on the deeply indented coastline of Crooked Harbor, east of Starling Inlet.

On May 27, we drove through the border checkpoint near Sha Tau Kok, and then on to the town itself, rolling up on the pier to park our vehicle. It was a hot and sunny day. The boatman whose services Michael had engaged was waiting for us, in shorts and broad rattan hat. We loaded everything aboard, the P4 rocking as Hasbian introduced his imposing weight. Then we were off, motoring east to the mouth of Starling Inlet, passing the abandoned village of Yung Shue Au, then southward into Crooked Harbor. Soon we were passing So Lo Pun, another isolated and abandoned settlement, eventually drawing up at the low concrete pier near Lai Chi Wo. We unloaded and dragged the equipment two hundred yards or so along the coastal path to a broad concrete apron next to a stream and an old temple just outside the village wall.

"I think we could set up camp here, Michael, don't you?" I said, lowering the generator to the ground.

"Yep, sounds good to me."

We stashed all the camping equipment next to the temple, then set out to establish our three trapping sites. The first of these was in the splendid mangrove forest at the seashore and the woodland behind it, which contained enormous coiling tendrils of the white-flowered derris climber. It reaches over a foot in diameter and dozens of yards in length, droops from the trees, throwing wide loops on the forest floor. An extraordinary spectacle and one not rivaled elsewhere in Hong Kong. Next, a site in the extensive, largely dry abandoned paddy fields in the valley bottom south of the village, in which were ominous signs of cattle, and finally in the large feng shui wood on the village's northern side.

That sorted, we proceeded to prepare our campsite, cooked a tasty dinner (canned meat balls and instant noodles) and retired to our separate tents, Michael and me in one, Hasbian in the other.

The night was full of strange noises, mostly emanating from Hasbian's tent: prolonged loud rumblings punctuated by short periods of snorts and whinnies. Hasbian emerged from his tent the following morning looking brightly revivified, which is more than can be said for his two bleary-eyed companions. Work had to be done, however, and we got on with it. An early discovery was that two of the three malaise tents in the paddy fields had been dragged down during the night, presumably by the cattle, of which it was now clear there was quite a large herd. We put them back up again and did some exploring.

There was a lot to see, particularly butterflies, of which we had recorded seventy-nine species by the end of the four days, our highest total to date. There were white dragontails at the stream, flitting close to the water, and — a first for the Biodiversity Survey — a spotted ace skipper (Isoteinon lamprospilus), in a shrubby area along the coastal footpath. We saw a porcupine in the evening, and heard barking deer and brown wood frogs — another locality record.

The following day, oxen roamed the fields, leaving all three malaise tents in disarray, and kicking over two yellow pans. We gnashed our teeth but were soon mollified by the discovery, in a marshy patch next to the coast, of a new dragonfly species for Hong Kong, Macrodiplax cora, the coastal glider.

That night, at about eight o'clock, more excitement: two masked palm civets in the feng shui wood. We heard them first then got them in the torchlight. They were on the hunt. Although they eat a lot of small fruits, and are important seed-dispersers, they are also predators of small mammals and even birds. A sudden squawk suggested that the pair in the feng shui wood had just nabbed one.

Packing up the traps before departure the next day, we again found the three malaise tents in the paddy fields already down and dissembled. Hasbian stepped forward and shook a fist at the doleful milling bovines.

"Clear off, you cows!"

Michael, Hasbian and I had decided to spend a month living and working on Lantau Island, over which it was now possible to drive, provided you had a permit for your vehicle, which we did. On 2 September, the three of us drove across the massive bridges now linking Lantau to the New Territories and took the new highway south-westwards along the northern coast of the island. We cut inland at Tung Chung, now a busy new town, at the farther end of which we had to show our vehicle permit. Hasbian gave a triumphant whoop as we drove beyond the check-point.

"Hooray! Lantau is ours, Boys!"

We drove up and over the old Tung Chung road between Lantau's two giant peaks and down to the south coast, then westward again to the small village of Shui Hau, which was to be our base for the rest of the month.

One survey target was the Chi Ma Wan peninsula on the south-eastern corner of Lantau. On 8 September, we parked our trusty vehicle at the detention center on the northern end of the peninsula, then worked our way southwards along the pleasant trail, setting up sites in the plantation woodland next to the small Chi Ma Wan reservoir, in an area of tall shrub land, and in disused agricultural fields at the tiny hamlet of Tai Long on the peninsula's southern coast.

The legendary Frog and Toad Pub, venue of the annual Mud Olympics, was situated in Tai Long. Hasbian was a friend of the proprietor, Joe Lee. After we had set our traps in the old village fields, he turned to me and Michael, "Fancy a pint?"

I did, but it was a week day and the pub was closed.

"There's nobody there."

"That's all right. We can just walk in and help ourselves."

"Are you kidding?"

"Nah, nah. Joe's always said if I'm ever here and the place is shut I can just go in and pour myself a beer."

It had been thirsty work. I looked at Michael. "Fancy a beer, Michael?"

He chuckled resignedly. "Sure."

I licked my lips. "Oh boy, this is gonna be great!"

Hasbian confidently led the way to the door of the pub and grasped the handle. It wouldn't open.

"Ah, right, of course. I guess we have to go round the back." That made sense. We went round the back. The gate was locked. Hasbian shook it, his jaw jutting perplexedly.

"Bollocks."

"Crap."

Hasbian now had the desperate look of a convict leading a jail-break that had been thwarted at the first barrier. I turned on him.

"You bloody sod! You and your talk of nice cold beer!"

It took a while to recover from that disappointment but we eventually settled into a pleasant rhythm of hard work surveying wildlife in the daytime and hard boozing in the evenings. Although we were working, it felt a lot like a holiday. The weather stayed hot and sunny; our office was the great outdoors.

All too soon, our month on Lantau came to an end. In the final week of our stay, Michael, Hasbian and I strolled out one evening to take dinner at a South African restaurant in the village of Tong Fuk, about a mile east along the coast from Shui Hau. A considerable volume of red wine of South African provenance was consumed. We tottered out, quite late, and began the return walk in the dark. Michael had had quite a skinful and appeared rather jolly. Suddenly, without a word, he took off, sprinting at full pelt along the road. We chuckled as we watched his manic frame disappearing into the blackness ahead. A month of enforced proximity with Hasbian and I had clearly taken its toll on this sensitive, sincere marvel of a chap.

"He's finally cracked," I remarked, in sudden consternation.

Hasbian nodded and burped. "Looks like it," he said. I looked at him mock-reproachfully.

"It's all your fault."

"Not at all. It must've been you."

We quickened our pace and followed our friend back to Shui Hau. We didn't want him to come to any harm. He was indispensable.

So now we were in October and there were just two fieldwork months left to us. We had reached this point disconcertingly quickly. There was so much still to be done. We decided to go out with a flurry of short surveys, visiting as many sites as possible and focusing on day-long visits to outlying islands, but first, on 18 October, we set off for what would be our final four-day survey on the remote island of Dung Ping Chau, the most far-flung of Hong Kong's many scattered islands, situated close to the Guangdong coast on the eastern side of Mirs Bay.

For a final time, we traveled to Ma Liu Shui pier, starting point of so many Biodiversity Survey adventures, to take the small ferry northeastward through Tolo Channel, past Chek Chau with its nesting white-bellied sea eagles, and onward across Mirs Bay. A voyage of several hours, in the course of which I noticed Hasbian's bag seemed unduly heavy and bulky.

"What have you got in there?" I asked.

"Essential supplies," he answered, tapping his nose with his forefinger.

We arrived in warm sunshine in the early afternoon, disembarking at the Lei Uk pier on the eastern shore, along which there was a scattering of low buildings, the vast majority unoccupied. Only two elderly gentlemen actually lived on the island, running the store there for the benefit, normally, of weekend visitors. Michael had rented us rooms at the store and we lugged our gear there first before taking a spot of lunch.

The island is less than half a square mile in size and its terrestrial habitats are not particularly diverse but we were able to find a secondary woodland site, a mixed woodland and shrub land site. This achieved, we returned to the store where the proprietor prepared us some dinner. I remembered, too late, that there was no beer to be had on the island. That was a blow as we could all have used a drink. Then Hasbian disappeared into our room, marvelously reappearing some moments later with a two-liter demijohn of red wine — one of his more successful dramatic entrances, greeted with cheering enthusiasm by Michael and me. It transpired that Hasbian had brought along three such demijohns, one for each night we would be staying on the island. Suddenly the prospect of the long evenings to be spent at the store was suffused with a rosy glow.

It had been apparent during the first day that there were a lot of butterflies on Dung Ping Chau. On the second day we started ratcheting up the species count in earnest, and by the time we left on the fourth day we had amassed a total of eighty-four species — the highest achieved at any location throughout the entire Biodiversity Survey.

A very pleasant coastal trail circumnavigated the island. On the third day I spent a lot of time walking this route. It was peaceful. It seemed as if we had the entire island to ourselves, which I suppose was indeed the case, more or less. It lay basking in Mediterranean warmth, and although the Chinese coast was less than three miles away, it may as well have been a thousand miles distant. Dung Ping Chau was a special place and I reflected that I could quite happily stay for weeks. Walking southwards along the raised western shore, the rest of Hong Kong a distant prospect, I suddenly perceived an odd-looking bird on the path about twenty yards in front of me. It was, unmistakeably, a Eurasian hoophoe — an occasional visitor to Hong Kong territory. About the size of a dove, with strong black and white barring on the wings and tail, a golden brown head and neck, a long slender slightly down curved bill, and a flamboyantly tall head crest, like a Mohican, tipped with black and white.

I savored the view through binoculars for a minute or so before slowly resuming my advance along the path. The hoophoe allowed me to within about fifteen yards before taking wing and flying another twenty yards or so in front of me, its broad barred wings giving it an almost moth-like appearance, again alighting on the footpath. I carried on following it in the bright sunlight, the only sounds a light breeze rustling the baking shrub land to my left and the blue sea languidly throwing waves against the bottom of the cliff on my right. The hoophoe continued to lead me on. This slow motion game of cat and mouse lasted for several hundred yards. It was quite delightful.

At the end of October, we drove to Sai Kung town and hired a sampan to take us to Bluff Island — a beautiful journey made even more so by the warming sunshine. We landed at a small cove on the northwestern shore and climbed up to the low saddle above it, leaving the light trap and generator on the beach. We set up camp at about 150 feet elevation on the ridge, which commanded a spectacular panorama of Rocky Harbor, Port Shelter, Basalt Island, Town Island and High Island. In the autumn sunlight the views were magnificent. A few yards away the land fell abruptly in a sheer cliff on the eastern side of the saddle, at the bottom of which the sea foamed noisily. It was a dramatic setting.

In the afternoon we explored the island, heading southwards up to the highest point at about 500 feet and encountering dense shrub land on the island's southern half. In the golden late afternoon light we ambled back to our camp and brewed up some tea. Hasbian remarked that he hoped we would also brew tea in the morning, as he was no lover of coffee. This proposition was totally unacceptable to Michael and me and was peremptorily rejected. As we sat on the grass beside our tents, sipping scalding tea, enjoying the scenery and animatedly discussing the relative merits of the two morning beverages, a pair of porcupines suddenly emerged from the low shrub land on the hillside above us, about fifty yards away. The conversation abruptly paused. The three of us watched, paralyzed in silent incredulity, as the two spiny creatures slowly waddled down towards us, side by side. They don't see well and we must have been downwind of them because they clearly couldn't smell us. They walked right past our camp, within a few feet of us, as we speechlessly gawped at them. Then they disappeared into the shrubby vegetation near the beach.

"Sheesh!" Michael said.

"Blimey!" I said.

"Shag a pig!" Hasbian said.

The Soko Islands were our next destination. This island cluster comprises Tai a Chau (the largest island in the group, just under half a square mile in size), Siu A Chau and a scattering of half a dozen or so tiny islets. These are the most southerly scraps of Hong Kong territory. The Hong Kong government had constructed a detention center for Vietnamese refugees on Tai a Chau in the late 1980s, but that facility had been closed down in 1996. Now, a year later, the Sokos were again deserted. To get there, we had first to take the ferry to Cheung Chau, which we did on the morning of 13 November, then hire a small wooden sampan.

The sampan Michael had hired belonged to a wizened elderly lady—perhaps in her late sixties, perhaps older—who cheerfully ushered us aboard her small craft at the pier. Then we began the long journey, which took a couple of hours, the old woman gabbling away with Michael, cackling and wheezing over whatever came to her mind. I wished I could have understood her better.

The November sun shone strongly but the day was pleasantly

mild. We sat on the open deck and scanned Lantau's Chi Ma Wan Peninsula and the island of Shek Kwu Chau with binoculars as we passed through the wide channel between them.

Presently the Sokos were dominating the view ahead, the smaller Siu A Chau lying a mile to the north of Tai A Chau, of which the highest point was about 400 feet; the hillsides of both islands covered in mixed low shrub land and grassland. We veered left to the larger island, where we intended to camp overnight, and disembarked at the broad landing stage on the island's northern end, where in previous years so many thousands of Vietnamese refugees had been offloaded. The old lady promised to return for us the next morning. We waved goodbye.

A narrow road ran southwards along the coastline and we walked along it for two hundred yards or so until we reached a vast concrete apron, four acres in size, which spanned the low-lying gap between the island's northern promontory and the bulk of the island to the south. Perhaps it had once been a natural tombolo. Later, however, it had been the site of a detention center, now eerily abandoned. The apron seemed populated by clamoring phantoms. Here, away from the eyes of the largely indifferent populace, riots had unfolded, traumas had played out, despair had set in.

We stopped, and gazed at the desolation around us, the vegetation sprouting through cracks in the concrete ground slabs, the outlines of hastily destroyed shacks with young vines and shrubs sprawling across them, the imprint of nameless facilities, already being reclaimed by nature. It was unsettling. There was no doubting the area still carried a powerful psychic charge. My imagination took off.

"This place is positively Ballardian," I murmured.

Hasbian nodded thoughtfully, "Yeah."

We carried on across the wide apron in the unflinching

sunlight and followed the narrow winding road up to the top of the hillock to the south. We dropped our tents here, then in the afternoon explored what we could of the island. We got through at least two bottles of wine that night, sitting on the hilltop next to our tents. It was Hasbian's birthday and would also be his last camping field trip of the Biodiversity Survey.

The next morning our cheery chatty sampan lady arrived punctually at the landing stage and we crossed over the water to the unspoilt island of Siu A Chau. There was no pier here, but the tide, already turning, was still high enough for us to jump ashore near a beach on the island's southern coast. The sampan lady then puttered to fifty yards offshore to wait for us while we conducted a brief wildlife survey.

We scrambled around on the low hillsides and along the shoreline for a couple of hours, recording, among other things, thirty-seven butterfly species.

Presently, from a low hillside, we noticed that our sampan had moved further offshore. Perhaps the ebbing tide was obliging the old lady to seek deeper water.

"Maybe it's time we got going," Michael suggested, a little surprisingly. It was only just past noon. We trudged down to the shore and called out to the old lady to come and collect us. She shouted something back to Michael then started her engine.

"Shit," Michael said.

"What is it?"

"She can't come in much closer. She's worried about damaging her boat on the rocks."

"Oh."

We watched as the sampan drew slowly nearer then came to a stop about fifty yards away. The old lady cut her engine then stood on the prow and beckoned us encouragingly with her arm.

Hasbian took off his backpack. "Well, nothing for it: we'll

have to swim."

"Yep." I looked along the beach and saw that among the piled detritus were two old polystyrene boxes that had been washed ashore. Both were still intact. "We can put our bags and binoculars in those and push them ahead of us."

"Good idea," Hasbian said.

I picked them up, emptied them of sand and started undressing. Hasbian put his things in one box and I put mine in the other. We were both poised on the shore, clad only in our undies. Michael stood fidgeting, looking a little embarrassed.

"Come on, Michael. What's up?"

He gave a sickly grin. "I can't swim."

I laughed. "Are you kidding? That's such a cliché in a situation like this."

"Seriously. I can't swim."

I looked at him searchingly. "Okay."

Hasbian was a strong swimmer. "You'll have to use one of these box lids as a float," he said. "Just hold on to it in front of you and kick with your legs. I'll push you along from behind. You'll be all right."

Michael nodded and got undressed, looking like a condemned man.

We swam out slowly, at Michael's pace. I was pushing one of the boxes, containing our precious binoculars, and Michael was clinging grimly to his float. All went well. We reached the sampan. The gunwale was nearly three feet above the water but there was a thin rope along the side and Michael grabbed this while Hasbian gave him a shove from underneath. He scrambled gratefully aboard and we lifted the box up to him. Next, I grabbed the rope and swung my other arm onto the gunwale, pulling myself out of the water. It wasn't easy and I was a little worried Hasbian, with his ample poundage, would be unable to replicate the feat. He was now swimming back to shore to collect the second box. A few minutes later he was back at the boat. His efforts had evidently tired him. After handing up the box he tried to heave himself up but after several seconds of sustained but ineffectual effort he slid back into the water.

"Shit, I can't do it!"

"Try again. We'll help."

Again he tried. I grabbed his arm. It slid through my hands as he fell away with a splash. He was tiring fast now.

"Come on! One more time!" He gathered himself, pulled on the rope again and I caught his flailing arm, gripped hard and tugged. Michael grabbed a hold of something too, maybe the other arm when Hasbian let go of the rope and slapped his hand on the gunwale. We all made an almighty effort. Somehow he got a foot onto the gunwale. We grabbed that too and hauled him aboard, flopping him down on the deck. He lay there for some seconds, gasping wordlessly like some enormous expiring fish. The old lady cracked a joke, cackling happily, and started up the motor.

Hasbian was shattered after his exertions and didn't move much for some time, but we all dried out quickly in the parching November sun. I stood tall on the prow in my underpants, enjoying the dry wind as we chugged back to Cheung Chau, the old lady making the odd remark and presumably looking forward to telling her friends all about her strange passengers.

WONDERLAND

Rachel Beresford-Davies

When I was six years old my family upped sticks from our semi in rural Hampshire to live in Hong Kong. We came back to England every other year, and the friends I'd left behind would sometimes ask me about my new home. Sitting on a hay bale, or on the low brick wall of someone's garden, or perched on a kerb with our knees around our ears, they would wonder what it was like to live in that place I went to when I wasn't with them. They weren't really interested, and I have no memory of ever replying. I wouldn't have known where to begin back then, and in truth I still don't.

My brother Graham has summoned me to his room. He is four years older than I am, an age gap that at the time felt like a yawning, unnavigable divide. I am seven, maybe eight, and given most of the time Graham barely acknowledges my existence, a summons to his bedroom is beyond unusual.

He is sitting on his bed tossing a tennis ball in the air in a nonchalant yet slightly sinister way. The floor-standing fan in the corner of his room is revolving at full tilt, which goes some way to drown out traffic noise from the four-lane highway our block of flats sits next to. The building is grandly named St George's Mansion. A slab of traffic-fume white behind black iron railings. Solid and serious. We are only four floors up, although during our six years in the building we will work our way to the sixth and finally the 13th, the top floor. There is a definite hierarchy to all this. The upper floors suffer less traffic noise, pollution, have better views, and by dint of all this, better occupants. We hold a relatively lowly status in terms of height, but at least our flat is not road facing. We don't even acknowledge those residents.

I walk into the room and stand still and straight. I know better than to touch any of Graham's stuff. He looks at me appraisingly for a moment or two.

"Shut the door," he says. I do so then wait, curious but wary. He sets the tennis ball aside and pulls something from his pocket.

"Want a chewing gum?" he asks, holding a shiny, white packet of Wrigley's Spearmint in his open palm. At this point in my life, chewing gum is the kind of thing other people do. Laughing, blonde females in television adverts mostly. It doesn't really feature in my life and there is something taboo about it — a notch down from alcohol but definitely above the sticky Sugas chew sweets we're sometimes given. I move closer to Graham to check its authenticity. He once had one of those joke packets, where a spring-loaded trap is activated if you take one. I'm not falling for that again. But these look genuine. He is watching me, like there's a right answer and a wrong answer here. I decide to play him.

"I like the yellow ones better." Juicy fruit. Vijay had some once on the school bus, and he folded three of them into his mouth at once with spectacular unrestraint, making the whole vehicle smell sweet and sugary. He allowed me a stick too, and we sat together in companionable silence, chewing our gum thoughtfully. We were best friends for about a week after that.

Graham ignores my juicy fruit preferences and hands me a neatly wrapped stick of spearmint gum. I examine it for a moment, admiring the crisply folded silver paper beneath the white sheath, the bold and simple print. For a second or two I am distracted by my admiration for this rare thing, until I remember that Graham doesn't generally just give me stuff. I close my hand over it before he can take it back.

"Thanks," I say, on guard.

"Wanna know where I got it?" he asks casually. I'm imagining Kam Wah, the grocery shop down the road where all food comes from. Our mother orders the contents of our kitchen cupboards over the phone in the morning, and they deliver them in the afternoon in a cardboard box, cheerfully announcing their arrival by shouting the shop name at startling volumes, sending our dustbin-rescue cat skidding across parquet flooring to some corner of safety. Only the fish man is louder.

Graham looks at me and shakes his head. "Nope. Wonderland. I shoplifted it."

This information hits me on a number of fronts. Firstly, Wonderland is my favorite shop in the whole world, so just the idea that Graham has been there without my knowledge ignites a small bonfire of indignation. Secondly, given the spectacular array of brightly colored, plastic toys, trinkets and battery-powered curios they sell, chewing gum seems a wasted choice. Thirdly, I'm not sure what "shoplifted" means, but it sounds like something our parents wouldn't approve of. I pull a face for wont of something to say. He asks coolly, Wanna come shoplifting with me?"

I shrug. "OK."

We inform our mother we're heading out to Wonderland. She's in the kitchen, looking flushed and warm, her soft skin glistening slightly from a perpetual sheen of perspiration. She wipes her hands on her pinny and passes us each a two dollar coin from her purse. In the lift lobby, Graham says, "You can give me your two dollars, you won't be needing it." I hand the coin over compliantly but make a mental note that I'm telling our mother if this whole stunt doesn't go well.

The shop is a ten or fifteen minute walk from our flat. To get there, we went past the smooth, concreted curve of wall punctuated with gutter outlets that hold Kadoorie Avenue in place, pass under the flyover and cross a complicated, multi-lane road intersection with breathtaking indifference. We are streetwise, but we don't realize it yet.

The shopping area of Waterloo Road is always busy. Not Nathan Road busy, but still a constant ebb and flow of locals carrying flimsy yet bulging candy-striped plastic bags, shouting at vegetable sellers or fidgeting at bus stops. Everyone seems to have a purpose, other than the old men who shuffle along with their hands behind their backs periodically clearing their throats to deposit gelatinous pavement oysters. Double-decker buses lumber between stops, jerking forward foot by foot or in short-lived bursts of reckless acceleration. Red and white taxis sound their horns and weave through the traffic to whoever is hailing them, no matter what. The clatter of mahjong tiles punctuates the general street clamor, and there is an assault of different cooking smells, but this sensory onslaught mostly goes over my head now. Very occasionally in this ocean of otherness I'll see another western child being towed along by a parent. We will silently acknowledge the other's existence, making cagey sideways eye contact, and feel suddenly self-conscious, reminded that we are different.

On the opposite side of the road, someone has turned their balcony into an aviary. It is on the second floor so is easy to see from the street, and I always slow to watch the colorful birds flitting from the netting to a branch and back again. They both fascinate and bother me, in a way I don't really understand. They are the lucky ones though. Mostly, songbirds are stored alone, in tiny, elaborate cages which dangle from balconies above the traffic and fumes. That is their home, when it should be the sky.

The entire sky. I find it so difficult to comprehend.

It hasn't happened yet, but in a couple of years' time a duck-egg blue budgie will fly in from who knows where and land on our verandah, somehow avoiding the cats (we acquired a second dustbin kitten, loud and insane), and hop willingly onto my finger. It seemed tame, so we kept it, duly buying a cage, a piece of cuttlefish and a box of Trill. For a while he seemed happy enough, until I decided he was lonely. Against her better judgment my mother took me to Mongkok market to find him a bright, emerald-green mate. That budgie sounded the death knell. She, or just as likely he, fell ill with a snuffling cold-like complaint, and no amount of vet-prescribed vitamin C fluid made any difference. It died, leaving me sobbing and heartsick as I held the small, stiffening corpse in my hands. Then another trip to Mongkok market to replace it. Repeat. Eventually, after the original duck-egg blue bird suffered the same fate, my mother decided enough was enough. They were all diseased from that market. I got through five budgies in all. It pretty much cemented how I was to feel about caged birds thereafter.

But none of this has happened yet, so I stand and watch the lively splashes of color in the balcony aviary, imagining what it would be like to stand among them or have one land on my head, until Graham hollers at me to catch up.

Other than Wonderland, none of the shops on this street holds any interest for me. They are mostly grocery stores or other utilitarian outlets, open to the street with goods spilling out like little lava flows at each corner. Wonderland, though, is air conditioned, meaning the door is always closed and the interior has a cool, hushed atmosphere, like the expensive shops in Ocean Terminal. Graham is standing at the door now, looking serious and thin lipped. He waits for me to catch up, then hisses, "Just do what I tell you," and pushes open the door.

The shop smells cool and clean, slightly bookish. We appear to be the only ones in here, other than the shop assistant who sits motionless and bored behind the cash register. I'm set on acquiring another Pippa doll to add to my growing collection. I know exactly where they are but Graham has halted halfway up the aisle, out of the shop girl's sight. I notice for the first time he is holding a white plastic bag.

"I'll hold one handle of the bag and you hold the other, and we can just drop things into it," he instructs. I take the handle and follow his lead by staring pointedly at an item on the shelf directly in front of me, in which I have no interest whatsoever. A small bouncy ball with dashes of color. I want to move along to the Pippa dolls, but Graham isn't budging. A row of fuzzy-haired Action Men peer down at us, but they're too high. Gradually, I become aware of the shop assistant's spectral-like presence. She has moved noiselessly from her seat and is standing in the corner, by the door, her eyes wide and expressionless. She has glassy-smooth black hair that hangs from a center parting and ends severely at her shoulders. She looks a little like one of my Pippa dolls. Same proportions, same rigidly fixed hair, same inscrutable features.

Graham shuffles along a step and the bag stretches between us. I sense a movement of air as the shop assistant passes behind, slowly and as though on coasters, and rounds the corner. Graham makes an immediate grab for an item and drops it into the bag. Bubblegum. Why the gum fixation?

"Take something!" he commands, wild-eyed. In a panic I pluck a bouncy ball from the shelf and let it fall into the plastic carrier. The weight as it rolls around the base of the bag sends a current of excitement through me. I'm about to see what else I can pilfer, but Graham is off, tugging the bag from my grasp and heading with purpose towards the glass door.

The Pippa dolls are just along a bit and higher up. I'm sure I could reach them. I hear the gentle suction of the door opening and a rush of traffic noise as Graham slides through a ten-inch gap of open door. Feeling somewhat cheated I dash after him, and notice as I do so the ghostly shop assistant, now back behind the counter, on the telephone. Her eyes dark, impenetrable pools settle on me as her fingers work the phone dial. The door makes a sharp air-sucking sound as it closes, securing me in the chilly tomb of playthings. The girl continues to skewer me with her inky gaze, standing with the phone held to her ear, not speaking. My mother usually opens this door. It's heavy, and has a habit of falling closed on you. I pull the handle with all my weight, wedge my foot in the tiny gap I manage to make and squeeze myself through a thin slice of air, back into the warm, comforting commotion of Waterloo Road.

My brother is up ahead, weaving his way through a throng of bodies and I walk as fast as I can to catch up, without looking back. Graham had advised we shouldn't run, it would make us look guilty, but I feel sure the girl is gliding just behind me, her doll's eyes black and lifeless, arms held stiffly out in front of her, at slightly different heights. The way I make my Pippas stand when they're being expressive. I break into a run and overtake my surprised brother. We sprint together back the way we'd come. The colorful balcony birds swirl excitedly around their enclosure as we pass, trilling loudly at our daring, but I don't slow down this time. Graham pulls me up at the road intersection and we stand panting among the small crowd. They regard us with detached curiosity, the way a cat might look at a tortoise. Just a couple of unruly gweilo kids.

Back home we skirt past our mother and head straight to Graham's bedroom to examine our ill-gotten gains. My brother tosses his gum on the bed, barely looking at it, then spends some time examining my ball, turning it this way and that in his fingers.

"Not bad for a first attempt," he finally says, and bounces it over to me. It goes wild, springing high into the air and rebounding off the ceiling and walls haphazardly. The tiny splashes of color seem to be brighter now the ball is in flight. It glances off one wall then another, darting swiftly around the confines of Graham's bedroom like one of the balcony birds.

Later on, I get knighted. Graham commands me to kneel before him and produces his five-dollar plastic sword from under the bed. For a second I imagine I'm to be executed, but then he lightly taps the sword on each shoulder and finally my head, proclaiming me a certified shoplifter. I sense our criminal partnership may have elevated my status to a degree, but even so, I was never invited to join him on further heists.

Eventually, that bouncy ball ricocheted one too many times off the living room wall, caught the revolving ceiling fan and soared, like a liberated songbird, right over the balcony into the car park below, never to be seen again. And that was fine by me.

LAI CHI WO: REMOTE WALLED HAKKA VILLAGE

Lynn Seymour

After three hours' trekking and bush-bashing in undergrowth, we arrived at the isolated village of Lai Chi Wo overlooking the scattered islands of Crooked Harbor in the northeast New Territories. Facing us were derelict buildings, broken walls and huddled houses in various states of disrepair with one incongruous modern house recently built. Narrow lanes crept in between the thick-walled homes and in what we thought was a deserted village, we were taken by surprise to see an old man sitting on a stool, washing clothes in a bucket. Without stopping his soaping, he sullenly replied to my questions but seemed to have a deep distrust of us. This was of no surprise to me as I had read that in the past people had lived in small communities housing members of a single clan and, in this case, the Tsang family, which goes back three generations, are the original inhabitants and consist of three families. Total: fifty people. Many rural villages were once walled for protection as a defense against bandits, pirates and feuding members of other clans. The actual level of threat was low but suspicion is an ingrained feature of New Territories rural life and outsiders are not warmly welcomed, as I clearly found out.

Mr Tsang volunteered his age as over seventy and that he was born in the village and had four children, three of whom had gone to university in the UK and one to Harvard, US. His younger brother-in-law, Tsang Tim Yau, was affable and willing to communicate. He proudly informed us that he was a British citizen and that nearly all the Tsang children had either been educated or gone to work in UK restaurants in the UK or had borrowed money from the family to open their own restaurants and now had several in Birmingham, Belfast and Dublin. He remembered going to the village school when there were 400 children but it closed thirty years ago when there were no more youngsters.

He owns the only village restaurant named Feng Shui Woodland. Many years ago, villagers were equally wary of dangerous unseen forces and took precautions, building virtually windowless houses to prevent the entry of evil spirits. Feng shui was an important element in this war with the supernatural, so the best site for a village was surrounded by hills, facing an open expanse of fields or water, with trees and bamboo planted in back to screen evil influences. It seemed appropriate that Mr Tsang's restaurant was so aptly named.

This was 2006 when his only customers arrived on Sundays on a ferry from Ma Liu Shiu, near Shatin, which people have to book in advance. I asked how he got his food supplies and he said he has to travel to Sha Tau Kok in the Closed Area on the border with Shenzhen. Anyone going there needs a permit and he sometimes stays a week until the next ferry arrives. They also grow their own vegetables.

We were joined by Mr Tsang's eighty-year-old aunt who had left her home in Sha Tau Kok to marry his uncle when she was twenty-two years old and had been in Lai Chi Wo ever since. She sat on a chair under a tree while Mr Tsang told us that every decade the village holds a huge celebration to the God, Guan Di, in the family temple. The next occasion would be in October 2009 when government officials and university students would attend and a Cantonese Opera would be held.

I looked around at the deserted surroundings and tried to imagine how different it would be at this special occasion or on Sundays when the village would come to life again with the sound of visitors enjoying a meal and perhaps children running around — all evoking memories of a community now left behind.

How to find Lai Chi Wo: From Fanling KCR take the 56K minibus that terminates at Luk Keng by Starling Inlet. The only access to the village is by foot, which takes about three hours on hiking trails. Continue by foot to Bride's Pool where you can get a taxi or bus. Total hiking time six hours.

DRUG MONEY LAUNDERING: THE HONG KONG CONNECTION

Stuart McDouall

What is money laundering? The theory of money laundering is simple. Placement which leads to layering which leads to integration.

Placement occurs when the proceeds of crime are placed into the public financial system via bank accounts, paying off legitimate debts, buying assets such as property, even casino chips. Layering happens when dirty money is mixed with legitimate funds, moving the proceeds of crime through multiple accounts, in multiple jurisdictions and using multiple banking instruments. Integration is the untainted or laundered assets integrated into the aboveboard financial systems, ready for use by the originating criminals. But the mechanics of money laundering are *not* so simple.

In 1989, leaders at the G-7 summit in Paris agreed, in a ministerial meeting, to set up a Financial Action Task Force to tackle an alarming rise in drug money laundering worldwide. The French insisted on hosting it in Paris. The FATF defined money laundering as the process of legitimizing assets obtained through illegal activity. They went on, in 1990, to make forty recommendations, the first of which was to develop a coordinated response by worldwide enforcement agencies and legal jurisdictions.

Hong Kong hit the ground running, following in the UK's

footsteps, formulating the first Drug Trafficking (Recovery of Proceeds) Ordinance, Ch. 405, enacted in December 1989. Police investigators from the Narcotics Bureau (CID NB) had, in the '70s and '80s, been increasingly successful in interdicting criminals who were trafficking in dangerous drugs on the international stage. But apart from cash seized as exhibits, alongside quantities of illicit drugs, it had never been possible for Hong Kong's enforcement agencies to go after the hidden assets of the convicted traffickers that they had put behind bars.

To give the reader an idea of the sort of money involved, foreign countries, including the US and Australia, already had forms of legislation enabling their courts to confiscate the proven proceeds of crime. In 1986, the US Drug Enforcement Agency arraigned twelve Columbian drug barons and, under the so-called Ricoh Statutes, they were able to freeze US$482 million in banks in five countries, including Hong Kong. But if you thought that was good, it was peanuts compared with a combined international law enforcement agency case, led by the DEA in '87, when 367 aircraft, 72 boats, 710 vehicles and just short of 1,000 buildings were confiscated in seven countries around the world. Not to mention a total of five tons of cocaine and other illicit drugs seized in more than fifty raids. But the drugs trade didn't stop there and traffickers, adept at staying one step ahead of the police, using ever-more sophisticated means of money laundering, defeated the best efforts of investigators within the constraints of their laws.

Thus it was that a team of government lawyers, led by Senior Crown Counsels Michael Lunn and Bill Boucaut, sat down, with their police counterparts from CID NB, Chief Staff Officer David Hodson and Superintendent Stuart McDouall, utilizing the experience of law enforcement agencies in Hong Kong and overseas, studied the legal successes and failures of major drug trafficking prosecutions. The imperative was to provide the Hong Kong Police with the teeth to investigate money laundering, to hold banks and other financial institutions to account and to enable the courts to freeze the assets of crime pending confiscation. More importantly, to create reciprocal agreements or channels of legal co-operation with foreign jurisdictions whereby external orders for the freezing and confiscation of the assets of crime can be implemented at the behest of another country. This was really time-consuming work but as the number of these agreements with "designated" countries and states proliferated, so money laundering avenues for the criminals were closing off.

Hong Kong has always been a consumer market for dangerous drugs, supplied by the big cartels such as Khun Sa's (1934-2007) Golden Triangle (950,000 square kilometers in Thailand, Myanmar and Laos) opiate empire and the South American, mainly Colombian, cocaine cartels. There are no such drug lords in Hong Kong, none of the hedonistic lifestyles of fortress houses, expensive cars, lavish living and high-rolling gambling. At street level, gangs that operated under the old Triad banner, were heavily involved in drug trafficking. But at the "wholesale" level of the trade, the principal traffickers were not triads and were smart enough not to draw the attention of police by flaunting their wealth. But having said that, Hong Kong, with its comparatively low tax regime and international-level banking status, attracted, and continues to attract drug money laundering business world-wide.

So it was with some fanfare, in legal and enforcement agency circles anyway, that Hong Kong's Drug Trafficking (Recovery of Proceeds) Ordinance came into effect on 1 December, 1989. And the new laws were retro-active in effect! At the same time CID NB unveiled its Financial Investigation Group (FIG), which had already been at work in Police Headquarters since

September 1989. That team of thirty detectives, selected by the commanding officer who was given *carte blanche* to retain experienced detectives in the force, began their work with a bang, so-to-speak, having half-a-dozen investigation files on Hong Kong drug traffickers, already in train. Also some international investigations, involving Hong Kong, were underway by Australian, Canadian and American agencies. And, because the legal onus was now on bankers and other financiers to identify and report money laundering activity through their portals, the FIG were conducting well-attended seminars for them on compliance with the law.

By year's end, the FIG had 29 investigations open and six local drug traffickers were up before the courts, their illegal assets frozen. Roughly 60% of those assets were cash deposits, easily traced, 15% in investments, 10% in ready cash and 5% in vehicles. The largest single asset, restrained by court order, was a Chinese sea-food restaurant worth then about $17 million. In another case a total of $161 million was confiscated in multiple forms of assets.

In Hong Kong, confiscated property and other investments are placed in the hands of the Government Official Receiver's Office. It soon became clear that many businesses had been set up or purchased because they were cash generators, e.g., restaurants or newspaper, tobacco vendor or corner shops. The term "money laundering" is derived from Al Capone's (1899-1947) practice of "washing" his ill-gotten gains by dividing the cash up through a chain of laundromats that he owned in Chicago.

The drugs trade, in Hong Kong and abroad, was on a steep learning curve in ways of hiding their assets, often advised by legal, financial and accounting professionals who claimed unwitting innocence. But as fast as the criminals learned, so did the detectives, adding their knowledge to training materials for the future.

In February1990, the NB FIG was in a position to take on the biggest wheel in Hong Kong's drug scene, Chan Fat (not his real name) and associates. He lived an unpretentious life with his family in the quieter climes of Saikung, yet his business connections and property portfolio encompassed the US, Australia and several Asian cities. He was a member of the Clearwater Bay Golf Club and his daughter attended the Pok Fu lam Horse Riding School.

Detective Chief Inspector Kenny Ip was the officer in charge of this case. Evidence soon came to light that Chan Fat's money laundering activities were exceedingly complicated, extensive and wide-ranging across the spectrum of international finance, requiring professional accounting knowledge to unravel it. Government accountants were called in but could not devote their energies full-time to police investigations. Cue local accountants Deloitte Ross Tohmatsu (now Deloitte Touche Tohmatsu) and their forensic accounting team headed by Fred Leung and Jim Wardell, partner and court-accredited expert. Fred moved his team into the FIG offices and began five months of grueling paper work, sifting through a global spider's web of intrigue. As caches of drug money were exposed, so the figures mounted, reaching spectacular sums: deposits of US$84.3 million plus HK$60 million in just one branch of the Bank of Credit & Commerce International (BCCI) Ltd in Hong Kong alone.

On 7 December 1989 at Kai Tak Airport, Chan Fat was arrested for drug trafficking by the FIG while he was waiting to meet his wife and children off a flight from Sydney. In the early hours of 19 December 1989, a large-scale police operation was mounted by the whole of CID NB. It netted most of the other important targets in the Chan Fat investigation. The following day, Crown Counsel applied for restraining orders in the High Court on assets against which sufficient evidence existed that they were the proceeds of drug trafficking.

Extradition proceedings were mounted in Hong Kong by the US to have Chan Fat returned to New York to face a variety of drug trafficking and money laundering charges alongside his associates already arrested in America. At trial, Chan Fat pled guilty to drug trafficking, the weight of evidence against him being overwhelming. Evidence showed that in 1987, alone, at least 420 units (about 316.5kgs) of pure heroin, with a market value of US$24 million, was "moved" by Chan Fat from Thailand to New York. Evidence exhibited in court included a yellow notebook in which Chan Fat had hand-written some of his drug trafficking transactions. For example (hand-writing in italics):

"Bought 60 units [of heroin] *at USD60,000 each."* The total investment cost, including transportation, would have been about US$3.6 million.

"After mixing (The purity level of the 60 units when shipped was in the order of 95%). After mixing (diluting with other substances) there was enough to make seventy units at the lower purity of 80%. *Consignment of 70 units sold* (to local criminal gangs in New York) *for US$85,000 per unit. Net profit US$2,350.000* in a single day.

The three years of Chan Fat's proven heroin trafficking in America generated vast amounts of cash that needed to be extricated from the US and laundered in Hong Kong. To arrange for this he used numerous tactics, including:

- Employing a New York remittance company "Piano" to set up the nominee "Wallon Trading Co" under the control of Chan Fat's mother, sister and brother. Piano then funneled remittances through the BCCI to Wallon Trading;

- Organizing a service for old people queueing up at the HSBC, Hang Seng Bank and China Bank branches in Chinatown who were invited to purchase as many as nine gift cheques of US$1,000 each, thus not reaching the STR (suspicious transacting threshold) of US$10,000. The usual handling charge of 3 percent was paid to the syndicate and bundles of these cheques were then posted to agents in Hong Kong who deposited them into Chan Fat's nominee accounts;
- Sending Chan Man (younger brother) to Singapore and Tokyo to set up nominee companies to receive remittances from New York.

The Court of Appeal presided over a number of judgments between January and December 1996. Ten judges ruled in separate proceedings against all of the accused, handing down seven- to twelve-year jail terms, plus fines.

At time of writing, what has happened to the principal players in this case?

Chan Fat entered into a plea bargain with the DEA, resulting in a guilty plea to all charges and, in return for information on his confederates, he was given four years in prison. He is back in Hong Kong now, doing business with Shenzhen.

Chan Man was sentenced to seven years imprisonment in Hong Kong. He also lives in Hong Kong.

Sybil Chan escaped arrest and an Interpol Red [wanted] Notice was issued and is still extant. It is believed she is living in luxury on a remote Pacific island where there is no extradition treaty with America, Australia or Hong Kong.

The BCCI went into liquidation in November 1991, after

serious irregularities were uncovered by both the police and banking regulators. Senior personnel were arrested and charged. Kenny Ip and Detective Inspector Evelyn Lam received the Governor's commendation, with the right to wear a red lanyard in uniform. Kenny was later promoted to Chief Superintendent. Then, after retiring, headed up security for a major bank. Since then he has been teaching Enhanced Competency Framework on Anti-Money Laundering and Counter-Financing of Terrorism, professional-level courses with Hong Kong University and School of Professional and Continuing Education. Stuart McDouall wrote that if there is such a thing as a *Super Sleuth*, then it is Kenny Ip.

David Hodson retired as Assistant Commissioner of Police, was awarded the Queen's Police Medal and went to Hong Kong University as an associate professor in social sciences. Now he is in and out of hospital with old age issues.

Stuart McDouall was awarded the Colonial Police Medal for Meritorious Service in 1995. Normally there is no citation but one was written: "For leadership and professional ability of a high order in commanding the Financial Investigation Group of the Police Narcotics Bureau between January 1989 and March 1992." He retired in 2005 as a Senior Superintendent and now lives in England.

Of the other inspectorate officers in the FIG, from the same era, two were promoted to commissioner rank. Five more were promoted to senior rank and/or left the police force to work in high-level offices in banks and credit card companies.

Michael Lunn QC became the lead crown prosecutor in all of the High and Appeal Court hearings in the K.M. Law case. Both he and Bill Boucaut are now retired.

Jim Wardell has retired and Fred Leung runs his own accountancy company.

A Muslim Discovers Masonry

Noorie Razack

My name is Noor Mohammed Razack and my friends call me Noorie. I was born on 16 November 1924, and I am a third-generation Indian Muslim in Hong Kong, the eldest child in a family of six, my parents, myself and my three younger sisters.

My family were well off. I don't know when my Grandfather, Mosa A. Razack, a devout Muslim from North India (now Pakistan), came to Hong Kong but I believe it must have been 1850-60. He was a member of the Hong Kong Stock Exchange and eventually became chairman. Grandfather also became a Freemason, initiated into Lodge Naval and Military, 848 SC, though I had no inkling of this until the '70s when I read a book by a Hong Kong Freemason, Kit Haffner, in which he mentions M.A. Razack.

Grandfather bought a mansion in the Mid-Levels where my father, Ahmed A. Razack, was born. He was a son of the first of grandfather's five wives. My father was educated at a missionary school on the Island, one of the best schools at that time. When he finished his education, he went to work in the Government Dockyards, becoming the quartermaster, a position he held until the fall of Hong Kong in World War II. When he married, my grandfather helped him buy a property in Leighton Hill, above Happy Valley. That was where I was born and brought up.

I was sent to a kindergarten near where we lived and, at age six, graduated to the primary section. Teaching was in Cantonese and I was given a Chinese name Shek Yue-man. I was good at my lessons and gained a place at the prestigious St Joseph's School. There I joined the Scout troop, the first in Hong Kong. I was in Form IV when World War I came to the colony in December '41.

Meanwhile, my father and mother moved the family to a spacious flat in Fort Street, North Point. It was from there, in the months before the war that I signed up with the Hong Kong Volunteer Regiment. After a week of training, I was posted to the Dispatch Corps as a bicycle messenger rider.

When the Japanese started shelling and bombing the northern shores of Hong Kong Island in the week before they landed in North Point, I was assigned to an ARP post at Quarry Bay School. I borrowed a cycle from a Chun Yeung Street shop and rode, in my Scout uniform, all the way there. I did my duty, as dispatch rider, for five days, without respite, until my commanding officer gave me permission to go home and see my family. That happened to be on the eve of the landing by the Japanese army on the island.

Early the following morning I awoke to the sound of heavy fighting about half a mile away, in the direction of the North Point power station. I was still in my Scout uniform when I walked outside and down the street to Fortress Hill Road. From there I could see lots of people milling about, some evidently panic-stricken, shouting, "They're coming!"

Realizing that wearing my uniform and an ARP helmet might make me an enemy target, I hurried home and took off my kit, disposing of it down the yard well.

My parents, who had brought in extra provisions, battened down the hatches, securing the front and back doors, backing furniture against them. I remember my sisters were crying.

Within an hour, the army arrived in our street, soldiers mainly of Korean and Taiwanese nationality under the command of Japanese. One of our neighbors was an Indian GP and I saw him attempting to drive away in his car, as if going to his clinic. But he was stopped and questioned by soldiers. They dragged him from his car and marched him to his flat. We all heard screaming and shouting. Not long afterwards the soldiers left. There was silence. Soon word began to go round that the good doctor had been beheaded. To this day I don't know if that really happened.

Around mid-day, all the residents of Fort Street, a few hundred of us, were ordered out into the road where we were roughly paraded, at gun point, into one long line: Portuguese, Chinese, Eurasians, Indians and a few British. A neighbor spoke Japanese and went on bended knee to plead with the Japanese Captain for their lives. That seemed to work for the officer warned the residents to go home and stay there, not to venture out on pain of death. All of us rushed home. The captain stationed several of his soldiers on guard in the street, then left with the rest of his men. As darkness fell on that first night of captivity, everyone locked their doors and windows. The soldiers began to visit the residential blocks trying to find food and any valuables they could steal. Not every household was targeted and my family was lucky. But imagine our terror when we heard a couple of guards, apparently Korean, forcing entry into the flat above ours. It was the home of a Chinese family, with three teenage daughters. We were friendly with them. We heard shouts and screams. The next morning my dad went upstairs to see if he could help. The parents had been hog-tied and their two eldest daughters raped.

Within a couple of weeks, relative peace was restored under Japanese rule and, a daily routine in our neighborhood began to emerge, one dominated by fear. The necessity for food and water, as well as medicines, became a daily torment as I and others ventured outside. We had to be alert to the presence of soldiers wherever we went, ready to bow before them or risk being beaten. On one foray, I learned that lessons in the Japanese language were being given free at local schools, sponsored by the military. I decided to enroll in a three-month course, thinking I could curry favor with the occupation forces and, hopefully, be in a position to help my family out in desperate times.

Up Fortress Hill Road there was a government rice-rations outlet manned by civilians but with soldiers marshalling the queues. Long lines of people of all ages stood in an orderly manner while troops watched them closely. It could be hours before one reached the head of the queue and, in the hot summer sun, people fainted. The soldiers never helped anyone. I remember one time when my eldest sister came back home crying. She had witnessed a Korean soldier pulling a rather fat Chinese man from the queue, berating him loudly then, in his anger, sticking his bayonet into the man's belly. That poor man was left writhing in agony in the road.

News from other theaters of the war was sparse and unreliable. Few people had radios. But in 1943, we all heard and saw American bombers flying over Hong Kong, the first glimmer of hope that the allies might have the upper hand at last. That presented another danger, of being killed by allied bombing. My parents had contacts and our whole family quietly slipped away one night, heading for Macau. The journey was fraught with difficulty and danger but we made it to the British Consulate there and registered as refugees.

In '43 to '45, I attended St Louis School in Macau that was run by the Catholic fathers of Wah Yan College. I picked up a reasonable grasp of Portuguese. A classmate and good friend was Edwin Wong Man-wai who later qualified as a doctor at Hong Kong University. Many years later, I discovered he was a Freemason and member of Lodge St John, 618 SC.

When the war ended, my whole family returned to Hong

Kong and I went looking for work, finding an opening in Chan Brother's Ship Chandlers. It was one of the partners there who advised me to change my Chinese name to Shek Ho-man, which I did. Grateful for the job, I worked hard and was promoted, being made ship's chandler to the hospital ship Maine moored in Victoria Harbor. My job was to engage Chinese crew for her and visit ships of the British Navy Auxiliary Fleet. I also arranged the repatriation of Indian and Chinese crews.

In 1947, I was given a special assignment, which I carried off successfully. My employers were so pleased that they gave me a letter of commendation which I have kept ever since. It reads: "*An outstanding case he attended to was the reception of a Japanese ship's company of about forty men who sailed the 'Carmen Moller' to Hong Kong on her rendition to the British Government. This was a ticklish job requiring crew disembarkation at Tai Kok Tsui, transporting them to Queen's Pier and then handing them over to the Military who took the sailors in, pending repatriation. Mr Razack intelligently carried out the instructions given to him in this affair with credit to himself and satisfaction to all concerned.*"

In those years with Chan Brothers I spent much of my time in the extensive dockyards along the foreshore from Murray Building (then on the waterfront) all the way to Arsenal Street. I met Jim Barber, an ex-navy officer, who told me something of Freemasonry: "... it's a society where you learn to be a good man." Jim impressed me but I thought it was a club for expatriates and took the matter no further. Later I discovered he was a member of The Zetland Lodge, 525 EC.

In 1953 I left the Navy Dockyards, looking for other ways to improve my lot. I visited a Chinese geomancer who told me that my birth elements were gold and *wood* and that I should change my Chinese name to Shek Yiu-fai. This I did, my third name change. I quickly found new employment at Moller's Shipping.

And on June 20, 1953, I left Hong Kong for my first trip overseas aboard a cargo passenger ship, the MV Soochow. I wore the uniform of ship's purser with the title "No 1 Writer."

The MV Soochow plied between Hong Kong, Port Moresby and Sydney. I did a couple of these voyages but decided that the ocean-going life was not for me.

I was home-sick and wanted to settle back into Hong Kong. I resigned on November 19, 1954, and was presented with a glowing testimonial from the ship's Captain:

"...Purser Razack has been a loyal and dedicated crew member. 100% reliable in the execution of his duties and, above all, trustworthy. He has shown initiative and team spirit, keeping good time and always with a smile."

It wasn't long, after leaving Moller's Shipping, that an assistant manager in Swire's Shipping, John Bremridge, contacted me, offering the post of Ship's Purser with Swire's. I politely turned him down. (Sir John Bremridge later became Hong Kong's Financial Secretary). I think he was a Freemason though I never found out which lodge he was in.

On September 1, 1955, I found a position with Metro Cars (HK) Ltd, which were the sole agents for Austin Motor Cars. Starting as a sales representative, it wasn't long before I was made a senior sales representative and I made the acquaintance of a departmental manager, Roger Pennels. He had come out to Hong Kong as a young man and married a lady of Malayan extraction named Wazira. We became life-long friends.

With my few linguistic talents I was made responsible for expatriate car buyers. Top salesman, an achievement rewarded with a new Austin Mini.

In 1958, I met my life partner, Linda, a divorcée with two children by her first marriage. She was a Chinese beauty, a part-time actress and model. I kept magazine photos of her to show guests at my home. In 1959 we decided to buy a flat in newly built Causeway Bay Mansions. My sisters were not enamored of her; they thought her improperly wed and not a Muslim. Her children never amounted to much. Her son went to live on the Mainland and whenever he was short of money he'd come to see us in Hong Kong and scrounge some cash.

Also in '59 I became a member of the Indian Recreation Club in Soo Kon Po, proposed by my then-ailing father. A top player in the Hong Kong Lawn Bowls Association, he had long been coaching me. A fellow member of the IRC was David Roads, an American foreign correspondent. We met occasionally at the bar. Many years later we met again as members of Lodge S. John, 618 SC.

I stayed with Metro Motors for ten happy years from '55 to '66. But I got itchy feet eventually and, on leaving the company, I was given a testimonial by senior manager Roger Pennels:

"Noorie Razack has been a faithful employee, always giving of his best and with the best interests of the company at heart. He is honest and hard-working. His customers are mostly British; they all like Mr Razack because of his pleasant manner and desire to be helpful."

Shortly after I left, my friend Roger moved to Zung Fu (Mercedes) as a senior manager.

On the lawn bowls circuit I was becoming well known as a decent player and was approached by two friends, members of the Craigengower Cricket Club in Happy Valley. They persuaded me to join their lawn bowls team. At that time membership was cheaper than the IRC (Indian Recreation Club) and the clubhouse was better situated at the Causeway Bay end of Happy Valley, near my home. Fast-forward to 1980, I was approached by Harry Turner, the President of the HK Lawn Bowls Association. I didn't know it then, but he was also a Freemason and a member of

Lodge St John, 618 SC. He offered me the post of Chief Coach. I accepted the offer and was re-elected, year on year until 2004, when I became ineligible due to age.

In May '66, I moved to Kian Gwan Company (China) Ltd, a rice hong but with a side line in cosmetics. Starting off as a salesman in the cosmetics department. I was promoted in '67, to Sales Manager. I got to know the Managing Director of Kian Gwan, an Indonesian called S.G. Liem who was married to a Dutch lady and domiciled in Holland. On his bi-annual inspection visits I was his assistant, usually taking him to lunch at the CCC, Craigengower Cricket Club.

In lunchtime conversation with him freemasonry was mentioned. Liem told me it was not an exclusively expatriate club and that, if I wanted to join, I only need ask my old friend, Roger Pennels.

While I was with Kian Gwan, I was invited to take up the agency for Rimmel Cosmetics in Hong Kong. I did so working from home until leaving Kian Gwan in March 1970. That same month I joined Henry David (HK) Ltd, an import and export company dealing mainly in cosmetics. I was their general manager and brought Rimmel with me to my new employers.

I still met up with Roger every now and again and in '72 I asked him if I could become a Freemason. Roger seemed pleasantly surprised and agreed to propose my membership. He found a seconder by the name of Si Min, a Chinese Malay friend of mine from the IRC. I duly attended a Lodge Inquiry Committee meeting and then was asked to wait for a year before I could be initiated. Then fellow Indian, Gary Harilela, was in the chair of Lodge St John, 618 SC. It was only then that I chanced upon many acquaintances, wondering at the coincidences leading them all to play a part in my life.

Leaving Henry David Ltd in '73, I tried my hand at yet

another line of work. I was taken on by Hastings & Co Solicitors as a clerk. In '74 I was made office manager, a post I held for 10 years, until my 60th birthday in '84. But I wasn't ready to retire and went on to work for another solicitor's firm, Susan Liang & Co, finally retiring in 1989.

I found out about a marketing enterprise in cosmetics where there is no shop. One just buys in products to sell to one's friends and acquaintances. So I started doing that from home but it was not lucrative. My friends told me it was pyramid selling. I kept on giving stuff away to my friends with no profit margin for myself. In retirement I also started attending public lectures, mainly on health and welfare issues. I enjoyed these, making more friends. Sometimes I invited them to have lunch with me at the CCC where we chatted well into the afternoon.

Freemasonry now played a big part in my life. I soon got a reputation for not missing a single one of our nine meetings at Zetland Hall every year. My party-piece was the North East Corner lecture to entered apprentice candidates. I never needed a prompt. I attended the socials, bringing my Linda with me to the annual Ladies Night, all done up to the nines. In 1985 came what I call my crowning achievement in life when I was elected as the Worshipful Master of Lodge St John 618 SC. In later years I couldn't afford those grand dinner dances but a few of my dear friends used to club together and pay for us. After my installation, at the banquet, all of my brothers there, about a hundred of them, stood to sing the Master's Song for me. I was so humbled and elated at the same time. I cried unashamedly.

Soon my meager savings began to run out and, in the millennium year, finding that I would not be able to afford the management fees for the building Linda and I lived in, I had to ask my Masonic friends if they could help me out. It was Stuart McDouall, almoner in Lodge St John 618 SC, who took up my case. The Far East Masonic Benevolence Fund came to my aid with an offer of a grant-for-life in exchange for a first charge on our flat. Linda was suspicious of the Masons' intentions but not me. I completely trusted them and am happy that the Masons should be reimbursed for looking after Linda and me for the rest of our lives. That generous monthly grant kept Linda and me, and then only me after she died, in board and lodging up until now.

After my Linda was taken ill and put into a care home, which the Masons paid for, I lived for a while on my own. I visited her every day in a tiny, windowless room shared with another elderly lady. She remained there for five years. In the last two years she never left her bed, became incommunicative and had gloves made with strips of stiff bamboo wired together so she couldn't scratch herself. When she passed away, I was finding it very difficult to look after myself properly. Some strangers from the Mainland pretended to look after me but actually just used my home and occasionally took my cash. My short-term memory was going. Linda's son came back, refusing to pay for his mother's funeral and still looking for cash. Lodge members Henry Aun and Raymond Teng told him he had no call on me anymore. Henry and Raymond supported me all the way, looking after me. They eventually found me the excellent care home where I am now living. I am one of the few men there. Most of the residents are widows with whom I like to chit-chat and occasionally we make up a foursome for mahjong.

Update: On November 20, 2021, Noorie celebrated his 98th birthday. A picture was taken of him grinning like a Cheshire cat.

Confrontation: Cultural Revolution Bombs in Hong Kong

Guy Sanderson Shirra

My time as a young cadet with Voluntary Service Overseas teaching in a secondary school in Sarawak in 1965/66 during the Konfrontasi with Indonesia gave me a taste for life in the Far East doing something "interesting and useful" and possibly adventurous. So my visit to the Crown Agents in London on my return from Malaysia proved fruitful. I was interviewed and was accepted as a probationary inspector in the Hong Kong Police and admitted as a member of Her Majesty's Overseas Civil Service, arriving Hong Kong on 6 January 1967.

After two months of intensive Cantonese language training with my expatriate squad mates, my police training with our local squad mates—the law and police procedure, drill, weapons training and self-defence, I started at the Police Training School in Wong Chuk Hang in March.

However, all the PTS bull ended in May with the outbreak of leftist-inspired demonstrations and later rioting in Kowloon. Local leftists, inspired by Mao's Cultural Revolution and the capitulation of the Portuguese authorities in nearby Macau, embarked on a campaign of rioting, strikes, murders, police revolver snatching and terrorist street bombing. This was not, however, officially sanctioned by the Chinese government in Beijing and in, particular, Chou Enlai, although they could not be seen to openly disown it.

On the surface, the CCP apparatus swung into full support with the formation of the All Circle Struggle Committee in Hong Kong. The Hong Kong Government response was immediate and resolute. The HKP was fully mobilized with several Police Training Contingent Internal Security (IS) riot companies immediately available, backed up by three Emergency Unit IS companies. Every division formed its own IS company supported by Light Striking Forces (LSF) at half platoon strength; two LSFs could quickly be combined to form an extra platoon. This was called force mobilization or FORMOB.

PTS formed two IS companies of trainees led by staff who were in the thick of the action but my own squad was too junior to be involved. The most we ever did was support Special Branch in performing a sweep and search of Queen's Pier for bombs prior to the departure of the Governor, Sir David Trench, on leave. For this we were in plainclothes and armed with the Webley .38 revolvers, mostly replaced by the better Colt .38. The Webley was so unreliable that we were not permitted to load a round in the chamber beneath the firing pin. We managed to complete this task without accidentally shooting ourselves or the Governor so I suppose it could be called a success.

One of the worst days of the Confrontation came on 8 July, 1967, while we were still cooling our heels at PTS. I was on the square talking to a IS company officer when a staff sergeant advised us to tune the IS radio to the NT channel. Police in Sha Tau Kok on the Sino-HK Border were calling for help after coming under murderous Chinese machine-gun fire that we could hear in the background.

Five police officers, three Chinese and two Pakistanis, were killed and eleven others injured. Inspector Dave Pitt attempted a rescue in a tin-can police armored car manned by Pakistani officers from EU NT before the Gurkhas arrived hours later to restore order. Dave was awarded a Colonial Police Medal for Gallantry for his exploits that day. Needless to say, this incident caused alarm bells to ring in Hong Kong, London and Beijing and many thought that China might invade. We certainly feared the worst for a time.

There was mayhem all along the border. In another incident on 4 December 1967, a constable was blown up by a British Army land mine outside the Pak Fu Shan border police post. Attempting to rescue him, Inspector Ted "The Leg" Stevenson was also blown up and lost a leg. He also later received the CPMG. Ted and the constable were rescued and given first-aid by Sergeant James Matchett from the Welch Regiment who received a George Medal for his valor. Altogether, during the so-called Confrontation, ten police officers were killed by shooting, chopping and bombing but the force, supported by the community as a whole, stood fast.

In one earlier incident in Sha Tau Kok, a Frontier police Land Rover was set on fire and destroyed. A molten lump of bodywork later adorned the Fanling Mess walls as a memento. However, if Land Rover UK had ever been informed of the outcome, they would have been very proud of their vehicle as, at the time of its destruction, it was reportedly carrying a ton or more of ammunition, furniture, files and equipment of every description from formations all over the NT. It was a truly remarkable, sturdy vehicle. All of its missing contents were conveniently written off, of course.

Another Confrontation memento adorning the walls of Fanling Mess was a poem by an officer commemorating *The Day the Irish Guards Invaded China*. At the end of the Sha Tau Kok Road leading into the fenceless border village, there was a twenty-foot sign in English, Chinese and Gurkhali reading, "Turn Left Onto Border Road Here!!" The illiterate Paddies in their Land

Rover drove straight on across the border and were the guests of the PLA for several days. London and the Governor were not amused.

The Confrontation, the counter-insurgency operation against local communists and their sympathizers, had begun in May 1967 but at PTS I was not directly involved. Bayview (later Causeway Bay) police station was surrounded by Dannert, or concertina wire on knife rests (a UK military barrier system) and blast-proofing sand bags. I lived in Eastern (later Wanchai) police station officers' mess, and the whole of Jaffe Road between the station and the quarters opposite was similarly reinforced and blocked off. But I digress.

I had passed out of PTS with a rather naive and bookish local officer whose name escapes me because he resigned after his first week of duty. Apparently, he misunderstood the purpose of his Official Diary and his first week included details of his breakfast, journey to work on the tram and meeting senior officers. An example: "Mr Ron Smith is a very nice man, so is Mr Jim Harris, but I do not like Mr Leary very much; he is fat and shouts too much." Leary was the chief inspector Bayview and if the DS was "God", then the CI was the Devil and he inspected and signed all Official Diaries every week.

CIs were few and far between and although they had three pips on their shoulders, they would never become gazetted officers, i.e., assistant superintendents and above, who were more usually second-in-command of divisions. Leary had a very large chip to go with his three pips as a result.

As the whole force was mobilized into full IS structure, the station was protected by sandbags, wire and guards. In the event of an attack on station, the guards would be reinforced by officers of any rank who would rush to the armory, grab weapons and run to take up pre-allocated defense positions. It was all taken very seriously. The attack-on-station alarm, I quickly discovered, was a wooden plunger on the floor beneath the Duty Officer's (DO) chair. In those days, the report room desk was high off the ground and imposing, so that the exalted DO could look down on the complainant from on high. The DO's chair was a throne-like high chair with a step to assist ascension thereto.

My second day was more of the same and my third day I understudied the DO. We had lost property reports and members of the public surrendering fire crackers; these were banned, and still are, as insurgents were making bombs or improvised explosive devices from them. We also had the occasional crime report. Or we would have done if the intending complainants had not usually been intercepted in the lobby by a lurking Criminal Investigation Department man. The complainants were usually to be seen leaving a while later having received "compensation" from CID or an assurance that their case would be investigated...

One complainant did get to make a report, though: my girlfriend and wife-to-be, Annie Yip. She had her handbag nicked in the cinema. On this occasion, CID reluctantly accepted the report and even took a statement from her. Perhaps with hindsight she should have accepted some compensation instead. Perhaps she did.

Another time a bloke turned up one night in his underpants screaming robbery. Once calmed, he revealed that he and his girlfriend had been having a "quiet chat" in his car atop Tin Hau Temple Road where they had been robbed of their belongings and clothes. Our hero then ran off, leaving his girlfriend up there alone. She was later found safe but not too well disposed towards her less-than-heroic beau.

However, returning to Bayview police station. On my first day as Duty Officer proper everyone in the station got to know me very quickly. I slid off the chair to go for lunch and stepped on the alarm. All hell broke loose. The alarm clanging, officers shouting, doors slamming and "God" arriving in the report room to get a sitrep. "Where's the DO?" he barked, not being able to see me because I was on my knees under the bench trying desperately to pull up the alarm plunger.

Unfortunately, this happened not once but twice. Not a third time. "God" decided that I needed a change of scenery. I thus progressed to going on duty in a patrol car. These were Land Rovers painted in the battleship gray paint inherited from the Royal Navy after World War II. They had a very high frequency radio connected to the Hong Kong Island Control Room and also BV Divisional Control Room. Only vehicles had radios in those days. Beat officers had nothing except a key to open police telephone boxes (also battleship gray), which were few and far-between. Much reliance was placed on borrowing telephones from shopkeepers and watchmen.

Only the IS command Land Rovers had blue lights and sirens. So responding to emergency calls was problematic. The universal technique adopted, not to be found in Police General Orders or General Duties manuals, was for the driver to drive like a man possessed in low gear, revving loudly and blowing the horn continuously with the crew leaning out of the windows yelling crudely at pedestrians and vehicles alike while beating frantically on the doors with long batons. Keystone Cops wasn't in it!

Many of the calls we got were bomb reports. There were so many because most of them were either false reports of innocent bags or parcels left in the wrong place or hoax reports. There were reports of articles designed to look like bombs, usually with "Comrades Keep Clear" written on them in red Chinese characters. However, a significant number were genuine IEDs mostly made from the gunpowder extracted from firecrackers and stuffed into pipes or tins and concealed in travel bags and other luggage. They were usually placed to cause maximum disruption to traffic or business, occasionally as booby traps and rarely thrown at police. Intelligence revealed that the communists were paying bomb planters US$40 for a hoax or US$200 for a genuine bomb.

On 28 August 1967, a British Army Explosives Ordnance Disposal officer, Sergeant Charles Workman was blown up and killed by such a device concealed inside a makeshift flagpole on Lion Rock. Senior Inspector Ron McEwen, our erstwhile chief drill and musketry instructor at PTS, who had begged to get back to front-line traffic duties, was blown to pieces in Wanchai on 5 November 1967 by a travel bag bomb he was trying bravely to move to a safe place.

Another IED blew up under similar circumstances outside the fire station in Wanchai on 3 September 1967, killing an off-duty fireman rubbernecking on his balcony. The explosion, again, was caused by a well-intentioned fellow resident of Eastern Mess, Colin Lamont. He tied string to the bag, retreated to what he thought to be a safe distance, pulled hard and up it went. Colin was hospitalized and eventually returned in one piece but full of small bits of bomb shrapnel. He would often find them in his mouth and drop them onto his side plate with a resounding ping during meals.

The worst incident I remember took place in North Point on 20 August 1967. The bombers must have been too cowardly to plant their device openly and instead stuck it in Ching Wah Street, a quiet cul-de-sac leading to a primary school. Here it was discovered by two children, sister and brother, eight-year-old Wong Yee-man and two-year-old Wong Siu-fan, who died when it exploded as they played with it. It was probably this incident, along with the immolation murder five days later of popular Commercial Radio talk show host Lam Bun along with his cousin Lam Kwong-hoi, which turned public opinion massively against the leftists and their supporters. Regrettably, none of these horrible murder cases has ever been solved.

I remember being dispatched about this time to a suspect package in the King's Road. We cordoned off the area, awaiting the combined Police and Army Bomb Squad, but some idiots in an office doorway refused to leave. I shut the sliding metal shutters on them and left them in the dark. Some people in the high rise buildings around us refused to close their windows (to prevent sniping or dropping objects) so I had to threaten them with my M1 carbine. The device proved to be genuine and went off with a huge bang when detonated by the EOD team. Prolonged screaming from behind the shutters resulted.

Most of the reports were false or hoax, as I have said. Probably ill-advisedly, most of us did our best to weed out these incidents so that the overworked Bomb Squad could deal with the most suspicious ones. We would cordon off the area then have a good look at the suspicious object. If we thought it was too small or too innocent to be a bomb, we would take cover behind a lamp post or something solid and prod it with a long bamboo pole. Once I climbed into a manhole to examine a very small package placed on the new Plover Cove water scheme pipeline. I survived this behavior but it was bloody stupid.

During one particularly bad period for bombs, someone twice left hoax bombs on the zebra-crossing and tram tracks outside the Victoria Park dog garden in Causeway Road. The intention was to disrupt traffic and it certainly succeeded. On night shift that week I decided to try and catch the bomber in the act if he struck again. An hour or so before dawn I climbed a tree in the dog garden with an excellent view of the location and sat there waiting with an M1 carbine. It started to drizzle. Then, just before dawn a crowd of elderly morning exercisers entered the garden and one old bloke wandered around looking for somewhere to hang his umbrella. He chose my tree and as he reached up he saw me grinning down at him. He let out a yell, dropped his brolly and scampered out of the park hollering "*Yau gwei! Yau gwei!*" (Devil! Devil!), followed by his stampeding companions. Needless to say, I abandoned the ambush and drove around my patch for an hour during which time the bomber struck again in exactly the same place.

We got lucky another night, though. "God" had put all our uniformed beat patrols into plainclothes in an attempt to catch the bombers. Some patrolled on foot but many were in concealed observation posts. One such OP was in the bushes on the slope opposite the HK & Shanghai Bank in Quarry Bay. Before dawn on 13 November 1967, they saw three men place a straw effigy of the Governor and several grenade-type bombs at the bank entrance and attempt to set fire to them. Officers had started to chase them round the corner into a side street when Shau Kei Wan Inspector T.K. Chan and I arrived. One teenager was arrested at the top of a staircase, and after enquiries by the Bomb Squad, a whole "Red Youth Fighting Group" underground cell was smashed with more genuine bombs and weapons seized.

To improve their cover, it was suggested that the teams disguise themselves as hawkers. Some attached themselves to licensed hawkers. I remember seeing an anguished fruit hawker observing the inept efforts of his attached constable trying to peal a pear properly. Leary issued others with a large quantity of toys from a relative's factory. After a day spent flogging toys, they reported for debriefing with no arrests, no toys and no money. Leary was not amused and did not repeat the experiment.

I was company radio operator and we were conducting a raid on union premises in Leighton Road, Causeway Bay. While the company had all the fun, I stayed with the vehicles, drivers and lorry guards parked near a tea shop. I was walking in front of a lorry when there was a loud bang and the windscreen exploded above my head. My stomach in my boots, I drew my revolver and started looking for a bomber as I assumed that an IED had been thrown at us. I checked nearby staircases and entrances, found nothing and came back to find the poor lorry driver sitting in a chair in the tea shop with most of his jaw missing. A passing citizen on his way to work also received minor injuries from flying glass. The lorry guard, tired as we all were after months of prolonged duty and little rest, had fallen asleep with his finger on the trigger of his Greener riot gun.

This was a fine weapon, nicknamed the *lofu cheung* by the locals. It was a 12-gauge single barrel, Martini action shotgun manufactured by W.W. Greener in Birmingham. It fired twelve .303 pellets from a brass cartridge and discouraged riot ringleaders most effectively. It had a massive kick and was usually only issued to larger PCs in deference to Isaac Newton's Laws of Motion.

Unfortunately, PCs being what they are, most had had their safety catches forced back on again so often (it was designed to be unloaded and reloaded if not fired) that they did not work. Sleeping Beauty accordingly pulled his trigger and the round went through the back of the cab, through the driver's jaw and through the windscreen over my head, the only time I have ever been shot at.

I was sent for a period to the Bayview Division Control Room, a centre opened especially during the Confrontation. This was normally staffed by an inspector, a sergeant and a couple of PC radio operator/telephonists. Our duty was to co-ordinate the deployment of IS forces in the division: LSFs, mobile patrols and fixed posts. One of the radio operators was a very sexy red tab

English-speaking WPC. I particularly liked the way she would say "Roger out" on the radio; it came out in a seductive drawl as "*Laja mao*" or "Dirty cat".

I remember one particularly bad evening on 10 December 1967, we received numerous bomb reports all over the division, badly disrupting traffic and population movement and tying up all of our resources. We cordoned off the areas as best we could. After HKI Control informed me that EOD teams could not be sent for some time, I stuck my neck out and calling myself "Chief Inspector Shirra", I called them back on the telephone demanding an EOD response. I got it but spent a day or two worrying that I would be carpeted by "God", or worse for impersonating a CI. I guess that they thought I was Leary. Eight real bombs and forty-nine simulated bombs were discovered in Bayview that day, 93.5 percent of HKI's reports and 85 percent of the whole Colony's.

Central Magistracy's Court No 1 was presided over by a famous magistrate, Paul Corfe. Before the arrival in court of any jurist, the clerk will call "Court!" and everyone will rise. In Court No 1's case, it seems that the clerk had a sense of humor because he instead always called "Corfe!", which is said to have greatly bemused His Worship. Anyway, Court No 1 was where all the leftist rioters, bomb throwers and similar types were always brought as it was a very large court with the dock in the center with direct access via stone steps to the cells beneath.

In one case, a leftist rock-thrower appeared and was tried and sentenced whereupon he launched into Mao Thought, hurled his flip-flops at Corfe (a universally popular method of showing one's displeasure with magistrates among the less well shod in Hong Kong), and then made scurrilous suggestions regarding how he should treat his mother, "*Diu Lei Lo Mo!*"

Corfe gave him an extra month for contempt of court. The court sergeant then hauled him off down to the cells but a further "*Diu*

Lei Lo Mo!" arose from beneath. Corfe ordered him brought back up and gave him another month. Astoundingly, this was repeated twice more with the by now-demoralized leftist receiving an extra four months. My colleague, the late Brian Coak, the prosecuting inspector of some experience and long service, later recalled this story in the mess. He had chatted with the Court Sergeant later and questioned the leftist's stupid behavior. The sergeant then told him "Well, Sir, just between you and me, the first *Diu Lei Lo Mo!* was his but all the rest were mine!" Brian later admitted that this was all a tall story for the Mess.

During the Confrontation, the Hong Kong public were four-square behind the government and police, particularly after the murders of the two little children and Lam Bun and his cousin and vast sums of money were donated for police welfare and police children's education.

The force as a whole was recognized in 1969 when it became the Royal Hong Kong Police, a name which became part of history on June 30, 1997.

In Memoriam

In memory of the Hong Kong Police and British Army who lost their lives in 1967: 8 July *Shot in Sha Tau Kok:*

Cpl 4009 Fung Yin-ping PC 7266 Wong Loi-hing PC 8868 Kong Shing-kay PC 3015 Khurshid Ahmed PC 3033 Mohamed Nawaz Malik

PTC D Coy No 12 Pln PTC D Coy No 10 Pln PTC D Coy No 12 Pln EUNT No 1 Pln EUNT No 1 Pln

All five officers murdered in Sha Tau Kok

9 July *Hacked/ricochet in Western* PC 9424 Edward Lam Po-wah

28 August Killed by bomb on Lion Rock Sgt Charles Workman RAOC

13 October Killed by bomb in Wanchai PC 6990 To Hung-

kwong
    5 November Killed by bomb in Causeway Bay
    S/Insp Ronald J. McEwan
    29 November Stabbed in Shek Kip Mei PC 8548 Sit Chun-
hung
    9 December Shot in Kam Tin, NT
    PC 3810 Lee Koon-sang
    The family of a murdered police officer at his funeral

Other Notable Murders:
20 August—Blown up by bomb in North Point WONG Yee-man, 8-year-old girl and her 2- year-old brother, WONG Siu-Fan 26 August—Immolated in Kowloon Tong LAM Bun, radio commentator and cousin, LAM Kwong-hoi

Confrontation Statistics
Deaths—51 (10 HKP, 1 Army, 1 Fire Services, 39 Civilian) Cause of Death:
    bombs, shooting, stabbing, immolation
    Bombs Reported—8,074 including 1,167 genuine explosive devices Injuries—212 HKP, 832 civilians
    Public Order Arrests—4,974
    Public Order Prosecutions—1,984 with 1,936 convictions
    Murders—73 (63 prosecuted)
    Attempted Murders—4 (4 prosecuted)

TOUCH AND GO

Mike Tinworth

The Men of the East was an elite invitational rugby team, much on the lines of the Barbarians. The team consisted of players who were based in, or had previously lived in Hong Kong, and played one match a year against the Manila Nomads. The rules of the fixture were that the winners had to host the next game, which possibly accounted for the fact that the Men of The East lost seventeen straight games. The mandatory Bloody Mary party immediately prior to the match may also have contributed to this ignominious record.

The prime motivator behind the team was Phil Godolphin, a great friend of mine who sadly died of cancer a few years ago. Phil wrote a novel that included some chapters based on his experiences with the Men of the East. The novel was never published, but Phil subsequently inserted these chapters into the magazine that he produced for each tour. The following story is taken from the 1984 magazine and concerns an incident when the return on the Philippines Airlines flight from the 1975 tour took off from Manila despite a typhoon warning in Hong Kong. As they approached Kai Tak, the typhoon had well and truly kicked in, and the landing was aborted four times before the plane turned around and headed back to Manila.

Abrams slept and the Road Runner started reading the English-language Manila Daily News.

"Hey, it says here there's a typhoon approaching Hong Kong. The Captain didn't mention it. I wonder what the weather's like there now?"

His wondering was interrupted by the static cackle of the intercom. The steward's warm voice announced "Ladies and Gentlemen, we are approaching some turbulence up ahead. Please return to your seats and fasten your seat belts until we have passed through it."

The warning was only a few minutes old when the plane jolted to right and left almost in rhythm.

"Damn!" said Abrams who hated flying in rough weather.

There was a time when he had found flying difficult, but the necessities of his job had altered that. It had been a difficult inner struggle with himself. The way he altered it was to go parachute jumping at Shek Kong, in the New Territories of Hong Kong. That first real trip had been terrifying but only initially. The sensation, miles above the flat green plains of Shek Kong, bordered by the dark mountains, had been fantastic. The feelings of exhilaration he achieved were incredible and he jumped whenever he could. It wasn't the jumping he enjoyed, it was the initial free fall. Simply marvellous.

This had cured his fear of flying but he still did not like it. The coziness of a small Cessna or Wessex helicopter was far more reassuring to him than large commercial jets and all his old fears, the sweating brow and palms, came flooding back to him as the Philippine Airlines Boeing seemed to drop suddenly. This was no ordinary turbulence, visibility outside the cabin windows was zero.

Abrams was white. Beckingham, who had managed a few moments of sleep, was delighted. "Come on, lads, remember we're British. Stiff upper lip. Let's have another beer!"

He did eventually get service as the unfortunate hostess staggered down the aisle. "I'm sorry, Sir. We are temporarily closing the bar until the plane is steady. Here are a few until then." She handed Jewell a dozen cans of San Miguel and Heineken and retreated to the comparative comfort of the rear seats.

The plane felt like a shuttlecock in some frantic game of badminton between the sky gods. And the gods were angry. The sky was black; the plane was falling, pushed and pulled in all directions. Several of the overhead luggage racks burst open and cases clattered onto the floor, ignored by their frightened owners. Many of the passengers had faces like unsmiling white clowns. There was little conversation.

The intake of alcohol had made Jewell very sleepy and he dozed off, oblivious to the panic rising in Abrams across the aisle. Abrams was terrified and felt very sick. He reached for the sickness bag and promptly returned the rice pudding he had eaten earlier.

There was a crash as some of the food trays lifted out of their metal containers and hit the floor. It was the worst trip Marsden had ever known and he considered the possibility that the plane could break up or the pilot lose control. The winds must be enormous. He looked at his watch. The plane had been airborne for eighty minutes. On the normal flight schedule they should have already commenced their descent into Kai Tak Airport but there was no word from the captain on their situation. Perhaps he had taken Abrams' earlier advice and parachuted out! There could be no way they could land in this.

What Marsden did not know was that they were very close to Hong Kong. The pilot was trying very hard to land and having to alter his descent path. Over Hong Kong, the No 10 tropical cyclone warning signal had been raised. This indicated hurricane force winds were blowing with a sustained speed reaching upwards of 64 knots and with gusts exceeding 120 knots.

The full blast of Typhoon Elsie was battering the south side of Hong Kong, trees in the Stanley, Deep Water Bay and Repulse Bay area being mercilessly stripped of leaves and branches.

Abrams was getting desperate. He was not a religious man but he nevertheless started praying to the God of his childhood days, silently whispering that he would believe in Him if He'd only get them down safely on land.

He began to imagine this situation was a sign that the God he disbelieved in was displeased with him. Were the heavens trying to punish him? There were many things Abrams had done in his life that might have earned the gods' wrath. Perhaps, as with Ebenezer Scrooge, it was not too late. Abrams was not about to become a convert but he was terrified. Perhaps he could avoid his own "Christmas yet to come", the plane crash, by mending his ways.

How? How could he change? Well there was the booze, the cause of most of his amoral life, for a start. He could give that up right now, but was that enough? No. What else? He pondered, still gripped by his terror of crashing. Would he never see Jill again? That's it! He'd make a pact with the Lord Almighty. Save me from this, he promised, and I will marry Jill. He had used, misused and abused her for years. They had lived together on and off for a long time. He'd make an honest woman of her. Let me live and I'll marry her. At that moment, he came as close to praying as he ever would, but his God was not listening; the nightmare flight continued for a full twenty minutes before the captain's voice boomed over the intercom. Abrams was sure the captain's voice was shaking as much as his own hands.

"Ladies and Gentlemen, I regret to inform you that Typhoon Elsie is currently over Hong Kong, We have attempted to land four times but the weather has made it impossible. Philippine Airlines deeply regrets the considerable inconvenience you have all suffered. We arc therefore returning to Manila. Please remain in your seats with the seat belts securely fastened."

There was a synchronized audible sigh of relief from the

passengers. There may be another ninety minutes flying still to endure but at least they would be going away from this terrible rage of wind.

It was at least half an hour before the plane returned to a steadier course. Abrams confirmed his promise to his God. No more booze, and he would marry Jill this year, if she'd have him. Beckingham was disappointed that the storm had gone, the only consolation was that he no longer had to clutch his beer to save it from spilling on his lap. He had enjoyed the hint of danger and his calm reaction to it. Marsden knew that although only Abrams had revealed his fear, they had all been frightened, even Beckingham.

As a postscript to this story, the plane duly arrived back in Manila, by now quite late in the evening and with no chance of attempting a return to Hong Kong until the storm had blown through. So our intrepid tourists were faced with an extra night in Manila, which on the surface might appear to be a bonus. However, they were all exhausted and slightly terrified, and had all spent what was left of their tour money on what should have been their last night there.

In the days with very limited availability and use of ATMs and credit cards, and with all the banks and moneychangers shut, they consequently found themselves having to negotiate a night in Manila with no money. How they did this is, as they say, another story.

Royal Hong Kong Jockey Club by DaiFoo & Seemafoo

Stuart Smith

In 1845, "You can't really have a colony without a horse racing club can you?" would have been the cry from the military and new colonials. The administration got the last laugh, however, by allocating them the stinking mosquito-ridden swamp of Happy Valley... From a low start, things very slowly improved for the Hong Kong Jockey Club. For many years the Club meandered in its amateur ways until going professional in 1971, with Royal patronage elevating the Club to the RHKJC in 1975. From there the quality of racing improved along with the betting turnover to such an extent that illegal bookmakers started to pose a real problem to the Club and society, hence, Off-Course Betting was established to provide a legal alternative. This is where I came in. Such was the success of the OCB systems, the manually operated apparatus for taking bets and paying dividends couldn't cope. These systems had been copied from Australian practice and a few of their operational managers, Brian Hatton, June Rothery and Bill Sargent, had come with them to set up and run it. In the early '70s, I was working as an engineer at a UK company, De La Rue, which supplied automated ticket-handling systems to lotteries and the like. The RHKJC placed an order for six of the systems and somehow, I got the job of installing them. In the words of Terry Smith (Dai Foo 'Big Smith'), who was the betting operations manager-to-be of the system,

"We opened a large box and out popped an engineer." So there I was, in mid- 1976, a fair bit of pressure being applied to get the systems installed and commissioned, ready for the start of the next season, and what the hell was a Six-up bet, let alone a Banker Double Quinella?

Terry Smith was in charge of sorting all this out on the Club side and having been in the HKP and ICAC for several years knew the ropes and decent bars. None of which prepared me for my third day in HK when he told me to bring my kit tomorrow as we were going for a run! "A what?" I asked. "Yes," a run around the racecourse, yes, in mid-summer." Well, I couldn't even manage one lap without stopping in pain and torment, welcome to Hong Kong… From that low point I slowly improved and even managed a bit of squash. We were lucky that we could use the Club's membership facilities, bars, restaurants, pool and squash courts. The running eventually became an addiction (to this day) and entry into the world of the Hash House Harriers, of which more later.

We got the betting systems working in time for the start of racing and what a difference they made. With an aggregate ticket handling capacity of 350,000 tickets per hour, we had fixed the problem. Volume was still growing, though, and we often worked until 2:00 a.m. on Wednesday nights after racing at the Valley. What to do then? We were too awake to go home so it was off to the bars in what is now known by the Hash as "Central East", often with me on the back of Terry's trusty 500cc Honda bike.

The expat Club staff were an interesting mixture of UK racing professionals, stewards, vets, handicappers, lunatics and the like, with a few Australian betting types and sundry contractors running odd systems like the photo-finish. In the background a new racecourse at ShaTin was under construction.

Rumour had it that one pile driver there just disappeared into a void mid-stroke such were the challenges. All this really was background noise as we were busy with twice weekly racing at the Valley. After racing, all the officials convened in the Official's Bar for a light ale or two. Now I really didn't qualify as I was not a Club employee nor an official, I was an engineer. Somehow Terry managed to wheedle our way into this inner sanctum but we had to keep our heads down… Apart from the free beer there was usually a substantial buffet laid on by the Club's excellent catering dept. The bar was basically a post-meeting office, everyone would tell everyone else of their race-day problems, which were carefully noted in the back of your programme and acted upon next day, an efficient system. But the Happy Valley bar closed one hour after the last race and the bar steward made a big point of serving last orders and locking the fridge with a large chain and padlock around it. We gave him ten minutes before sliding the chain off, back over the fridge, and continued drinking into the night.

One of my jobs was the care and maintenance of the starting gates used to start the race. Little did I know about the politics involved, I thought it was just a simple case of mechanics and a bit of electrics to make sure all of the horses started at the same time. No. This being high-stakes horse racing, games were played, and the gates were in the middle. The mechanism of the gates was pretty simple, a common trip bar allowed the individual gate latches to all trip at the same time. Sounds easy? But the jockeys had discovered that a bit of pressure from the nose of the horse at the right time and in the right place on their gate delayed the opening of that individual gate, which could now be blamed for the horse's poor start, all of which ended up in the steward's inquiry room. Often the poor tote engineer got the blame for incorrectly setting up gates, my defense to which was a slow motion film made before the meeting showing all the gates opening simultaneously, back to the jockey. Another trick was for the jockey to kick the horse just before the starter opened the gates to panic the horse into crashing into the gate and breaking out early in order to get a good start. I had an assistant given to me by my boss to help look after the gates. He was the oldest technician on our staff, Mak Chuen. Such was his help that things were a lot worse when he was around. My boss and I made some discrete inquiries of the personnel department as to his age as he looked as though he could be due for retirement. Personnel promised to check. Back they came a few days later with the news that, according to their records, he had three different ages on file, none of them making him eligible for retirement yet. This was probably due to his having Club quarters, a valuable bonus. One trick pulled by a cocky trainer was to claim that the gates had been struck by lightning just as they were about to open, electrifying his horse and causing a bad start. Nonsense of course but a good try. From then on, though, we had to place a spike in the ground at each start and wire it to the gates... The day I was relieved of the gates' responsibility was a great one... They were taken over by Harry, a talented local maintenance technician. Just before one particularly important race, a horse reared up and entangled his front legs in the gates. Normally this would have caused a race postponement and probable bullet for the horse. Not for Harry however, he whipped out his hacksaw and proceeded to start cutting out the gate to free the horse, then his blade broke. No problem, Harry produced a replacement and cleared the problem. An envelope later, from the horse owner to Harry, was rumored to be quite thick.

When I arrived at the Club, communications were far from those of today. We didn't have a telex machine that was only available through the Club's accountant, Peat Marwick. To send a telex one had to firstly get it typed, that took a day through the

Club's secretaries. Next the typed copy was sent by messenger to Peat's office in Central, another day. Then Peat's office prepared a paper tape and sent it, usually the following day. If I got a reply from UK the same week then that was considered fast. Phone calls to UK had to be made by going to the Cable & Wireless office in Central and paying cash for three minutes or so then either going into a booth there or booking the time for a call and going home to receive it. I remember once going through all of this to urgently contact my UK office for some spares. When the phone in UK was answered I asked for my boss. Whoever picked up the phone in UK just said "Not here" and put the phone down. Back to C&W in Central to book it all again.

Things got slightly better years later when the club got a fax machine. This was located in, and controlled by, the much hated admin department. They loved being able to read all our faxes and exert some control over us. My then boss, Peter Frankowski, found some project funds and bought our own departmental fax machine. The din from admin when they found out is probably still echoing around Happy Valley. Peter delighted in finding flaws in the system and to this day recounts the phone call he found on the Club's fixed assets register, for all of $5. I had a number of my staff working outdoors at Shatin in far from ideal circumstances early on. They quite reasonably asked for a fridge so they could have cool drinks after working outdoors all day in the summer heat. I consulted my boss and was soundly rejected for no apparent reason. I waited a couple of weeks and put in a requisition for a "battery storage machine type AQ437-67R" under an open project budget. It was approved instantly, of course, and my guys got their fridge. It was two years later that my boss discovered the ruse. Peat Marwick early on also had an operational role at the race course on race day, they organized all the staff and generally ran the operation. Several of the Club's executives were employed around the track and were paid directly by Peat's office. This was handy, of course, as they could have the funds paid into a separate bank account that their wives didn't know about.

Peter Frankowski was an interesting character. He came to the Club just after me as a computer systems project manager, the ultimate goal being to unite all of the Club's betting systems into one computer hierarchy. Peter's background was slowly drawn out of him over the years, from exiting central Europe during the war clinging onto the underside of military trucks to a brief Olympic performance and a role in the moon shot. If you added up all of his stories, he was around 150 years old. His main methodology in managing projects was to get every task into a computerized jobs list, known as the PTT, and to hold people to them. I remember during one particularly fraught project meeting and Peter yelling at someone, "If you can't give me a date then give me a date when you can give me a date!" Much as we hated him much of the time, he did get things done.

Another of Peter's institutions was the end-of-work beer session in the clubs' members bar, Tattenham Corner. Over the years, these stretched from "a quickie" to a full-on multi-hour drinking session where the Club's and world's problems would be fixed in extraordinary depth. When these extended to five evenings a week, something had to be done as it was all getting a bit tedious. One of the betting operations managers, Daryl Plowright, and I hatched a plan; we'd go drinking somewhere else — and not tell Peter... So was founded the "501 Club", so named as it started at one minute past 5:00 p.m. What happened was that Darryl and I chose a bar in the area and my secretary was given a list of internal Club phone numbers to call at 3:00 p.m. on Friday afternoon. This led to a bunch of confused secretaries around the Club as they received the coded message, "501 Bull & Bear" for their boss. Eventually, of course, Peter noticed that his Friday night sessions were getting a bit thin but he never inquired as to what was going on. Incidentally, the 501 continues to this day, run by the Hash House Harriers with no HKJC involvement. The formula is much the same, a different location each week, with a special negotiated rate for Carlsberg as the 501 can now command as many as thirty attendees.

Terry and I continued to run, mainly at lunchtimes, as we skipped lunch, got some exercise and had a respite from the terrors of the office. We had a number of routes around the Valley, up through the graveyard, along Shiu Fai Terrace and up to Bowen Road which had superb views over Happy Valley, Mid-Levels, the harbor and Central. For longer runs we'd go up the Peak or over Black's Link to the Cricket Club, Jardine's Lookout and back down. These longer runs were too hot for mid-summer but were superb in their scope and challenge, I mentally re-run some of them to this day. Such was the humidity for most of the year we would attend afternoon meetings dripping wet. Terry had meanwhile joined a mysterious running club called the HK Hash House Harriers, The Hash, and tried to get me to join as well as he seemed to think I'd fit in as it was described as a drinking club with a running problem. I resisted for a while as I was sure I wouldn't be able to keep up the pace with these athletes. Eventually I caved in and have had assorted liver problems ever since. The core idea of the club was to "provide gentlemen with a bit of exercise on a Monday night to compensate for the excesses of the weekend." Although a great idea, never in the ninety years of the Hash's Asian existence has it been achieved. The run was usually an hour or so and had been set during Monday afternoon in chalk and flour by the hares. There were "checks", "check backs" and other devious markings designed to give the fast runners a good stretch and let the slower members have time for a rest while it was sorted out. As such, it was too short for any real exercise. After the run, the grandmaster assailed his audience with trumped-up charges of misdeeds, which required the guilty party to down-down, a cold can of Carlsberg in one swallow. This hardly improved one's health as one had another two or three, while cheering on other miscreants, hence, negating all positive aspects of the run. Then there was the curry afterwards where a few more were consumed followed by "one for the road", ha-ha, in some dingy dive on Lockhart Road, by which time it was past midnight, ensuring a hazy start the next day. However the Hash did provide insight into how the rest of HK's expats lived and worked and also got us into some interesting countryside. As the scope of employ of Hashers was quite diverse we often had some site engineer get us access into tunnels or bridges that were about to be opened or MTR stations under construction. To this day, the friends made on the Hash are lifelong friends and rarely a day goes by without hearing from, or of, one of them. Membership of one Hash grants access into any other Hash in the world so when you move around you are always ensured of friends with similar outlooks and lunatic ideas.

The Club had a policy of employing ex-British army generals as its chief executives, few of these had any racing experience but they were all good managers with a wealth of people experience. General Penfold had arrived a few years before me and had inherited the Shatin project from his predecessor. Asked on TV how the Club was going to afford such a vast development he replied, "It'll be paid for by the end of the first season!" This wasn't quite so as funds were tight and Shatin's costs considerable, it even had its own internal railway station. So tight were funds that we delayed installing a couple of escalators until the second season, by which time, of course, all was well financially. General Penfold was a practical no-nonsense type.

When there was a noise problem with the ventilation system in the new stables, the consultants told him the noise level was perfectly acceptable. Penfold was having none of this. He sent out his secretary to buy a book on acoustics, got a sound level meter from somewhere and went out to measure the din... The consultants folded and fixed it pronto. The infield at Shatin was planted and landscaped following the guidance of Mrs Ursula Penfold. In celebration of her efforts the tunnel entrance was fitted with a sign triumphantly naming it in Chinese characters. When asked to translate it, a proud local proclaimed that it was called "Ursula's Underpass". More suitable wording was soon found.

The Clerk of the Course was an ebullient Irishman by the name of Noel McCaffrey. One of his claims to fame was that he ran the last mule train in the British army. Now the Clerk of the Course has many duties on a race day, one of which is to make sure that the grass track looked pristine. But growing grass in an old swamp at summer temperatures in HK isn't easy. Somehow though it always looked pristine. Eventually, some eagle-eyed executive rumbled Noel. "Why did horses returning from the track after the race have green hooves?" "No idea," Noel said, knowing he had been caught. The grass had been sprayed early on race day mornings with green vegetable dye, he eventually admitted. Noel, apart from being a Kowloon Hash man, had a number of party tricks up his sleeve, two of the more interesting were his ability to hypnotise chickens and identify the sex of horses, blindfolded. I once watched him consecutively take six chickens and "talk to them", whereupon they entered a trance-like state. Noel laid them down on their backs, totally out of it. Just as in the movies, a clap of the hands brought them out of their trance and back to normal. Noel once performed this trick for a charity fund-raising event on the bar of the HK Football

Club, raising thousands of dollars. Sexing horses involved blindfolding Noel and slowly bringing the horse close to him, he then ran the back of his hand over the horse's nose and correctly told you male or female — impressive. How it was done is a secret that remains with Noel... This trick was not, however, done in the bar of the HK Football Club.

Another redevelopment saw Happy Valley track and grandstands blitzed in the three-month close season. So tight was the schedule that as the last punter left the last race at the end of the season, the diggers moved in at 10:30 p.m. Every part of the track and stands had something done to them, all in the three months of the close season. Now the photo finish system was for some odd reason operated by an independent contractor who had it operated by his technicians Derek Dutton and Dougie Marson. We in the tote supplied them with occasional technical help when needed; otherwise, they looked after themselves. At the end of the close season redevelopment, we had a trial race night in which we got a few horses and ran a few races with the tote, TV, photo finish and all other systems to make sure that it all worked before the first race day. All went reasonably well so the season started as normal. I can't remember what triggered it but about half way through the season, Derek Dutton came up to me and started asking detailed questions about what had happened during the close season, had we moved his cameras or what? No, I replied, we had carefully not touched anything as the photo finish system wasn't in the scope of works for redevelopment. After a bit I found out that Derek was worried about the accuracy of the photo finish system alignment to the track. The cameras need to be perfectly perpendicular to the track and exactly on the finishing line. Hmm. I got the track drawings out, old and new, and noted that the track alignment had indeed had been moved slightly, so let's get the surveyors in. Sure enough, Derek's hunch was correct; the cameras were no longer exactly on the finish line, so time for a quick re-alignment before the next race day. The racing department went bonkers wanting to know how many and which race results were now wrong. Derek slaved over half a season of pictures for days and came up with only a couple of place changes with no winners being incorrectly assigned. I think the racing department made some discrete changes to the official results and the event got lost in history.

Policing of the racing was a critical task to maintain the honesty of racing in the face of the hordes of crooks trying to pervert the course of racing integrity. The stipendiary stewards were a panel of racing experts, sometimes even ex-jockeys, who managed the integrity of racing and watched every second of training and racing to ensure fair play. Their powers were considerable, they could end a trainer's or jockey's career forever if the offense deserved it. Normally, though, a fine or a few days suspension were the sentences. The stewards had their own high-quality film camera system to monitor the races, based on 16mm film and professional Ariflex cine cameras. Early in the days of professional racing at the Club, a visiting jockey from the UK, Lester Piggot, thought that he'd play a few games on this "back country track" but was astonished to be summoned after his first race to appear before the stewards. He was even more astonished to find that they had some fine pictures of him poking the adjacent horse to his in the eye with his whip halfway down the straight, all played back to him in exquisite detail on the large screen in the steward's inquiry room. Jim Marsh was the chief Stipe a few years later, an Irish steward of much experience in the UK and Europe. He had crossed paths with Lester on many previous occasions and wouldn't let Lester so much as breathe deeply without hauling him in for an inquiry. Jim knew of Lester's reputation as a tight wad and issued penalties to Lester in the form of significant fines rather than banning him for a few race days, knowing that this would hurt Lester the most. I attended three farewells to Jim, one in Hong Kong, the next in Macau and his final in Riyadh, all but the last were enveloped in a haze of Irish whisky.

Another key area of racing integrity was drug testing of the horses. With so much money at stake it was imperative that the horses were clean. This was all run by the racing chemist, pipe-smoking Dr David Crone. Of course, like all these things what looked simple at first, wasn't. From the urine sampling through to the analysis, the whole process had to be completed at haste with security and accuracy. There was one incident when a mafoo (stable hand) couldn't get his horse to fill the bottle in time so he filled it himself. The racing chemist duly reported the horse to the Stewards as having "a bit of a coffee and beer drinking problem". The mafoo was surprised to later have his escapade replayed to him from the stable CCTV cameras. In another caffeine case, the answer wasn't so simple, after weeks of analysis the stewards came to the conclusion that someone in Australia, where the horse food came from, must have thrown a cup of coffee over a bale of hay, such was the sensitivity of the analysis. One of the more interesting places to visit was the secure room in the racing chemist's laboratory where he held a sample of every known doping drug to calibrate his analyzers. Some interesting stuff there!

Much as we loved HK, I was becoming slowly disenchanted with the pace and noise so it was time to look around, but where to from here? Tough decision as Lyzah and I really only wanted one more move so this was to be our final one. Lots of options, but they all had a disadvantage... Northern Europe, too cold... Southern Europe. I didn't fancy learning another language. The Philippines: doubtful safety for a Gweilo. As for the rest of Asia, the interesting countries didn't allow foreigners to own land. Oz was high on the list but after a visit, Lyzah declared it to be "too big". I would have loved to go to Southern California, having spent some time there on Club projects and the tech scene was amazing, however, it would have been back to eight-day weeks. We had visited New Zealand a few years earlier on a Hash trip so decided to re-visit it, spending two weeks around Auckland. All looked good but we couldn't find a suitable house; the criteria was simple, sea view, local running and within one hour of Auckland, and then... On our last full day we noticed an interesting bit of land in West Auckland, Huia. The agent took us out there, warning us of the steep drive, promptly getting stuck on it in her 4WD. Well, stunning sea view, right in the bush and only thirty minutes from town, perfect... But it was only land, no house... Not being ones to make snap decisions we slept on it and visited again on our way to the airport. Verdict, even more stunning! So we committed ourselves to it on the spot. Subsequent visits sorted out an architect, builder and we were off. Of course the builder's estimate of a three month-build were way out; it took us a year just to do the design and approvals, but eventually we made it and it has, indeed. been bliss!

THE CHATER COLLECTION MYSTERY
Edited by Stuart McDouall

This tale of wonder and mystery, surrounding the life-time legacy of Sir Catchik Paul Chater, a gentleman entrepreneur who lived in Hong Kong in the late 19th and early 20th centuries, is succinctly captured in a "case investigation" conducted by a former Assistant Commissioner of the Royal Hong Kong Police, Angus Stevenson Hamilton, QPM, etc.

As a younger superintendent of police, Angus was seconded to the staff of the Governor of Hong Kong, Sir Murray Maclehose, GBE, KCMG, KCVO, between 1978 and 1982. Already a seasoned detective when he took up the office of aide-de-camp, Angus took a personal interest in rumors, being aired *soto voce* by government officials, as to the disappearance of a large part of Sir Paul's valuable collection of Chinese art and artifacts during World War II.

Angus researched known facts relating to the accumulation, housing and eventual disappearance of this fortune in paintings and sketches, engravings and furnishings, porcelain, pottery and jade. Apparently no valuation of the full collection was ever completed.

Catchick, who became a prominent British-Indian businessman, living and working in Hong Kong for most of his life, was one of a family of 13 children born in Calcutta to his Armenian parents, Mr Chater and his wife Miriam. Catchick's father was a government servant in British India.

Orphaned at the age of seven, Catchick was taken into care and, exhibiting intelligence, won a scholarship to a Calcutta College. In 1864, as a youth of 18, he moved to Hong Kong to live with the family of his sister Anna and her Armenian husband. He adopted the Christian name of Paul.

Paul Catchick Chater started work as an assistant in the Bank of Hindustan, China and Japan. A while later, with a grounding in finance and a chance liaison with the well-established Sassoon family, he set up business as an exchange broker, the beginnings of an incredible success story. He went on to build a business empire in the food industry — dockyards and warehousing, land reclamation and building development, *and* setting up the world's first electric power station and urban grid. At the age of fifty, Paul Chater was wealthy, a philanthropist, a grand officer in English Freemasonry and a highly respected citizen of Hong Kong. He was appointed to the Governor's Executive Council and, in 1902, he was knighted by King Edward VII at Buckingham Palace.

Among his many interests, Sir Paul was a connoisseur of the arts and an antiquarian of distinction. Most of the valuable original paintings that Sir Paul bought were landscape scenes of Southern China trading ports in the 18th and 19th centuries. In 1901, he began the construction of a fine family home at No 1 Conduit Road, in the mid-levels, half way up the Peak, with a view over Victoria Harbor. He named his grand edifice Marble Hall and it was here that he housed his famous collection.

Sir Paul died in 1926, bequeathing Marble Hall and its contents to Hong Kong. His wife lived on in the house until her own death in 1935 when the property passed into the ownership of the Hong Kong Government. The collection was subject of a book by author James Orange at which time the collection stood at 430 items, from paintings to porcelain.

Sir Cecil Clementi, the Governor of Hong Kong in 1935, inspected the property and its magnificent collection, personally directing that the items be disbursed around the Colony for the people of Hong Kong to admire. Recipients included Hong Kong University, the City Hall Museum and Government Secretariat. Some of the collection was left in Marble Hall, which was renamed Admiralty House, becoming the official residence of Hong Kong's Commander-in-Chief of the military garrison. More valuable items were displayed in Government House.

Due to the vagaries of South China weather, hot and humid summers, typhoons and winter monsoons — air-conditioning not being widely available in the early 20th Century — much of the more perishable pieces, paintings and silks, books and scrolls, carved wooden furniture, required regular maintenance plus restoration work. In 1935 a Hungarian artist by the name of Von Kobsa Nagy was entrusted with this work, aided by his assistant, Sinn Chi Lam.

The speed with which the Japanese army swept down through South China in 1941 caught everyone by surprise, not least the Hong Kong Government, had to scramble in preparation for invasion, hastily building defense lines, gun emplacements, and munitions dumps plus air-raid shelters.

These preparations included a system of underground tunnels running from Government House to Lower Albert Road, opposite the Secretariat by a few hundred meters. An access shaft in the basement of the house was sunk about fifteen meters, leading to a dual tunnel system comprising a small generator room, a bomb shelter, first-aid area and stores and admin rooms. Apparently the plans for the tunnels did not take into account the possibility that the foundations of GH, already creaking at the seams, might be further compromised. At about the same time tunnels leading from under Flag Staff House, the residence of the

Commander of British Forces in the Victoria Barracks complex, were being dug less than half a mile away.

When Angus was appointed ADC in 1978, he became responsible to the governor for administration and all operations relating to Government House. In other words he had the run of the house and grounds. He was in a position to access the wartime tunnels beneath GH and carry out exploration of his own. He found them of safe construction, uncluttered with the debris one might have expected after five years of war.

One of the first things Angus checked on was the rumor that the tunnels under GH and Flag Staff House were designed as escape routes for the Governor and the CBF in times of emergency. One GH tunnel was said to exit in some hidden spot at the lower end of Ice House Street. Angus found no evidence of this. If it had ever existed, it was certainly well blocked up now. What Angus did find were spacious tunnels and rooms, one housing a generator for electricity.

It was a different story with the tunnels under Flag Staff House. These did not appear to have been much disturbed since they were last used in 1941. In 1979, when Angus first saw them, there was a skeleton of a cat in one corner. Round the walls could be seen some loose telephone lines. In the center of the room was a large, square pane of glass, supported upright in a wooden frame, with some words, lines and arrows, drawn with crayon, still visible. It was quite obvious that signals staff wrote up information, as it came in by telegraph, on the sheet of glass in mirror script, which the chiefs of staff could read from their side of the glass.

Sir Mark Young, GCMG, was Governor of Hong Kong from 10 September to 25 December 1941, and again, after the war, from 1 May 1946 until his retirement in 1947.

Sir Mark succeeded Sir Geoffrey Northcote as governor

and must have been aware of the threat of war in the Far East and the possibility of it engulfing Hong Kong. In consultation with the War Office and the Commander-in-Chief of British Forces, Major General Maltby, he set about putting Hong Kong on a war-footing, throwing up such defenses as his limited resources allowed. It was only a few months later that reports of a 50,000-strong Japanese army, massed in Canton, was ready to invade Hong Kong. On the 7th of December it was Maltby who informed the governor that the enemy was at the border.

As luck would have it, a copy of a closed file, dating back to 1945 and belonging to the PWD, was found in the Government Secretariat in the 1970s. An examination revealed useful information about GH, the former Admiralty House, Flag Staff House, City Hall and other government buildings. Among its pages, like silver threads gleaming in a black cloth, were clues as to the existence of the Chater collection.

City Hall had a number of items from the Chater collection on display in the years before the war. From the contents of the PWD file, an allusion to the secreting of those items in a basement under Western Market was found. It was also ascertained that the bulk of the Chater porcelain collection, also on display in the City Hall, had been moved in boxes to Government Stores in North Point. And it was discovered that paintings undergoing restoration in North Point stores, shortly before the invasion of Hong Kong, were packed into cases or trunks and deposited in a government furniture store in Arsenal Street, Wanchai. Precious paintings and silks displayed in Admiralty House were presumed destroyed, either by enemy bombing or a fire that raged in the house shortly after the enemy occupation had begun.

Information was also gleaned from memories of former civil servants, tapped into years after the end of the war. According to Mr John Deakin, custodian at GH in 1941, Sir Mark Young directed that steps be taken for the safe-keeping of the GH Chater collection, plus some family silver and other valuables of his own and that of Captain Batty-Smith, his ADC. Angus studied the architectural plans of Government House, looking for the locations of possible strong rooms or places in the basement that could have been made into secure hiding places. But there was nothing. All furnishings and fittings had been dismantled and removed, seemingly long ago.

The mystery deepened when it was learned that, just two days prior to the land invasion, Captain Batty-Smith had asked the Hungarian artist, Von Kobza Nagy and a Mr Harmon of PWD, to arrange for the safe storage of precious items from the Chater collection in the house and grounds of GH.

This came to light in 1943, when the editor of the China Mail newspaper visited the terminally ill Von Kobza Nagy, a friend of his, in hospital and Nagy told him his secret. Nagy knew that the Japanese were about to rebuild part of GH under the guidance of a former PWD engineer, an internee of the POW camp at Stanley. The foundations needed to be made safe after the air-raid shelter had been built among them. Nagy continued, "I'm afraid they will find the secret chamber where we hid the best of the Chater collection." And to another friend, an Austrian, he described how the paintings had been taken out of their frames, rolled up, sealed in metal containers and buried in the gardens of GH.

On of Nagy's assistants was a Mr Fung Ming who had been told by his boss of plans to secure pictures from the Chater collection. Fung visited Nagy when he was dying in hospital and the latter swore Fung to secrecy. But all Fung seemed to know was that pictures had been hidden in the tunnels under GH.

The Governor, Sir Mark, was obliged to surrender the colony to the invaders on Christmas Day, 1941, just 106 days after his appointment as the governor. Two months after the capitulation,

Lt General Resuke Isogai arrived to take over the administration of the territory. Isogai chose not to live in GH, as it was traditional Japanese practice to always work from home.

Isogai ordered repairs to the GH foundations and retained an architect to create a fusion of Japanese and Western-style architecture in the remodeling of GH. A civil engineer from Japan, named Seichi Fujimura, was contracted to lead the project. While the foundations and the state rooms on the ground floor only needed repairs, the upper storeys were dilapidated, needing to be re-built. Japanese-styled furnishings, cornicing and roofing were added plus a Shinto tower in traditional form, rising above the house.

In August 1945, when the battle of the Pacific had been won by the allies, Rear Admiral Cecil Harcourt and his fleet sailed into Victoria Harbor and, on 16 September, 1945, formally accepted the Japanese surrender from Vice Admiral Fujita and Major General Okada. After securing the territory, the British navy released the POWs from the camps in Kowloon and on the Island. Among them were Messrs Gimson, the former Colonial Secretary, and John Deakin, the former custodian of GH. Gimson ordered Deakin to make GH habitable for Admiral Harcourt and his staff.

David MacDougall, who had managed to escape from Hong Kong at the outbreak of war, returned and took over as head of the Secretariat with Claude Burgess as his deputy. The latter, having heard various rumors of the missing Chater collection while he was a POW, and having talked to Deakin about it, planned to recover it. Burgess had known Von Kobza Nagy before the war and was convinced that the latter would have tried his very best to preserve the collection for posterity.

When Burgess came across information about part of the collection being buried in the garden of GH, he informed

David MacDougall who convinced Admiral Harcourt to allow exploratory digs by PWD staff and GH gardeners. Much fruitless digging was done, turning the admiral's flower beds and lawns into what looked like a cratered battle field. An irritated Harcourt summoned Burgess to his office and told him to call off the search and take his men with him. After Sir Mark Young's resumption of his gubernatorial duties, having recuperated from the privations of a POW camp, he could shed no further light on the fate of the Chater collection formerly displayed in GH.

After both McDougall and Burgess had retired in 1947, a fresh perspective, that of Senior Administrative Officer Austin Coates, was brought to bear on the vexed question of what had happened to the Chater collection. He found out from staff who had served in government stores, that Japanese soldiers had loaded all the boxes of porcelain, 987 pieces, and taken them to the naval dockyard. Coates also located John Deakin, still living in Hong Kong, and learned that, when he was refurbishing GH for Admiral Harcourt, he had seen that the underground storerooms had been demolished with new ones built. That was Seichi Fujimura's work rebuilding parts of GH. There was no sign of the Chater collection.

The controller of Government Stores, before and after the enemy occupation was W.J. Anderson. Coates found it was Anderson who, in 1946, was tasked by MacDougall to investigate and report on the whereabouts of the Chater collection. In his report was information gleaned from former staff at the Government Secretariat and at the University of Hong Kong, that the Japanese military, taking possession of the works of art and other valuable items, had been advised by them of the antique value of those pieces. A Japanese art expert, Ogura, was tasked to collect those items. He disappeared from Hong Kong before the end of the war. Initially soldiers had been placed on guard duty in those buildings but when they were withdrawn, after the most precious pieces had been taken away, all the rest had been stolen in a looting spree by residents.

Anderson had also interviewed a Mr J. Braga, from Macau, who said his father had been lent a number of photographs of former Hong Kong governors and that two paintings had recently turned up in a Macanese antique shop. Although they may have been part of the Chater collection they were found to be of little value.

Coates initiated inquiries with staff of General Douglas MacArthur, Supreme Commander of allied forces in Japan. He named three of Lt General Resuki Isogai's senior staff in Hong Kong, during the war years, and three more officers of the Japanese Army HQ. Circumstantial evidence linked all of them to the Chater collection. And at Coates's request, the art expert, Ogura, was traced. Under questioning, he admitted he had an interest in the Chater collection, having read the catalogue put together by James Orange all those years ago. But he denied all knowledge of the collection beyond a few pieces that he had seen hanging on a wall in the HKU library. His statement is at variance with intelligence from three separate sources that he was the principal agent in the disposal of a large part of the art collection. MacArthur's staff got no further with him.

GH underwent three major refurbishments between the end of the war and 1980. First, Sir Alexander Grantham, in 1947, had air conditioning installed throughout the main building and had the interior decoration restored to a more western appearance. Second, in 1962, while Sir David Trench was in residence, minor decoration work and up-grading of the air conditioning was carried out. Third, the most comprehensive works were undertaken under the governorship of Sir Murray MacLehose. He, his family and GH staff were temporarily housed in Flag

Staff House. All the roofing woodwork was renewed and tiles replaced. The old air conditioning plant was modernized as were the kitchens and the electrical and plumbing works. The gardens were extensively redesigned. "And in all that time," says Angus, "the only buried treasure found was an unopened bottle of brandy." It wasn't for want of trying! Angus used the opportunity to tackle the basement, foundations and tunnel systems in both GH and Flag Staff House, having the works contractor at GH drill exploratory holes in four apparently solid granite blocks that were part of the foundations. There were four remodelled store rooms in the basement and Angus had those walls tested as potentially hiding treasure. Again negative.

Sometime after the refurbishment had been completed, Angus was informed that British Forces HQ had ordered "bug cleansing" electronic sweeps to be carried out in GH. Angus mentioned to the officer in charge his aim to locate at least part of the missing Chater collection. The "bug cleansing" did include making structural cavity searches, requiring the approval of the CBF, General Sir Roy Redgrave. Angus obtained that through the ADC. Two days were allocated for the team to work in the basement and foundations of GH but their equipment's limit of penetration in concrete was two feet. A blank was drawn.

Angus was the last of a line of treasure seekers since the end of the war, certainly the first to have made such a thorough search of GH and its grounds. His conclusions, partly based on the work of Austin Coates and Claude Burgess, are:

There is evidence that
- The hierarchy of the Japanese forces were complicit in appropriating the porcelain collection and, most likely other looted items, storing it at the naval dockyards before shipping it out of Hong Kong in 1942, presumably

to Japan.

- In the summer of '42 the cargo vessel, MV *Lisbon Maru* under the Japanese flag, was chartered to convey 2,000 POWs from Hong Kong to Japan in appalling living conditions. As it passed through the Taiwan Strait, a US submarine sank it with a torpedo. The US Navy had no knowledge of the ship's human cargo. The other cargo it could feasibly have been carrying was part of the Chater collection, the porcelain, as there is no evidence that it was ever landed in Japan.

- Less valuable items of the Chater collection did begin to surface after the war, in shops in Hong Kong and Macau.

- Only one painting found in Japan has been identified as part of the Chater collection. There may be others that have not been identified. Most likely that one painting and others were Ogura's contribution to the thievery.

- Von Kobza Nagy mentioned items being hidden in a secret chamber in GH basement and pieces being buried in the gardens. If that was true then it is highly likely to have been uncovered during Seichi Fujimura's rebuilding of the foundations and upper floors of Government House in 1942-43. A locked door of a basement storeroom would have posed no obstacle to the contractors. Likewise the tunnels under GH certainly would not have escaped the attention of Seichi Fujimura.

- The evidence found in the PWD file, pertaining to GH, is that officials had two to three weeks before the invasion in which to secrete items from thieves.

They even had time to make sealed metal tubes for storing painting canvases. "And," remarks Angus, "how is it that the governor, Sir Mark Young, resident in GH at the time, apparently had not an inkling of any of these specific plans to save the Chater collection?"

- Are there any more leads left? Angus mentions a note in the PWD file which seems to imply that some of the more precious items were stored in a strongroom, perhaps concealed in an air raid shelter, in the house or grounds of the Colonial Secretary's house on the Peak. The present Chief Secretary has an official house, built in the 1920s, on Barker Road on the Peak, too. Is it the same one? No one seems to know if a search has ever been carried out at that house.

- Finally, another little mystery. There is circumstantial evidence that British regimental silver was wrapped up in oilskins and buried in a deep hole in the grounds of Flag Staff House. In the days before and during the invasion, the Commander of British Forces was in residence. Angus has had a good look around but not with his spade, mindful, perhaps, of the furore over the digging-up of the governor's lawns in 1947.

VIA IMPERIAL
Rod Olsen

At the conclusion of university studies, the great magnet of London has for years lured many young Kiwis and Aussies away from their home countries. Like pilgrims heading for a holy place, their mecca, was often around Earl's Court, and at some stage they would likely travel around Europe in a camper van in search of further enlightment. When it came time to return home, or their money was running out, they were often found gathered around Bush House (the former headquarters of the BBC World Service) at the Southern end of Kingsway. Here, especially during weekends at the end of a European summer, all available car park spaces would be occupied by camper vans for sale by pilgrims returning home.

My personal pilgrimage took a different course in that I came to London and later Hong Kong to work full time. Leaving New Zealand in 1969, I was committed to a two-year assignment with a global accounting firm. The plan at the end of two years was to return to New Zealand bringing the benefit of London experience and the wishful thinking of finding a fast track to a partnership perhaps.

It seemed a good plan at the time, but it never came to fruition. Hong Kong became the centre of my world; I never did make it back to New Zealand, instead spending more than twenty years with Cable & Wireless as my employer. Nor did I ever get to own a camper van.

On showing up in London for my first day in the office, at cobbled Ironmonger Lane in the "City," I met first with Wing Commander Nightingale (retired), the head of personnel, and received my first lesson in etiquette. I was proudly wearing my new brown pinstripe suit, brown shoes and a colorful tie. The Wing Commander (retired) didn't mince words in suggesting, "We don't wear our country clothes to the office, Old Boy. You look like you are off to Ascot. "

Suitably chastened—but a fast learner—I forever thereafter blended in with only a kiwi accent to give me away. Even that changed over time apparently. Kiwis visiting London told me so and on a holiday visit back to New Zealand I was told I "sounded like a bleeding Pom".

As a kiwi chameleon I had blended in sufficiently to be trusted with my first client after eight weeks at Ironmonger Lane. A Slough Industrial estate-based manufacturer of something or other, run by a sleazy character who wore a monocle, smoked cigars, and drove a Bentley. The cigar smoke in his office was a helpful foil against the smell from the Mars Bars factory next door which pervaded the entire Industrial estate. The client had not had a good year and the clean audit needed to support bank financing didn't stack up with the audit findings. Here is where diplomatic skills were added to my recently acquired etiquette skills. A consultancy contract to restructure and refinance the business was awarded and my manager was delighted with the increased fees that year. He got a bonus for it—not me. Another learning curve moment.

Towards the end of the two-year assignment came an invitation to join a new department in London, specializing in computer audit and investigations. The firm were setting up two such departments (the other in New York) with the objective of consolidating expertise and subsequently spreading it out across their other offices around the world. So, my two year secondment was extended and I was posted to Hong Kong in 1972 to build the first computer audit team there.

Here began a relationship with the Far East and Hong Kong in particular — which has endured for more than fifty years.

In accepting the new opportunity, my focus was on a new adventure. I failed to think through the proposed reporting structure and was naive about related office politics. It was decreed that I was to report monthly in writing to both the worldwide senior partner for computer audit in London (my direct boss) and the senior partner in Hong Kong. It didn't occur to me that they might have opposing interests, which could leave me exposed as "piggy in the middle".

Sure enough, there emerged a difference of opinion between my two bosses. For London, my role was seen as essential to the firm's global reputation. The view in Hong Kong was that the investment in computer auditing could be made more slowly over time. I was held back from recruiting planned additional staff and began receiving conflicting directions from my two masters. A team arrived from London to intervene. Piggy was indeed in the middle and though better understandings were reached, my enthusiasm and confidence were severely dented by the way it had been so badly managed.

Up the creek without a paddle just nine months after arriving in Hong Kong was nerve wracking but fortuitously a former client from London appeared on the horizon with an interesting proposition. Its timing and challenge provided a perfect opportunity to escape the logjam and its internal politics.

Back in London, a previous assignment had involved valuation of a business to enable two investors to buy a controlling interest in it. The business was that of sole UK distributor for Iskra

Commerce electronic components (effectively the Yugoslavian state electronics industry). The new investors planned to expand the business by adding a wider range of complimentary products from other sources.

Distributors live by their reputation for fast, efficient, reliable delivery but since buying control of the UK distributor, none of these goals had been achieved. Supply of product had been unreliable and it had proved difficult to expand the business as planned, let alone attract the trust of other component manufacturers to distribute their products. The benefits of rebranding had also been squandered by the poor delivery record.

The challenge put to me was to replicate the entire product range from Asian suppliers; develop reliable delivery programs and have every product carry our own brand. From a small office in Wyndham Street, Hong Kong, ably assisted by three brilliant engineers with manufacturing and production-line expertise and a small admin team—we had largely achieved this in two years. From a Hong Kong base, we had product supply chains from Osaka, Tokyo, Kyoto, Seoul, Inchon, Taipei, Kaohsiung, Singapore, Penang, Kuala Lumpur, Manila and Hong Kong. We were the first to ever persuade Matsushita to supply a product with someone else's brand on it other than their own. Standard Chartered Bank stood by us with letter of credit facilities that underpinned and enabled our rapid growth and good relationship with suppliers.

The travel schedule was hectic but having joined the hash house harrier group in Hong Kong, I found that all the locations I visited around the region also had their own hash groups. A social network across Asia through running resulted in many enduring friendships.

The job done, I somewhat reluctantly spent time back in France helping establish distribution channels in Europe. Anticipating bouts of homesickness for Hong Kong, this sad sack had taken with him to Paris hours and hours of tape recordings from Ray Cordeiro's late night radio show "All the way with Ray."

Eventually the lure of the East (and Uncle Ray) got the better of me and I succumbed by responding to a head hunter who chased me down in Paris.

The lure was to fill the role of Finance Manager, Hong Kong for English telecommunications company, Cable & Wireless (C&W), which then provided all of Hong Kong's external telecommunications. While certain about returning to Hong Kong, there was much less certainty in my mind about the prospective employer and the job.

Like some British Banks and great Trading Companies, C&W was a true product of Empire. It had its roots firmly implanted in many places that were painted pink on maps; all connected by undersea cable networks and later satellite networks. Compared to the smaller and riskier business world I had come from, C&W lived on a different planet. Its management style was risk averse, and paternalistic. Management was almost entirely expatriate; engineering led and prepared at a moment's notice to be shipped off to another location if so instructed. In return the Company provided fully furnished accommodation, paid local income taxes, school fees and generally took very good care of its staff. At most of its stations outside the UK the local C&W manager ranked alongside the local British ambassador or high commissioner and the local British bank manager, as important and influential members of the community. Some said that C&W were better at the art of diplomacy than the diplomats, not least because its planning horizons were longer term, and its managers were normally "on station" much longer.

In a book on the history of the company, one manager who joined it at the end of the World War II and retired as Regional Director for the Arab World in 1981, describes a working life spent entirely as a member of the expatriate cadre, which made up most of C&W's body of engineers and managers.

"It was cradle to grave, the Company. You were there for life. When you went to a place overseas, someone met you off the ship, or at the bottom of the runway ramp and took you through. Somebody helped with your visa, you had a house waiting, which may have needed furnishing, or you went in to a mess.

You had a basic set of rules and regulations:

- "Overseas staff are reminded of the necessity of daily evacuation of the bowels."
- "Juniors are reminded of the dangers of loose living. In the event of any trouble, consult the Company's Medical officer."
- If your mess bill, which included the drinks you signed for, went above a certain figure you were called in to see the assistant manager and explain why your bill was so high—although his was probably twice as high! You didn't expect to become terribly rich, but you knew you were taken care of and you'd have a good pension at the end of your time."

The company was then owned by the British Government, having been nationalized in 1947 just after the end of the war. At its Head Office in London, its most senior management were appointed to the "Court of Directors", rather than the Board. The Bank of England has a Court of Directors. So too did the East India Company in its day. The Chairman and Court of Directors were looked upon as civil servants by their single Government shareholder. As such, their levels of pay were then severely constrained to conform to a Government-mandated civil service pay freeze. I was shocked to learn the full-time Chairman was being paid just £12,000 per annum while Executive Directors earned £10,000.

Beyond the boardroom (courtroom?), however, the company was free to pay commercial market rates and incentives, which meant that managers all around the world were being considerably better rewarded than their bosses in London. It was not a situation conducive to attracting talent to the top.

The thought of working for a government-owned business, run by engineers, and lacking the motivating ingredients of profit, growth and related incentives was not particularly appealing. Gold-plated engineering—the best there was—had priority over normal commercial yardsticks.

In the end, an urge to return to Hong Kong and to many friends there, won the day over the uncertainties. Taking a chance on the job seemed low risk and being on the spot, in Hong Kong, in the event things didn't work out, seemed the better option.

Little did I know then that I had Maggie Thatcher on my side and was embarking on a fascinating twenty-two-year journey in which not only the missing ingredients became strongly embedded in company culture but also change and opportunity proved to be ever-present stimulants and companions.

Hong Kong was the revenue generating jewel in C&W's crown at the end of the 1970s, but its legal form was as a branch rather than a locally incorporated subsidiary company.

Like all C&W entities around the world it reported to London headquarters via what was known as the monthly Cash Statement. C&W, Hong Kong branch (CWHK) did not have its own Balance Sheet or Profit and Loss account and no one in Hong Kong had any accurate idea about its overall financial performance. Least of all its branch accountant. The Cash Statement consisted of many pages of numbers (all completed manually) which had to be back in London within five days of month's end. Only in London, was there a complete picture of the C&W group's overall financial position as cash statements from around the world were gathered and consolidated every month.

With privatization looming, under the Thatcher government, this way of reporting had to change and not just in Hong Kong. A local subsidiary would be essential. The franchise from the Hong Kong Government had only eight years to run whereas the planning horizon for new investment in submarine cables, buildings and satellite facilities extended out to twenty-five years. The Hong Kong Government well appreciated the need for long-term planning and preparation for privatization. They were amenable to a franchise extension and asked, not unreasonably, to see the last five years' accounts for CWHK.

Back in London, arms went up in horror. "Impossible" they said. "It can't be done. We can't separate out Hong Kong from the rest of the global network. Bear in mind, these were engineers who had no training in the subtle art of creative accounting). In due course, accounts were produced, heavily laden with caveats and qualifications as to why they did not truly reflect the value of the global network that CWHK enjoyed access to. The decades of experience and intellectual property had not been valued and the cable ships, which were dotted around the world had not been included, yet they were critical to protecting Hong Kong. The Hong Kong Secretary for Economic Services, on receiving these accounts, observed that CWHK was probably making 110 percent of the C&W group's profit. But beyond that, there was no greater interest or curiosity. The accounts were filed for the record and not referred to again during the ongoing constructive dialogue with Government about franchise extension and privatization. It is possible they may have been influential, however, in Government electing to become a 20 percent shareholder of the new CWHK subsidiary.

Pre-privatisation, this was a sharp lesson to C&W that the impossible was possible and that it needed a longer-term strategy to better balance and protect itself from the vulnerability of having too many eggs in the one basket.

C&W was an early candidate for Margaret Thatcher's privatization strategy because of its prior history as a private company. The plan to privatise C&W was announced in 1980 and the British Government sold the first half of its C&W shares in November 1981.

The task of preparing for and enabling privatization was an enormous one. Suddenly the Hong Kong branch accountant had a very different job description from the one he had signed up for.

CWHK was by far the largest business unit in the C&W group. Every aspect of its business in Hong Kong required adaptation to the new legal structure of a subsidiary company. Every license it held from the Hong Kong Government; every land lease and property title, customer contract, employee contract, vehicle registration, submarine cable contract agreements with telecom operators in every country in the world, —and on and on. The list seemed endless. To add complication, many of the contracts to be transferred to the new legal entity also needed renegotiation. The tenure of CWHK's license to operate in Hong Kong needed extension to be compatible with substantial new upcoming investments in submarine cables and new buildings. Typically, renegotiation of a franchise extension was a project measured in years — not months.

One agreement that became problematic and threatened the privatization timeline was that governing revenue sharing between HK Telephone Company (HKT) and CWHK. It had been the norm for many years that revenue earned on international calls was shared between the two operators in an agreed ratio. Originally, the ratio may have been based on the relative value of assets deployed in making international calls but spotting a vulnerability, HKT demanded a larger share and to make their case stronger they ceased paying CWHK. So important was CWHK to world-wide C&W cash flows that this situation not only threatened the whole C&W group; it also threatened the process of privatization.

Maggie was not pleased. The Governor was requested to intervene. CWHK and HKT agreed to an arbitration process and, hey presto, all was resolved with a new 60 percent C&W/40 percent HKT ratio arbitrated by the Postmaster General. Neither side was particularly happy with the outcome, but we moved on and solved the conundrum another way later.

There were key changes of personnel as C&W lined up for privatization. Apart from the logistical challenges, there were also massive challenges for a corporate culture that was completely unsuited to the listed company environment of the London Stock Exchange. A New Chief Executive came aboard with both Government and Public Company experience. New non-executive directors were appointed and an executive director responsible for new business development. The non-executives were no longer favorites of the Chairman but people with relevant backgrounds and skills who brought real added value.

This was beginning to feel like a very different company.

Change and opportunity were in the air. After a visit to Hong Kong to sign off on final details before privatization—the new CEO asked what was the most important thing we had to do next in Hong Kong. My reply was, "take over HKT." Unfortunately, others had their eye on the same prize and just a few months after privatization, Hong Kong Land made a move that made them owners of a circa 35 percent stake in HKT. The opportunity had passed—at least for the time being.

The early 1980s had seen Hong Kong Land diversify from its usual property interests, with its purchase of significant shareholdings in HKT and Hong Kong Electric Holdings Ltd. In 1982, Hong Kong Land acquired the last major site available in Central and began construction of the first phase of Exchange Square.

In the same year, however, the property market in Hong Kong plunged dramatically, and in the following two years rentals fell substantially. This became a period of financial adjustment for Hong Kong Land as it sought reorganise itself and reduce its debt burden through asset disposals and restructuring measures. Hong Kong Land sold its international properties as well as its non-core assets in Hong Kong, including its interests in HKT and Hong Kong Electric.

The buyer of the HKT holding was C&W. But C&W needed more than a 35 percent holding to be able to fully consolidate HKT into the C&W group. The next largest shareholder group in HKT spoke for a sufficient block of shares to get C&W to a more than 50 percent holding. Agreement with them on terms was reached over a long weekend and the Hong Kong Government was briefed to ensure there were no objections. A full bid was launched at the opening of the market after the long weekend and resulted in acceptances from shareholders that took C&W's

holding above 75 percent. There followed a restructuring that brought CWHK and HKT together under a new holding company, Hong Kong Telecom, which retained a listing on the Hong Kong Stock exchange and later sought listings on the New York Stock Exchange as well as the Pacific Exchange, then in San Francisco.

For anyone attending the Canton Trade Fair in the 1970s communications were very poor. Getting an outside line to make any call required a booking and that could sometimes take days. Long distance calls from city to city across Guangdong Province or within China were difficult enough but international calls were even a rarer events.

It was in C&W and HKT's best interest that the network across the border should develop as rapidly as possible. To the extent that calls were between Guangdong and Hong Kong, both parties would share the new revenue generated. C&W worked with China to complete the eastern section of the Guangdong Microwave project. A few months later the western section opened, effectively linking twenty-five cities in Guangdong Province, which was then emerging as an expanding hinterland base next to Hong Kong. HKT donated and helped install analogue telephone exchanges that were surplus to requirements in Hong Kong because they were being changed out to digital exchanges. When they were reconnected across the border, they instantly earned new revenue ahead of China's own evolving digital network plans.

The Shenda Telephone Company, was a joint venture partnership set up between China Telecom 51 percent and C&W 49 percent to build new telecommunications infrastructure in the Shenzhen Economic Zone north of Hong Kong. In 1983, when announced, it was the first such Telecoms joint venture in China and was followed by another to service the needs of the offshore oil industry in the South China Sea.

In negotiations preceding the formation of Shenda much time had been spent on reaching agreement as to how the company would be managed and governed. The western model of a Chairman, a Board of Directors and a Chief Executive all meeting regularly to monitor progress against plans was certainly one way of doing things and it was fair to conclude that C&W brought a lot of experience of cross-cultural management to the table.

But it would be equally fair to say the idea of a non-Mainland CEO and other senior managers was unfamiliar territory for our partners. Building trust was critical.

Meanwhile building the network for the Shenzhen Economic Zone proceeded at pace. At times as many as 2,000 HKT staff were crossing the border daily to toil long hours building the fiber optic network. They became street theater as local workers took time out during their two-hour lunch breaks to watch them at work.

Soon enough the time for the first board meeting drew near. The pre board dinner the previous evening was amongst other things a way to enable any difficult issues to be discussed informally and to ease any related concerns. Likewise, it was a way to socialize and get to know each other better. There was much joviality and Mao Tai.

Next morning at 10:00 a.m. the Board convened, broke for lunch and by mid-afternoon had completed its business. All in all, the conclusion was that the management and processes were working well and that we were making good progress as partners.

It is a normal thing that board meetings and decisions are recorded by way of "minutes of the meeting" and that those minutes would form the first item on the agenda of the following meeting — for agreement.

A month later, following a jovial dinner the night before, the board sat duly around the table — the meeting is opened, and up comes item 1 — Approval of the minutes of the previous meeting. Normally a one-minute item is recorded as "The minutes of the previous meeting were approved".

But whoa! — not so fast. "I don't agree to that" — "I didn't say that" — "But what I meant was this" — went on until lunch time and then into the afternoon — with the result that the meeting was adjourned — with minutes still not agreed — until a future date to be agreed.

Game set and match to the East.

We did eventually find a modus operandi that worked better and ensured that our partners promptly briefed the company's Party official before and after each meeting. Something they seemed to have neglected for that first meeting.

The Commonwealth Telecommunications Organization traces its origins back to 1901. In 1969 it devised The Commonwealth Telecommunications Organization Financial Arrangement (CTFA). The name alone indicating it was designed by a committee. Well intended, no doubt, but the CTFA proved to be a cumbersome bureaucratic concept that sought to share the costs of communicating between Commonwealth countries. The logic being that by averaging costs across the entire Commonwealth the smaller less efficient countries could benefit from the economies of scale enjoyed by larger countries. Typically, the eventual settlement of who owed whom how much ran at least three years behind the actual year costs were incurred. The arrangement was terminated in 1992 in the face of withdrawals by Canada, Australia and New Zealand.

C&W was the operator in many Commonwealth countries

and shared a seat with British Telecom in the British delegation at regular conferences of participating CTFA countries. Within the C&W delegation CWHK was always represented because of its size, efficiency and the fact that it was a net payer to the Commonwealth. Typically, these conferences lasted two weeks — often in exotic locations.

One eventful meeting involved a two-week sojourn in Lusaka, Zambia. There would have been more than fifty delegates and support staff in attendance. At the end of the first week delegates were invited to sunset cocktails and dinner on a boat on the Zambia side of the Zambezi River. The border with what was then Rhodesia ran down the middle of the river. On the other side of the river were Rhodesian gunboats making sure that we and a few stray hippos stayed on our side of the line. There were rebel soldiers still active on the Rhodesia side and we had been assured the gunboats and the Zambian troops, also visible on our side of the river, were there for our protection.

The second weekend was also eventful with game driving on the Saturday and flights back to London on Sunday.

Departure from Lusaka was chaotic. Delegates had checked out of their rooms in the afternoon for an early evening Air Zambia direct flight to London. Then came news of flight delay until after midnight. No one could get back into their rooms, so the bar did a roaring trade until eventually transport arrived late at night to get us to the airport. After take-off we could see for a while a lot of flashing lights below. We took little notice at the time. Most were in need of sleep. On waking we were landing in Rome with the captain explaining we needed to refuel. An old Africa hand on board said this always happens on the non-stop flight to London. He told us what would happen next and to anticipate up to two hours on the ground as the duty-free shop was not yet open. Sure enough the entire crew disappeared from the plane, returning ninety minutes later—each of them with a two-liter bottle of whisky. Back in London, on arrival, morning papers carried the story of an Air Zambia flight which had been fired upon by Rhodesian rebel forces after a late night take off from Lusaka.

Back in Hong Kong, the efficiency and scale of CWHK meant that it had a significant impact on lowering average costs across the Commonwealth. It was not surprising therefore that we had many visitors to Hong Kong from Commonwealth countries. Often, they came requesting an advance on monies that might be owed to them when the accounts for a particular year were finally audited for settlement. The finance minister from one African country more than once appeared, claiming that their main office building had burned down and all their records were lost. The first time this happened we were able to supply him with copy records before his flight departed Hong Kong. The second time (yes, the next building burnt down too—such bad luck!) we had the records delivered to his hotel room before he got back from our meeting. From another country, the minister always stayed in the Peninsula Hotel and used one of their Rolls Royce's for getting about town. He wore fine white robes, gold watches and much jewelery. He also loved banqueting and somehow always forgot to pay his hotel bill when leaving town. The hotel knew we would pay—and of course deduct from any dues to his country under the CTFA.

After C&W bought control of HKT there were a number of management changes. The former Managing Director HKT took on a wider regional role for C&W. I succeeded him at HKT to manage integration with the rest of the C&W group. Together we made a number of visits to other operators around the region to introduce ourselves and explain our new roles.

One of the more interesting visits was to Fujian Province where, after formal meetings in Fuzhou, we headed up in to nearby mountains with our hosts to visit an ancient Buddhist monastery and temple.

Uniquely among his fellow monks, the Abbot at the Monastery spoke excellent English and showed us around before lunch. Of particular note were bullet damaged walls and idols, particularly in and around the Temple. It was explained the damage came from gunshots fired by Red Guards during the Cultural Revolution. Angered that the remoteness of the Monastery had kept it away from the public eye and related Red Guard scrutiny, the attack was meant to warn and scare the monks in to leaving. No one had attempted to repair the damage. It seemed to be regarded as a badge of honor by the monks who had stayed on.

We were also shown many ancient parchment scrolls and advised that the Chinese characters on them were painted from the blood of the monastic artists. It had not faded, we were told, because prior to cutting themselves the monks had heavily dosed up on salt. There was no such thing as air conditioning at the Monastery but its location on the mountain side was favourably disposed to a perfect humidity which in turn had helped preserve the ancient scrolls and many ancient books in the Monastery library.

During a "light" sixteen-course vegetarian lunch, I remarked how surprised I was, and complimented the Abbot, on how up to date he was on current world affairs. There seemed nothing he was not familiar with or about which he did not have a well-informed opinion. He grinned and replied that he had a secret, which he would show me after lunch.

True to his word we later strolled to the cell which was his sleeping quarters. He invited me in and lifted the pillow. Beneath it was a small transistor radio and earplug. He said it was tuned to the BBC World Service.

In C&W's long history, carefully nurturing its relationship with host Governments was always a top priority. Diplomatic skills were as important within C&W's management hierarchy as they are for any nation state. Historically those Governments were mainly within the British Commonwealth of nations but increasingly since privatization in 1981, C&W had become a more diverse multinational corporation. New business in the USA, Japan, Macau, Latvia, Belarus, Germany, Israel and China had been won since 1981. A new business team was exploiting opportunity from telecoms' deregulation in the European Union. New businesses in Australia, New Zealand and the UK were developing rapidly.

In the run-up to the 1997 change of Hong Kong sovereignty, it was natural that dialogue would take place with China regarding the post 1997 landscape. Negotiations, discussions and sharing of views—began more than two years ahead of the 1997 handover date against a background in which Citic had already become a 20 percent shareholder in Hong Kong Telecom in 1990 and had two directors on its board.

Unique among Hong Kong utility companies, the C&W group had widespread public ownership around the world. C&W plc, the parent company, was listed in London, New York, Tokyo, Frankfurt, Zurich and Hong Kong. Subsidiary companies also had widespread public ownership. Hong Kong Telecom was listed in Hong Kong and on New York and Pacific exchanges. Australian subsidiary, Optus, was listed in Sydney and New York. UK subsidiary C&W Communications PLC was listed in London and New York. One of C&W's largest shareholders (10 percent) was the German industrial giant Veba, which at the time was a primary strategic partner in Europe for exploiting deregulation there. Beyond public listings the shareholder registers of both parent and subsidiary companies included a multinational array of Pension Funds, Insurance Companies and other serious long-term investors with a keen interest in China.

Accordingly, while Directors had the ability to invite, share ownership, and enable board appointments, they were tightly constrained by corporate governance, legal requirements and multiple country listing rules, as to the terms of any such events. Breach of any constraints held significant personal risk of litigation by regulators or disgruntled shareholders.

Investment Bankers for both sides of the negotiating table understood this and its implication that any transaction that might be agreed would be subject to full disclosure and must pass the test of market norms.

Subsequently two teams of experts met in all sorts of exciting places — Amsterdam, Paris, London, Shanghai, Berlin — but made little progress as 1997 fast approached. In parallel siren voices came from many different places spreading a confusion of messages. Their origin was not always clear, particularly when delivered via intermediaries. The Joint Liaison office, the Ministry of Telecoms in Beijing, the Ministry of Radio, Film & Television in Beijing, Citic, China Telecom — and British voices — Ministers, former Ministers, former Prime Ministers, Ambassadors — the list went on. All had an opinion to share, a threat to be warned about; a helpful suggestion that was impossible or had not been thought through. Smooth transition was the most frequently expressed objective.

It took two years to gain a consensus that sticking to market norms was in the best interests of all parties. Both C&W and HKT were jointly developing business interests outside Hong Kong and the world's capital markets were watching closely.

With just two weeks to go before the handover—in May 1997—it was announced that C&W would sell 5.5 percent of its holding in HKT to China Telecom at the last ninety-day day average market price.

The sirens immediately ceased amid quiet applause of a victory for common sense and pragmatism.

Many of the C&W businesses in the Asia-Pacific Region were as far away as you can get from a head office in London. Apart from Hong Kong, they included Fiji, Vanuatu, the Solomon Islands, Tonga, the Cook Islands, Japan, the Philippines, Indonesia and Macau. Each one of which has its tales to tell. Here is a small selection of what goes on far away from "Head Office":

New Hebrides, in the South Pacific, became independent as Vanuatu in 1980. Prior to that it was a rare form of colonial territory in which sovereignty was shared by Britain and France. Under the Condominium there were three separate governments— one French, one British, and one joint administration that was partially elected after 1975. Other than the Joint Court, everything existed in pairs. Cynics called the Condominium 'the Pandemonium', as the dual administration produced amazing duplication. There were two police forces with their own laws, including road laws, two health services, two education systems, two currencies, and two prison systems. Additionally, there were separate British and French governments, which meant two immigration policies, two courts (apart from the Joint Court), and two corporation laws. Inhabitants of the islands were given the choice of which government they wanted to be ruled by. The result was an inevitable clash of foreign policy and a colonial mentality.

C&W had a 50/50 joint venture here with look alike, France Cable et Radio; the French equivalent of C&W. Small time diplomatic gamesmanship and one upmanship were given ample opportunity through the 50/50 relationship as no one had control. The joint venture agreement provided that the two partners rotate the general manager role every three years to give some semblance of balance—but a lot can happen in three years.

In the first year of a three-year term under French management, the board met, as usual, to consider and approve the annual budget for the following year. The manager's house was adjacent to a lagoon and a separating protective wall apparently needed repairs that were provided for in the budget. Said budget was duly approved by the board.

A year later when visiting for the next budget review the board were surprised to see a new jetty adjacent to the manager's house with a smart new power boat tied up alongside.

The same French manager went one better in year three of his appointment. He married the prime minister's daughter—so C&W did not get their man back in to the driving seat until there was a new Prime Minister, several years later.

C&W owned a number of bungalows at Shouson Hill in Hong Kong on a site which also housed the cable landing station for submarine cables entering Hong Kong via Deep Water Bay. A new General Manager's house was later built on the site. At the time the wife of the incumbent General Manager was heavily involved with local amateur dramatics.

It took a sharp eye to detect that the raised platform in the dining area of the new house, which looked out over a large lounge, also had a curtain around it. It quite literally doubled as a stage.

The London-based architect's department, which supervised all building projects around the world, didn't have eyes sharp enough to spot this one—much to the delight of the General

Managers wife who now had her own place to play with her amateur dramatic friends.

There were two coups in Fiji during 1987 - in May and September. At that time C&W managed Fintel, the international telecoms operator for Fiji. It also deployed a submarine cable repair ship from Suva. Some C&W staff, in Fintel management roles, as well as the captain and cable ship officers all lived in Fiji with their families.

The second coup resulted in Fiji declaring itself a Republic, abrogating its constitution and removing the Governor General from office.

All international telecommunications were cut for a time. Soldiers surrounded the earth satellite station making things particularly difficult for the British Ambassador to communicate with London.

But all was not lost for him. Cable ships have their own independent satellite communication systems.

C&W involvement in Philippine telecommunications dates back to colonial times in 1878 and links to early submarine cables in Hong Kong. In more recent times, the Marcos era reshaped ownership of the business, (known as Eastern Telecoms Philippines Inc or ETPI), so that so-called cronies owned 60 percent and C&W 40 percent. C&W managed the business and also maintained a submarine cable repair ship in Manila. It was a strategically important seat at the table on ASEAN (Association of Southeast Nations) matters and long-term satellite and submarine cable planning.

In 1983 Benigno S. Aquino Jnr, a former Philippine Senator and aspiring Presidential candidate, was assassinated at Manila airport on return to the country from self-imposed exile in the

United States. His assassination is credited with transforming the opposition to the Marcos regime from a small, isolated movement into a national crusade. It is also credited with thrusting his widow, Corazon Aquino into the public spotlight and her running for president in 1986. Although Marcos was officially declared the winner of the election, widespread allegations of fraud and illegal tampering on Marcos's behalf are credited with sparking the People Power Revolution which resulted in Marcos fleeing the country and conceding the presidency to Mrs Aquino.

The Presidential Commission for Good Government (PCGG) was established by President Aquino in 1986, with a primary mandate to recover ill-gotten wealth accumulated by Marcos his immediate family, relatives, subordinates and close associates, whether located in the Philippines or abroad.

Not surprisingly ETPI came under the purview of the PCGG. Largely due to its C&W management it was well and tightly run but that did not stop an invasion of locust swarm proportions for months on end. They all seemed to have new Mercedes cars and expected a parking space in the building plus a desk to work at. Most of the type of things they were searching for would have required sign off by one of the C&W managers so it became a bit of a witch hunt. I was indebted to the then British Ambassador, the late Sir Robin McLaren, for his assistance in thinning out the invasion and bringing some kind of normalcy to a day in the office at ETPI. His message about impugning the reputation and integrity of a century old British Company and its management of ETPI seemed to hit the mark and the PCGG retreated.

But The PCGG commission is still active today, thirty-five years later.

"Travel broadens the mind, but you must have the mind." So apparently said G. K. Chesterton, the English philosopher and writer. I began these anecdotes with reflection on leaving my country of birth more than fifty years ago. I called it a pilgrimage to the unknown for little did I know of my destination nor the adventures, challenges and particularly the learning that lay along the way. One thing led to another, but travel was a strong motivator.

Hong Kong, which was largely unknown to me when I first set out on my journey became a mecca. Its ever-changing face has been with me for 65 percent of my time on earth. I share my experience of it and relationship with it - with a huge number of friends and colleagues. Yes, it is changing — but it has always been changing, and more particularly adapting to its challenges. Long may it continue to do so.

British Foreign Secretary, Lord Palmerston could not have been more spectacularly wrong when he said of Hong Kong in 1841, it is "a barren rock with nary a house upon it — it will never be a mart for trade".